Social Work, Immigration and Asylum

of related interest

Research in Social Care and Welfare
Issues and Debates for Practice
Edited by Beth Humphries
ISBN 978 1 85302 900 4

Deportation is Freedom!
The Orwellian World of Immigration Controls
Steve Cohen
ISBN 978 1 84310 294 6

Immigration Controls, the Family and the Welfare State
A Handbook of Law, Theory, Politics and Practice for Local Authority, Voluntary Sector and Welfare State Workers and Legal Advisors
Steve Cohen
ISBN 978 1 85302 723 9

Community Care Practice and the Law
Third Edition
Michael Mandelstam
ISBN 978 1 84310 233 5

'Race', Housing and Social Exclusion
Edited by Peter Somerville and Andy Steele
ISBN 978 1 85302 849 6

Racism and Mental Health
Prejudice and Suffering
Edited by Kamaldeep Bhui
ISBN 978 1 84310 076 8

Meeting the Needs of Ethnic Minority Children – Including Refugee, Black and Mixed Parentage Children
A Handbook for Professionals
Second Edition
Edited by Kedar Nath Dwivedi
ISBN 978 1 85302 959 2

Mental Health Services for Minority Ethnic Children and Adolescents
Edited by Mhemooda Malek and Carol Joughin
Foreword by Kedar Nath Dwivedi
Child and Adolescent Mental Health
ISBN 978 1 84310 236 6

Social Work, Immigration and Asylum

Debates, dilemmas and ethical issues
for social work and social care practice

Edited by Debra Hayes and Beth Humphries

Foreword by Steve Cohen

Jessica Kingsley Publishers
London and Philadelphia

First published in the United Kingdom in 2004
by Jessica Kingsley Publishers
116 Pentonville Road
London N1 9JB, UK
and
400 Market Street, Suite 400
Philadelphia, PA 19106, USA
www.jkp.com

Library of Congress Cataloging in Publication Data
Social work, immigration and asylum debates, dilemmas and ethical issues
for social work and social care practice / Debra Hayes and Beth
Humphries [editors] ; foreword by Steve Cohen.— 1st American pbk. ed.
   p. cm.
Includes bibliographical references and index.
 ISBN 1-84310-194-7 (pbk.)
 1. Social work with immigrants—Great Britain. 2. Great
Britain—Emigration and immigration—Government policy. I. Hayes,
Debra, 1960- II. Humphries, Beth, 1940- III. Cohen, Steve, 1945-
HV4013.G7S63 2004
362.87′53′0941—dc22

                                    2003027297

British Library Cataloguing in Publication Data
A CIP catalogue record for this book is available from the British Library

ISBN 978 1 84310 194 9

Contents

Breaking the Links and Pulling the Plug

Steve Cohen

First, let me state that of course the Refugee Council recognises there is a role within immigration policy for a strategy of returns... We accept that enforced returns will be necessary. (Refugee Council)

The process of removal needs to be open and in order for it to be effective there needs to be close liaison between local authority asylum teams, private accommodation providers and immigration officials. (Sheffield City Council)

The removal enforcement authority's efforts are often ineffective for the following reasons...lack of communication and liaison between the Home Office enforcement authorities and the local authorities. (Oxfordshire Social Services Department)

These statements were all made in written evidence to the House of Commons Home Affairs Committee on Asylum Removals, which published its report on 8 May 2003. They show that a watershed has been reached in the development of immigration controls. Voluntary sector agencies, local authorities and workers in both sectors, particularly those involved in issues of welfare, have a clear decision to make – to continue to collude in the enforcement of immigration controls or unambiguously to oppose such controls. There is no third way.

However, evidence submitted to the Home Affairs Committee repeatedly suggests there is a third way – namely the implementation of 'fair' controls and the development of 'humane' removals. But controls can never be 'fair' to those subject to them. Nor can they ever be 'humane', in that the inevitable end game of all immigration control is forced, compulsory removal accompanied by the threat or actuality of legally sanctioned violence. There cannot be immigration control without there also being legitimised the use of physical restraints to arrest those deemed unwanted here, the policing of detention centres for those imprisoned without charge or trial, and the forcible manhandling of those to be deported.

The strength of immigration restrictions resides in the fact that they are a total system. They are not simply about exclusion and deportation. They are also about internal controls – which include not only the physical policing of migrants, immigrants and refugees but also their economic policing through making entitlement to an ever increasing array of welfare provisions dependent upon immigration status. Though the Home Office is responsible for controls, it is only the hub of a huge wheel the spokes of which stretch out through the country and internationally. A vast array of workers who thought they were being employed to undertake socially useful work now find they have been conscripted into being agents of immigration control. Amongst those finding themselves in this invidious situation are those responsible in some degree or another for the provision of benefits, housing, medical treatment, education and social services.

Paradoxically, the fact that it constitutes such a total system is also immigration control's weakness and a source of potential vulnerability. It means there are numerous points at which controls could be completely undermined if those administering them refused to cooperate. That is, if those administering them decided to pull the plug on controls. This would, of course, require the active support of the trade union movement in the protection of its members. Many trade unions now voice criticisms of immigration controls and are prepared to assist individual anti-deportation campaigns. However, all unions support the principle of controls and none has agreed any policy of non-compliance to protect their members who refuse to collude in controls. A debate is much needed on how best to form pressure groups within the unions on this issue and in formulating what non-compliance/non-collusion would mean in practice. Of course, the direct opposite to collusion is also possible. Instead of cooperating in controls, many welfare workers are in a position positively to help those threatened by them. Social workers, for example, have the training and the facilities to provide welfare reports as an aid in contesting individual deportations. Again, a debate is required to legitimise this provision professionally.

There is one Home Office department that is central to these issues and which is rapidly becoming the dominant force within immigration control. This is the so-called National Asylum Support Service (NASS). NASS has managed to place welfare, or rather the lack of it, at the centre of Home Office enforcement and to sow confusion amongst many welfare workers. New Labour established NASS in 1999 to enforce a modern poor law for asylum-seekers. This is a poor law outside welfare state provision based on forced dispersal into often sub-standard accommodation, itself generally contracted from local authorities, at maintenance 70 per cent of income support level. Others subject to immigration control but who are not asylum-seekers are excluded from even this poor law. Some welfare agencies and local authority consortia argue that because NASS is dealing in 'welfare' then it is to that extent a benevolent organization with which there should be cooperation. The primary forms taken by this cooperation have been the acting as agents for NASS's forced dispersal scheme and the sitting on joint committees with NASS representatives. However, this misses the point. NASS is dealing with the *withholding* of welfare. It therefore has a crucial role in the whole enforcement process – that is, starving out migrants, immigrants and refugees. Indeed, this is how NASS sees itself. For instance, NASS has recently established an office in the North West. This includes an 'investigation team' whose role is to track down those allegedly working here 'illegally'. NASS has asked the voluntary sector to cooperate in this and supply names. A NASS pamphlet on *The New Asylum Support Scheme*, issued in March 2000, is quite clear that NASS is not neutral when it comes to the expulsion of failed asylum-seekers and particularly the expulsion of failed asylum-seeking families with children. The pamphlet states: 'It is, therefore, important that we develop our removals capacity to ensure that we can effectively remove such families from the country.' The lesson here is that immigration control can never have a benevolent face.

Local authorities and voluntary sector agencies are placing themselves in a politically impossible position by cooperating with NASS. This is particularly the case with voluntary sector organizations. These are well-suited to be the allies of asylum-seekers, but instead many are increasingly being viewed by refugees as antagonistic to their interests. This perception is correct. For instance, a letter dated 1 April 2003 from the Immigration and Nationality

Directorate deals with the provision of emergency accommodation to asylum-seekers by voluntary sector organizations. The letter says that where NASS support is refused because an asylum application is made out of time then 'the voluntary sector will be expected to evict the individual the following working day'. This is the end result of collusion with NASS – the forcible eviction of refugees. Organizations entering into this collusion are increasingly becoming the subject of protest by asylum-seekers and their supporters. In June 2003, 20 asylum-seekers went on hunger strike in protest against conditions at Nayland Rock Induction Centre in Margate, Kent. The centre is contracted to NASS but overseen by Migrant Helpline, which places asylum-seekers there. In July 2003, the Refugee Council was lobbied by Legal Action for Women in protest at the Council's involvement in the refugee dispersal scheme.

Rather than cooperating with NASS, it would be far more principled and effective to break all links with it. It is only by refusing to collude in the system organisationally and individually, by pulling the plug, by breaking the links, that it is possible to argue and fight for what is in the best interests of all migrants, immigrants and refugees. That is, the full restoration of all benefits and the end to controls. It is to these urgent debates that this book addresses itself.

Chapter 1

History and Context:
The Impact of Immigration Control
on Welfare Delivery

Debra Hayes

Introduction

This book has been written at a time of heightened concern about the presence in the UK of those defined as 'asylum-seekers'. We are bombarded daily with scare stories and negative images which serve to demonise this group and help to justify their unequal treatment. This book is an attempt to explore current arrangements for dealing with asylum-seekers, and others subject to immigration controls, by examining their draconian nature within the context of a history of ever more restrictive and racist controls. The book also attempts to consider the impact and implications for social work and social welfare practice, as this group increasingly presents for services and help. A significant theme throughout is a concern with both the *role* and *function* of professionals in social work and welfare, as they become entwined within processes which police, monitor and control those subject to immigration controls. It is a call for us to stop and think about the seriousness of this collusion and to consider strategies for resistance, as well as the development of good practice.

The book continues a commitment by the Department of Applied Community Studies at Manchester Metropolitan University to researching, writing about and developing good practice in social welfare with those subject to immigration control (see Batsleer and Humphries 2000; Cohen, Humphries and Mynott 2002; Cohen and Hayes 1998; Jones 1998). A significant theme throughout all this work has been the exploration of the relationship between immigration control and the welfare state. Much of the work has been done in collaboration with the Greater Manchester Immigration Aid Unit and we would want, in particular, to acknowledge the influence of Steve Cohen in this. Many of the contributors are first-time writers, students and practitioners confronting these themes in their work and at the forefront of developing good practice. We are mindful of the lack of literature to guide, influence and help practitioners struggling both practically and ethically with this and hope the book will be the first of many to confront what is becoming one of the biggest challenges the profession has faced for some time. Our responses to this issue will tell us much about the current state of social work and its values and purpose. This first chapter will provide a historical introduction to the relationship between immigration control and welfare and the second will focus more specifically on this particular moment in social work itself.

A century of control

All migration is courageous. Whether through coercion, persecution, war or indeed poverty, the past and present movement of people around the globe is littered with scores of painful stories, many too awful to recount. But they are also stories of strength and hope, of survival in the often unwelcoming atmosphere of places like the UK. To tell these truths, to humanise these journeys is, of course, problematic – not so easy then to justify that inferior and cruel reception. Much simpler to present the group en masse as scroungers, illegals, criminals, bogus, terrorist, diseased and a myriad other negative stereotypes. We can then more comfortably stomach a dehumanising immigration and asylum system which contains, controls and excludes.

The movement of people geographically is, of course, part of human history and controlling it a relatively recent historical phenomenon, some one hundred years in the UK (Hayter 2000). Calls for controls have always been posed in racist terms, from the 1905 Aliens Act and its preoccupation with Jewish refugees fleeing pogroms in Eastern Europe, through to the attacks on black Commonwealth immigration in the period following World War II to present-day constructions of asylum-seekers.

> What was to become one of the most important expressions of racialised nationalism in the developed capitalist countries in the twentieth century

was the entrenchment of immigration controls. Racism was everywhere integral to the development of immigration controls. Particular groups of immigrants were racialised and presented as a threat to the supposedly finite material resources of the receiving nation, as well as its 'culture'. (Mynott 2002, p.18)

Those 'outsiders' we currently wish to control continue to be presented as a drain on the resources of the nation, despite their economic contribution. This allows us not only to justify refusing people into the country at all, but also their exclusion from the normal welfare services/resources available to citizens. Those citizen 'insiders' are then encouraged to see themselves as part of and benefiting from nation and as fundamentally different from and superior to the 'outsider', who should not enjoy the same rights. Who those 'outsiders' are remains the product of racism – but it is no longer a racism simply targeted at black people, it now encompasses new layers of the world's poor and dispossessed.

There is a new racism abroad in the land, even more virulent and devas-tating than the ones we have seen before. And this is the racism that is meted out to refugees and asylum-seekers irrespective of their colour. This is the racism that is meted out to Romas and Sintis and poor whites from Eastern Europe. This is the racism that pretends to be based on the fear of strangers and gives it the respectable name of xenophobia. (Sivanandan 2002)

Today we talk about 'asylum-seekers'; even the 'refugee' tag is less frequently articulated, as though to underline that these are seekers only, the majority of whom will not be accepted as genuine refugees. They are rather false, bogus and not genuinely in fear of persecution. We talk about 'economic migrants' as a way of discrediting asylum claims, as though a purposeful fight for economic survival is somehow less worthy and more damaging to *our* economic security. In the past we used words like 'immigrant' or 'alien' and it is important to consider whether these semantic shifts are significant. In truth, each fits a particular historical or political purpose: many of today's asy-lum-seekers would have had citizenship rights within the countries of their former colonial masters. In the 1950s and 1960s many would have been con-structed as 'immigrants', until waves of immigration restrictions developed since the 1960s in most of the richer nations around the globe moved the goalposts. Ugandan Asians, for example, fleeing persecution under Idi Amin's 'Africanization' programme, had British passports until they were systematically removed by the Commonwealth Immigrants Act 1968. This overtly racist piece of legislation subjected all holders of UK passports to immigration controls unless they, a parent or a grandparent had been born, adopted or naturalized in the UK (Hayter 2000, p.53).

From the Commonwealth Immigrants Act 1962, which took away automatic rights of entry to Commonwealth citizens by introducing work vouchers, through the 1968 Act described above, and on to the Immigration Act 1971 and the British Nationality Act 1981, the process was fairly relentless. The 1971 Act effectively brought primary immigration from the Caribbean, the Indian subcontinent and Africa to an end by creating the categories 'patrial' and 'non-patrial'. Patrials were free of restrictions and predominantly included British or Commonwealth citizens born in the UK, or with a parent or grandparent born or naturalized in the UK. This actually increased the number of people entitled to enter Britain, but they were mainly white. This period of increased controls culminated in the 1981 Act, which amongst other things abolished the principle of *ius soli*, which had entitled anyone born on British soil to citizenship. Citizenship now comes through the blood-line so is gained through having parents who are British. This legislation over a 20-year period succeeded in eroding those citizenship rights for people from the Commonwealth, and all but ended black immigration for settlement.

So we are left to talk about asylum-seekers. The four nationalities currently topping the asylum statistics (Refugee Council 2002a), Iraqi, Zimbabwean, Afghan and Somali, all have a particular colonial history which continues to shape their future. When we begin to scratch the surface, the distinction between fleeing harsh, oppressive regimes and crippling destitution seems at best meaningless and at worst a convenient distortion. What is clear from the asylum statistics is, whatever media mythologies persist, it is global crises which force the movement of people across national boundaries.

Nevertheless, the strength of the anti-immigration position can be evidenced by the ease with which the far right has grasped the issue. 'The asylum seeker issue has been great for us. This issue legitimates us' (Nick Griffin, leader of the BNP, quoted in *The Observer*, 13.10.02).

When considering the content of the Nationality, Immigration and Asylum Act 2002, it seems New Labour are all too aware of the support which can be gained by breeding a popular nationalism based on fears of immigration. The measures contained in the Act were initially outlined in the Government White paper *Secure Borders, Safe Haven: Integration with Diversity 2002*

(Refugee Council 2002b). The requirement of applicants for British citizenship to pass an English language test and the introduction of a citizenship ceremony involving an oath of allegiance confirms this narrow view of nation. Parts of the Act concerning the withdrawal of even subsistence level support for some asylum-seekers have caused the most alarm and have been subject to legal challenge. What is most worrying is that the Government should actually construct legislation that aims to drive vulnerable adults and their families into homelessness and destitution. Further features of the Act concern the setting up of accommodation centres, where asylum-seekers will be housed and where their health and educational needs will also be met. The provision of education for children outside of the mainstream has been most controversial and takes onto a new level the idea of exclusion from normal welfare.

> There is an explicitly racist justification for these education measures. It was given by David Blunkett in a radio interview and he refused to withdraw his words on the Bill's second reading – that schools are being 'swamped' by asylum-seeking children. (Cohen 2003, p.32)

Accommodation centres generally illuminate the Government's thinking – asylum-seekers should be set apart from normal society and be denied the opportunity to engage and participate in communities whilst their claims are being processed. The new Act is the latest in a long line of increasingly restrictive immigration controls which have now succeeded in completely separating and excluding those subject to control and have further strengthened the ideology which constructs that group as costly, dangerous and damaging to the national interest. The next section of this chapter will explore more fully the historical processes that have firmly and inextricably linked these two themes of immigration and welfare together.

Welfare and Nation

Any conversation about immigration or asylum inevitably ends up confronting the thorny question of cost. The social cost of those constructed as *outsiders* is presented in entirely negative terms, with little consideration given to the benefits brought by waves of immigrants who have paid taxes, brought labour and skills and generally contributed a richness created precisely by difference. Nevertheless, the idea that *we* should prioritise *our* own in terms of who we help and support seems so obvious and commonsensical that those challenging the anti-immigration position are often left floundering, unsure how to break down this monolithic ideology. Working with both black and white students on social work, youth work and related degrees, I see this clash of ideas regularly. I accept that, whilst the far right persistently presents asylum-seekers and 'immigrants' as a drain on the public purse, the majority to the left of them still struggle to see humanity globally, and are deeply influenced by an idea of nation which makes it appear natural for us to restrict *our* resources to *our* own.

To make sense of this, it is necessary first to unpack the ideology underpinning the existence and delivery of welfare. It then becomes all too transparent why those constructed as *outside* of nation have always also been placed *outside* of welfare. Just who is constructed as *outside* is, of course, not a simple question of blood or geography, but is rather a political question, steeped in racism and Britain's Imperialist past. In fact, the centrality of nationality for claims upon welfare existed long before large-scale black migration to the UK. The cost of relief arising from the administration of the Poor Law was the responsibility of the claimant's parish of origin, leaving Irish families most vulnerable because they did not 'belong' to any parish. In the event of sickness, old age and unemployment they could therefore not make a claim, thus creating a useful pool of cheap labour. Additionally, in the event of claims for relief, towns had the 'power of removal' to the parishes of origin, again affecting the Irish most acutely (Williams 1989, 1996). What we can see from the history, both of welfare reform and immigration control, is that both are influenced by a particular ideology of improving 'the nation' and its stock (Cohen 1996, 2001, 2003; Hayes 2000, 2002).

In the second half of the nineteenth century, Victorian curiosity and concern about the attitudes and behaviour of the urban poor took a more serious turn as a result of social disorder and Imperial decline (Marriott 1999; Searle 1971). As the role of biological science gained prominence on the back of Darwin's theories of natural selection, classifications emerged and from this time 'race' increasingly came to refer to a biological type of human being (Miles 1989, p.32). Heavily influenced by 'Social Darwinism' it was a small leap for reformers to call for social intervention to encourage reproduction among the 'fit', as well as discouraging reproduction among the 'unfit'. These ideas came to fruition around a concern with the 'health of the nation', which led to open attacks on both the poor and foreigners.

> The pathological condition of the urban poor was seen as evidence of a
> degenerative process within the imperial race, and the savagery of

colonial subjects as a characteristic degeneration from the ideal white race. (Marriott 1999, p.87)

Many of the prominent social reformers of the day, like the Webbs, Booth, Rowntree and Stopes, who were greatly influential in emerging welfare reforms, were extremely concerned about the alleged deterioration of the British race. Creating a working class fit for both work and war became the primary purpose of welfare; this resulted in a preoccupation with both rooting out the undeserving poor and foreigners who, in openly eugenicist terms, diluted the British stock.

Britain's international dominance was seen to rest on the cultivation of the fitness of the British race, and the fostering of national unity. Welfare reform was seen as central to this. (Cohen 1996, p.32)

Early welfare reforms at the turn of the last century had an explicit purpose: to improve the ability of the nation to compete with its emerging rivals in global markets and global conflicts. Clearly then, welfare is essentially for those considered deserving *within* nation and we see emerging at this time an alliance between Social Darwinists, Fabians, welfare reformers and lobbyists against the immigration of 'aliens'. The great Liberal welfare reform programme of 1906–1914, which included the 1908 Old Age Pensions Act and the 1911 National Insurance Act, emphasised the necessity for breeding an imperial race in the UK if the Empire were to remain both British and strong (Semmell 1960, p.28). These two key pieces of legislation contained both residency and citizenship requirements, including the loss of entitlement for those women who married 'aliens'.

Not coincidentally, it is precisely during this period that the first immigration controls emerge in the form of the Aliens Act 1905. The refugee question, more accurately, concern over Jewish refugees fleeing Polish and Russian pogroms, had entered public debate at the end of the nineteenth century (Gainer 1972; Garrard 1971). The poor Eastern European Jew became the focus of an intense lobby for controls, which looked in microscopic detail at the behaviour and habits of this group (Hayes 2000, 2002). As Jewish refugees became linked with the social problems of urban life, attention focused on their likely social cost. In these early discussions about how immigration controls might work, the question of 'means' became key. Newly created immigration officers would need to make judgements about who was likely to be a burden on the rates. Here we see the centrality of the question of welfare in immigration control. At the heart of the machinery is the need to let in only those who will be economically useful to the British nation and those not likely to require welfare. The Aliens Act 1905 did not apply to travellers in first and second class facilities, only those in the poorest steerage conditions. Decisions about undesirability focused on the diseased, the insane, the criminal and those likely to be a burden on the public purse. In practice, immigration officers and medical inspectors made crude judgements at the point of entry by asking people to empty their pockets. In the early operations of the Act, the vast majority of rejections were on the grounds of insufficient means, i.e. they could not prove they could support themselves and their families without help (HM Inspector of Aliens 1906, p.767).

A glance at the other main category of rejections, those on health grounds, indicates a conflating of the two issues. Medical rejections were often quite vague, reflecting a concern with economic productivity without recourse to the public purse (Hayes 2002). There is a powerful resonance here for those subject to immigration control in the present. Immigration rules now prevent entry to anyone who may have 'recourse to public funds', again illustrating the powerful link between immigration and welfare. Also of great significance was the establishment of 'internal' controls under the Aliens Act. The provision to deport aliens found to be in receipt of parochial relief was again an obvious forerunner to present-day arrangements. By focusing on this period at the turn of the last century when the first social insurance schemes were established to improve the conditions of the working class, we can see clearly how aliens were certainly not to benefit from that protection. The state employs a two-pronged attack here: first, by building into newly created welfare systems arrangements to exclude aliens and second, by building into newly created immigration controls barriers to those who might require assistance.

A comprehensive and universal welfare state?

The period following World War II, when the welfare state was created in a wave of hope and optimism, coincides with a period of significant immigration. These black immigrants in the post-war period, unlike the Jews before them, did have citizenship rights as well as a strong ideological connection with 'Mother England'. Surely then these citizens would benefit from this golden age of welfare? In reality this was not the case and these citizens were treated as short-term visitors, migrant workers who, it was hoped, would return home and not require the benefits of long-term settlement. For example, in the post-war housing programme, black citizens did not access state housing and were left to the whims of the private market via institution-ally racist allocation policies (Ginsburg 1989). Since the creation of the NHS there have been arguments about the problem of usage by those not entitled to the benefits of free, universal health care. In 1982 the NHS Charges to Overseas Visitors regulations were imposed, which restricted treatment to those 'ordinarily resident' in the UK. Whilst this did not formally affect many Commonwealth citizens, there were well-documented examples of illegal exclusions and requests for passports from black citizens (Cohen and Hayes 1998; Gordon 1983). In addition, this paved the way for more and more mechanisms to be introduced into the NHS to police recipients of free services.

The Education Act 1944 excluded from educational grants students 'not ordinarily resident' and in 1967 differential fees were introduced for overseas students (Cohen 2002). In terms of social security we have already noted a long history of excluding outsiders from basic safety nets. Gordon and Newn-ham's groundbreaking research (1985) showed that the practice of requesting passports by Department of Health and Social Security staff fell most onto black claimants and most significantly involved workers in the welfare state in the internal policing of immigration.

> What developed during this period was a system in which discrete and separate agencies of the state were advised or encouraged to play a part in the enforcement of immigration controls. (Gordon and Newnham 1985, p.70)

This issue of drawing other workers in state agencies into the internal policing of immigration is an important one and should concern social workers and related professionals. This will be returned to later, but the pattern was certainly established in the 1980s and has continued apace since.

In the 1980s then, we begin to get some acknowledgement of the exclusionary workings of the welfare state, both in terms of formal exclusions and also the discriminatory and often incorrect exclusions experienced mainly by black citizens. Before moving on to discuss asylum-seekers and restrictions on welfare, it is important to grasp that the layer of people subject to immigration control in the UK is broader than those asylum-seekers. Consequently, while the different and inferior arrangements for asylum-seekers discussed later are of most significance in this book, there remain considerable welfare restrictions for many long-term residents. The history of increasingly restrictive immigration control in the UK, particularly since the 1960s as described earlier, means citizenship rights have been removed from groups of people who previously had them, for example, people from former colonies.

> Citizenship is regulated by the 1981 British Nationality Act which became operative on 1 January 1983. For most white people citizenship is not problematic. For many black people it is extremely problematic. The absolute right of abode is anything but absolute. (Cohen 2001, p.46)

Anyone who is not a citizen with the right of abode is subject to the immigration rules which control who can come and stay before, during and after entry. At the heart of the operation of the rules is the issue of maintenance and accommodation; applicants wishing to stay or join family must show they will be maintained and accommodated adequately without recourse to public funds (Seddon 2002, p.328). The list of those things considered to be public funds is ever increasing and currently includes: income support, job seeker's allowance, housing benefit, council tax benefit, working families tax credit, local authority housing, child benefit, disabled persons tax credit, attendance allowance, severe disablement allowance, invalid care allowance, disability living allowance (Cohen 2001, p.49). Additionally, claiming public funds without settlement can jeopardise status because it would be interpreted as an inability to accommodate and maintain one's family. Here again we see the absolute centrality of protecting public funds via immigration control and restricting access to a large range of benefits to non-citizens. To underline the reality of this, long-term residents in the UK must satisfy these conditions if they are to reunite their families by bringing dependants into the country. These may be children, grandparents, extended family and spouses or fiancées. In addition, even for those with settlement, claimants of job seeker's allowance, income support, housing benefit and council tax must satisfy the 'habitual residence test'. This was introduced in 1994 and has had a disproportionate effect on black and Asian claimants.

> Advice agencies in Birmingham and Yorkshire in 1997 reported that 90% of their cases involving the test were minority ethnic claimants, whilst other agencies gave examples of unfairness, bias or overt racism. (Patterson 2002, p.169)

The interpretation of whether someone is habitually resident is open to the judgement of the worker assessing the case and regular trips abroad will be interpreted in a problematic way. Regular trips abroad are often a feature of the lives of those citizens living in divided families who are, of course, overwhelmingly black.

In addition to these restrictions on access to welfare, an 'efficiency scrutiny' introduced by the Tory administration in 1993 was a purposeful attempt to improve a largely ad hoc system of internal immigration control to create a more systematic and universal system. The scrutiny essentially focused on key central and local government bodies and their relationship with the Home Office's Immigration and Nationality Directorate. This recognised that much information about immigration status and claims on welfare was in the public domain via agencies like the Employment Service, the NHS, the DSS and local government, but was uncoordinated. The Government have explicitly made those agencies accountable for 'identifying claimants who may be ineligible for a benefit or service by virtue of their immigration status; and to encourage local authorities to pass information to the IND about suspected immigration offenders' (Home Office 1996). Clearly, there are significant issues here for workers in welfare who are drawn into this internal policing of immigration.

The shift to asylum

As migration for long-term settlement has all but ended in the UK, as well as across Europe, attention has shifted to asylum-seekers. As discussed earlier, these categories are simply constructs which fit particular historical circumstances. Current ideology, which constructs the economic migrant as an organised traveller wishing to gain from the British labour market and the British welfare state, also constructs the asylum-seeker as a poor, burdensome and costly addition which *we* can ill afford. These constructions have allowed a completely inferior system of welfare to be legitimised for asylum-seekers, again underlining the inherent link between the control of immigration and access to welfare. It was not until the 1990s that we had specific legislation concerning 'asylum-seekers'. The Asylum and Immigration Appeals Act 1993 and the Asylum and Immigration Act 1996 began to restrict the social rights of asylum-seekers, e.g. by withdrawing welfare benefits from in-country asylum applicants (Sales 2002). The 1996 Act shifted responsibility to local authorities and eventually the Labour Government introduced the 1999 Immigration and Asylum Act. This key piece of legislation formalised this category ' asylum-seeker' and removed entitlement to a range of non-contributory, family and disability benefits from persons subject to immigration control. This list of benefits is essentially the same as those considered to be public funds (see above). The Act extended the use of vouchers to this group and created a system of compulsory dispersal. A new centralised agency was created, the National Asylum Support Service (NASS), which enters into arrangements with both voluntary organizations and local authorities regarding arrangements for asylum-seekers. Subsistence is given by money or vouchers to the value of 70 per cent of basic income support, meaning asylum-seekers live well below that level considered subsistence. Housing is organised via consortia of local authorities and voluntary organizations, with asylum-seekers being dispersed into zones across the country on a no-choice basis.

> The 1999 Act represents a watershed. Part VI of the Act, 'support for asylum-seekers', constitutes a qualitative leap in the link between welfare and immigration status. It accomplishes this by reducing assistance to asylum-seekers to a form of Poor Law. (Cohen 2001, p.24)

A further concern relating to the operation of the scheme involves the level of surveillance asylum-seekers are subjected to. NASS must be informed in the event of a whole range of changes in people's lives, including temporary periods of absence from supported accommodation. Later in this chapter and more fully in the rest of the book, the complex repercussions of this inferior welfare arrangement will be looked at. Relevant local authorities have established asylum teams, whose responsibility it is to sort out accommodation, money and other basics like schooling and GP services, but what is already clear is that lack of more in-depth practical and emotional help is having devastating consequences for asylum-seekers. Ideologically and practically separating a group of people out from mainstream services is having profound effects on their day-to-day life experiences and is contributing to a climate of hostility to this group.

The Immigration and Asylum Act 1999 has redefined to some extent the role of local authority social services, most significantly in the community care arena. Many care in the community functions are now dependant on immigration status with exclusions for those 'subject to immigration control'. The detail of this will be explored in further chapters. Research by Roberts and Harris (2002) shows the consequences of disabled asylum-seekers not accessing mainstream disability benefits, but also the need for community care assessments to be done to ensure optimum access to resources. Recent Appeal Court rulings have reaffirmed local authority responsibilities, for example, when community care needs arise out of illness (*Community Care* 24.10.02). Refugee Council research has also shown how social services departments have not been providing appropriate help to asylum-seekers discharged from hospitals because of financial costs (*Community Care* 20.3.03). Much of this indicates that for ill, disabled and older asylum-seekers, accessing community care provision is by no means straightforward and it has taken the courts to 'persuade' local authorities of their responsibilities to this group.

> This issue was considered in the Westminster City Council v NASS court case in April 2001 and again in three further cases in Spring 2002 involving disabled asylum-seekers and the London Boroughs of Enfield and Lambeth. All four cases confirmed that local authorities have a responsibility to meet the needs of disabled asylum-seekers. In the latter cases this extended to providing residential accommodation. (Roberts and Harris 2002, p.6)

Similarly, at the moment school age children of asylum-seekers are entitled to education, including a school place, free school meals and, following means testing, support with travel and school uniform. According to Neil Remsbery of the National Children's Bureau (*Community Care* 19.9.02), some social services departments have argued that they cannot offer this support, but they have a responsibility, including the provision of special educational needs assessments and support, where relevant.

Research concerning the health care needs of asylum-seekers (BMA 2002; Burnett and Fassil 2002; Johnson 2003) indicates that whilst many asylum-seekers are healthy on arrival, dispersal put incredible strains on health, particularly for older people and pregnant women. Accessing suitable health care support remains a significant issue, with health care needs invisible in the decision-making processes regarding dispersal. General practitioners are also treating asylum-seekers without access to medical histories as a result of high mobility. The cost and availability of interpreting and translating services were issues frequently raised by medical staff. The health problems which asylum-seekers develop are recognised as predominantly to do with poverty and poor housing conditions, as well as those originating from physical and mental torture or other conditions from which they have escaped.

> There is evidence to suggest that the health status of new entrants may worsen in the 2 to 3 years after entry to the UK...dispersal has left asylum-seekers marginalized and impoverished and insufficient resources have been allocated to the NHS in dispersal areas to meet the special health needs of this group. Living in poverty, with severely

restricted freedom compounds their physical and mental problems. (BMA 2002, p.6)

Yet the debate surrounding asylum and health has focused not on poor health provision, but on exaggerated claims regarding the burdens being placed on the NHS. In similar language to that targeted at Jews at the turn of the last century and black migrants in the period following World War II (see Cohen and Hayes 1998), asylum-seekers are blamed both for bringing in diseases like TB and for using up valuable health care resources. In January 2003, the Shadow Health Secretary Dr Liam Fox wrote to all primary care and hospital trusts in the UK, suggesting that British citizens were being denied access to treatment on the NHS because of 'preferential access' given to asylum-seekers (Kundnani 2003). He pursued the idea of 'health tourism', suggesting asylum-seekers and migrants choose the UK precisely because of the NHS.

> What these scare stories ignore is that, since the 1980s, doctors and hospitals have been forced to question new patients about their immigration status, to prevent non-emergency hospital treatment being given to 'illegals'. Doctors have been given the added burden of having to become immigration police and asylum-seekers have been subjected to a second class service. Numerous reports have documented the cruelty that has been meted out by the system to asylum-seekers. (Kundnani 2003)

Add to this the increasing reliance by NASS on accommodation provided by private sector landlords, against some of whom there have been allegations of poor standards, malpractice and even profiteering (Shelter cited in CAB 2002, p.9), and it is not difficult to see why health care would deteriorate. Citizens Advice Bureaux (CAB) research gives examples of accommodation without cooking facilities, mice-infested properties and families contracting scabies from NASS-provided accommodation, not to mention numerous examples of racial abuse and harassment (CAB 2002, p.16). Complaints against private landlords who have contracts with NASS have involved:

- landlords classifying unrelated single adults as a family to circumvent the law on multi-occupancy
- landlords buying up cheap property and quickly recouping their outlay
- asylum-seekers left without support or information on local community services. (*Manchester Evening News* 29.9.00, cited in Cohen 2001, p.215)

As refugee support agencies have become overwhelmed by the volume of people needing support, other agencies like CAB have been left picking up the pieces (CAB 2002). Their research shows the delays and inefficiencies of the NASS system leading to devastating destitution on the part of asylum-seekers. Some of these involved people with serious mental health problems.

> The creation of what is essentially an entirely separate welfare support system for asylum-seekers inevitably carries the potential for problems at the necessary interface between that system and other public services, such as health and education. (CAB 2002, p.23)

Implications for social work

The experience of restricted rights and poorer access to welfare for many long-term residents subject to immigration control has largely gone unnoticed in most social work arenas. An exception has been in criminal justice work, where the commission of offences can lead those without citizenship to be at risk of deportation (see Cohen 2001). That harsh reality did lead to the development of models of good practice and some of those issues will be further developed in a chapter of this book. Whilst the restrictions in access to health, education, benefits and housing outlined in this chapter have impacted greatly on the lives of this group, social work as a profession has intervened only minimally. What has forced the issue onto the profession's agenda has been to some extent the construction and separation of this category 'asylum-seeker' and the scale of the imposed destitution. Now social work finds itself confronted with an inescapable reality as dispersal places *real* people with very real problems into areas without networks or traditions of support. The asylum-seeker's journey ends up in isolated and hostile terrain and essentially life under a Poor Law system. So, whether it is unaccompanied children defined as 'in need' under the Children Act, older or disabled asylum-seekers beginning to present for community care assessments, or indeed the presentation of mental health problems likely to be significant for this group, the work is now emerging in and across the full range of social work contexts. In statutory, voluntary and private settings and within mainstream and specialist provision this process is occurring. Workers in these agencies are often unprepared to deal with both the practical and ethical issues this raises, and there exists no serious or systematic preparation on social work courses or in practice settings. All of this leaves workers ill equipped to manage the complex situations of those subject to immigration control and their differing needs and entitlements.

A further theme within this book is a concern with the growth of internal immigration control systems and the role of welfare professionals within them. We have seen in this chapter how housing, DSS and health workers are now part of the infrastructure of enforcement, and this raises questions about ourselves. The provision of information to the IND, the gatekeeping of services to asylum-seekers and others subject to immigration control, the monitoring of status and movement by this group, are all tasks beginning to fall to social care workers. Further chapters in this book will consider in more detail the implications of this, but essentially social work now has a choice: we can campaign, defend and battle for service users who have immigration problems or we can simply be part of the Home Office internal immigration infrastructure. We can develop models of good practice or we can simply implement the new 'Poor Law'.

The purpose of this book then is to offer practitioners in social work and social care a framework for understanding the relationship between immigration control and welfare delivery and the changing role of social work within that and, most importantly, to improve social work interventions. Some of this will be done by exploring the tensions inherent in the work by using case study examples in different practice settings and by offering models of good practice. Over the coming years we expect many articles and books will be produced in this area. However, at the moment there is no substantial literature for workers to draw from and this book attempts to kick-start the process. The contributors are all academics, practitioners or student practitioners who have a track record of engaging with this work. The team not only have an emerging expertise in the practicalities of this work, but a clear position of opposition to immigration controls and a first-hand understanding of their destructiveness. We are informed by historical and political frameworks, which hold that immigration controls are inherently racist, not only in terms of whom they exclude, but also in terms of the internal policing of all black residents in the UK who must account for their right to welfare. The somewhat depressing history of immigration control outlined in this chapter has another side to it: a history of resistance. That resistance is most often located in those communities directly affected but, for over a hundred years, has drawn in others who see the chaos, destructiveness, pain and irrationality of immigration control. Social work and related professions now need a louder voice in that battle for resistance.

References

Batsleer, J. and Humphries, B. (eds) (2000) *Welfare, Exclusion and Political Agency.* London: Routledge.

BMA (2002) *Asylum-seekers: Meeting their Healthcare Needs.* London: BMA Publications Unit.

Burnett, A. and Fassil, Y. (2002) *Meeting the Health Needs of Refugees and Asylum-seekers in the UK.* NHS Publications.

CAB (2002) *Process Error: CAB Clients' Experience of the NASS.* CAB Publications.

Cohen, N. (13.10.02)'How frightening are they?' *The Observer.*

Cohen, S. (1996) 'Anti-Semitism, immigration controls and the welfare state.' In D. Taylor (ed) *Critical Social Policy: A Reader.* London: Sage.

Cohen, S. (2001) *Immigration Controls, the Family and the Welfare State.* London: Jessica Kingsley Publishers.

Cohen, S. (2002) 'The local state of immigration controls.' *Critical Social Policy 22,* 3, 518–543.

Cohen, S. (2003) *No One is Illegal: Asylum and Immigration Control Past and Present.* London: Trentham Books.

Cohen, S. and Hayes, D. (1998) *They Make You Sick: Essays on Immigration Controls and Health.* Manchester: Manchester Metropolitan University and Greater Manchester Immigration Aid Unit.

Cohen, S., Humphries, B. and Mynott, E. (eds) (2002) *From Immigration Controls to Welfare Controls.* London: Routledge.

Community Care (19.9.02) 'Seeking education.'

Community Care (24.10.02) 'Council loses fight over cancer sufferer.'

Community Care (20.3.03) 'Discharged asylum-seekers not getting support.'

Gainer, B. (1972) *The Alien Invasion.* London: Heinemann.

Garrard, J.A. (1971) *The English and Immigration: A Comparative Study of the Jewish Influx 1880–1910. London: Oxford University Press.*

Ginsburg, N. (1989) 'Institutional racism and local authority housing.' *Critical Social Policy 8,* 24 (3), 4–19.

Gordon, P. (1983) 'Medicine, racism and immigration control.' *Critical Social Policy 13,* 7 (1), 6–20.

Gordon, P. and Newnham, A. (1985) *Passport to Benefits: Racism in Social Security.* London: CPAG and Runnymede Trust.

Hayes, D. (2000) 'Outsiders within: the role of welfare in the internal control of immigration.' In J. Batsleer and B. Humphries (eds) *Welfare, Exclusion and Political Agency.* London: Routledge.

Hayes, D. (2002) 'From aliens to asylum-seekers: a history of immigration controls and welfare in Britain.' In S. Cohen, B. Humphries and E. Mynott (eds) *From Immigration Controls to Welfare Controls.* London: Routledge.

Hayter, T. (2000) *Open Borders: The Case against Immigration Controls.* London: Pluto Press.

HM Inspector of Aliens (1906) *Annual Report,* Cd.3473, 1xvi.

Home Office Circular to Local Authorities in the UK (1996) *Exchange of Information with the IND of the Home Office*. Ref. IMG/96 1176/1193/23.

Johnson, M.R.D. (2003) *Asylum-seekers in Dispersal: Healthcare Issues*. Home Office.

Jones, A. (1998) *The Child Welfare Implications of UK Immigration Policy*. Manchester: Manchester Metropolitan University.

Kundnani, A. (2003) 'The hate industry.' *Institute of Race Relations News* 6 March, via website www.irr.org.uk/2003/march

Marriott, J. (1999) 'In darkest England: the poor, the crowd and race in the nineteenth century metropolis.' In P. Cohen (ed) *New Ethnicities, Old Racisms*. London: Zed Books.

Miles, R. (1989) *Racism*. London: Routledge.

Mynott, E. (2002) 'Nationalism, racism and immigration control.' In S. Cohen, B. Humphries and E. Mynott (eds) 2002/2002)

Patterson, T. (2002) 'From safety net to exclusion: ending social security in the UK for "persons from abroad".' In S. Cohen, B. Humphries and E. Mynott (eds) 2002/2002/)

Refugee Council Briefing (Dec 2002a) 'The Nationality, Immigration and Asylum Act 2002: Changes to the Asylum System in the UK.'

Refugee Council Newsletter (Dec 2002b) 'Nailing press myths about refugees', via website: www.refugeecouncil.org.uk/news/myths

Roberts, K. and Harris, J. (2002) *Disabled People in Refugee and Asylum-seeking Communities*. Bristol: Policy Press and Joseph Rowntree Foundation.

Sales, R. (2002) 'The deserving and the undeserving? Refugees, asylum-seekers and welfare in Britain.' *Critical Social Policy 22*, 3, 456–478.

Searle, G. (1971) *The Quest for National Efficiency*. Oxford: Blackwell.

Seddon, D. (2002) *Immigration, Nationality and Refugee Law Handbook*. London: JCWI.

Semmell, B. (1960) *Imperialism and Social Reform: English Social and Political Thought 1895–1914*. London: Allen and Unwin.

Sivanandan, A. (2002) 'The contours of global racism.' *Institute of Race Relations News* 26 November, via website: www.irr.org/2002/november

Williams, F. (1989) *Social Policy: A Critical Introduction*. Cambridge: Polity Press.

Williams, F. (1996) 'Racism and the discipline of social policy: a critique of welfare theory.' In D. Taylor (ed) *Critical Social Policy: A Reader*. London: Sage.

Chapter 2

The Construction
and Reconstruction of Social Work

Beth Humphries

Introduction

As part of the task of setting the context of this book, it is necessary to examine the changes that have been wrought in social work over the past 20 years. I have described this elsewhere (Humphries 2002) as a move 'from welfare to authoritarianism', which, although it is a useful title for a piece on the increasing involvement of social work in internal immigration controls, implies that at some time in the past social work was benign, and somehow has moved to being an oppressive arm of a totalitarian state. The truth is more complex and more subtle than this, for social work has always been a tool for disciplining the poor as well as a profession genuinely concerned with their welfare. It could be argued (as do Jones and Novak 1999) that the social democratic welfare state should be seen as a brief departure from a more ruthless form of social policy that has characterized the state's response to some of the poorest people in society. This book describes the treatment meted out to people subject to immigration control in the contemporary context, but we should not be surprised to learn that ideas about the 'deserving' and 'undeserving' poor and restrictions on their mobility, the criminalization of their character and the withholding of the means of their survival, are old themes, reworked as expedient to the requirements of capital in each era of British history.

Social work: a short history

It has been argued that immigration policy in this country has become a new Poor Law (Cohen 2003), but what exactly does this mean? O'Brien (2000) charts a history of social systems from the late Middle Ages, the themes of poverty, 'idleness' and destitution, and his chapter is worth reading for this longer history. Throughout this period, concerns running through these systems were of the cost of the consequences of poverty, and of the 'threat' posed by the poor and the unemployed, especially since the emergence of capitalist relations of production. A series of Poor Laws in the 15th and 16th centuries progressively emphasized family responsibility – parents became responsible for children, for grandparents and for disabled relatives. They also restricted the mobility of the poor in order to control the flow of labour, and magistrates had powers to remove poor people away from the cities. In the 19th century the old Poor Law was regarded as not ruthless enough (Novak 1998) and further legislation brought a new social discipline. The Poor Law Amendment Act 1834 introduced workhouses, one of the most feared and hated aspects of the changes. None of these themes is unfamiliar in relation to current policy on refugees and asylum-seekers.

The rapid expansion of towns as a result of industrialization created new problems of poor housing, unsanitary living conditions and ill health. The resulting misery, disorder and disruption caused both concern and fear amongst the middle classes. The responses to social problems, then, formed the structure that would dominate the provision of personal care well into the 20th century (Clarke 1993). Institutions that classified people as 'normal' and 'abnormal' swallowed up many working class people defined as deviant on grounds of age, gender, disability, 'race' and sexuality. Meanwhile, the 'deserving' poor – those outside the walls – needed to be taught how to behave as good citizens. This was the role allocated to voluntary visitors and later, to social workers. The move from volunteer to full-time paid workers as part of state agencies took place during the first half of the 20th century. With the expansion of welfare came opportunities for a kind of professionalism, dependent largely on working in state bureaucracies:

> The new bureaucratic professions…do not resist the extension of state power…for they have no choice but to be public employees. On the contrary, they generally welcome the extension of state power, for it is the only source of such power as they themselves possess; indeed these occupational groups owe their very existence to the power of the state. (Reade 1987, p.126)

As a result, the specific power associated with social work came to be that of gatekeepers controlling access to resources, and using the firm but gentle means of casework to evaluate need and decide upon who should be allocated resources and under what conditions. Their statutory power and their claim to expertise reinforced this position, so that social workers have always experienced a tension between a genuine desire to help, and a very real position of inequality and power over those they called their 'clients'. When Cohen (2003) speaks of a new Poor Law for those subject to immigration controls, he alludes to the modern form of a system that classifies, criminalizes and removes from society those constructed as destitute or dangerous. He is referring to the administering of a less-than-poverty-line income, and for those designated as 'deserving', an obligation to live by values that require re-education about 'British culture' and allegiance to the British queen. Social workers are amongst other state officials who oversee this system.

We are living in a period post-welfare state, but even during the post-war period of the welfare state, humanitarian motives did not drive welfare policy. Rather social work and other 'caring' professions held out the promise of changes in the behaviour of the very poor and the way they raised their children; thus the poor would become less reliant on the state and its resources. Policies towards de-institutionalization for example, although couched in the language of the desirability of 'care in the community', sprang primarily from increasing alarm about the cost of residential care.

So the ways social work has been constructed over time demonstrate this mix of humanitarian motives on the one hand and the willing arm of the state to control the behaviour of certain social groups on the other. Indeed, they are so intimately intertwined, it could be argued that at times 'care' *is* control. At different junctures one or the other presses for dominance, a continuous struggle that is an important dynamic in the on-going construction of social work. Powell (2001) emphasizes the importance of this struggle: 'Social work's capacity to survive depends upon its legitimacy as an authentic "humanising voice", rather than simply a conservative profession conveniently wrapping itself in the rhetoric of the market' (p.161).

The social work business

Although concerns about cost and activities related to controlling the poor have always been a feature of state provision, over the past 30 years there has been a seismic paradigm shift, resulting in a lurch to a neo-liberal position. Since 1979 when the Conservative government came to power, the welfare state has been transformed. Drakeford (2000) described the essential aims of government as: to extend the rationalities and technologies of the marketplace to the provision of public services; to reduce the burden of social responsibility accepted by the state and to transfer the delivery of those residual services, for which it retained an obligation, away from public bodies and towards voluntary or independent providers. The compliance of social work in making welfare subject to economic imperatives was part of a Conservative modernization agenda, continued and intensified by the New Labour government. The belief is that economic objectives can be met through welfare, thus bringing a business mentality to social care and social work.

Although social workers have liked to believe that they work in a semi-autonomous profession, steered by its internal values and theories, in fact the occupation has always been driven by the changing global and national economic context. Nevertheless, before 1979 the dominant discourse was one of welfare as distinctive in that it was funded out of taxation and did not involve payment by its clients. Since then however, welfare has increasingly been regarded as a commodity and the culture of capitalism, business thinking and practices has transformed it into a commercial enterprise with a goal, as far as is possible, of making a profit (see Harris 2003). Community-based services are now purchased rather than provided directly by social services departments and new purchaser/provider structures and markets have been widely established. As Fine and Leopold (1993) have observed:

> Free market economics seeks to sweep aside all the political and social objectives that distinguish public from private provision in order to subject all economic activity to the iron-clad rules of the market...public provision is treated simply as an alternative to private sector provision. (p.300)

In other words, public provision as an *ideal* is now irrelevant in any decisions about procuring care. It is not a matter of choosing between ideologies, rather the calculation is one of cost-benefits prescribed by market economics.

The business legacy left by the Thatcher regime has been adopted by the New Labour government, which has developed it and elaborated on its detail. Although the rhetoric of New Labour deals in ethical principles and the aim of 'social justice', its claims to the moral high ground are based on the needs of global capital: 'It insists that the greatest wrongs are now being done by those who rely on collective provision, not those who exploit the skills and energies of their employees' (Jordan 2000, p.2). The role of social work is increasingly dealing in the business of *ascertaining eligibility* for services, not in bringing humanitarian values or those pertaining to 'rights' to bear on any particular situation. Agencies have been transformed into technological machines, where workers are limited to classifying customers into packages of care. A key aspect of this is that admission to services is highly conditional on increasingly narrow criteria of eligibility.

Chris Jones' research reported vividly the ways organizational changes have affected work in state organizations. As an interviewer, he said he

> was regaled by talk of budgets, and not only about their appalling paucity to meet the needs of clients, but also the manner in which budget management and control has become the key concern of the agency, stripping out its welfare ideals in the process. This was no series of disjointed factors…but an inter-connecting series of processes that created a new working environment within state social work: a new type of highly regulated and much more mundane and routinized relationship with clients which could not be described as social work. (Jones 2001, p.552)

It is not surprising then that the behaviour of social workers towards people subject to immigration controls appears to have little concern for the ethical questions raised by their being drawn into policing immigration status, or the morality of their complicity in leaving asylum-seekers without money or accommodation, or the politics, the quasi-market mentality (Jordan 2000). The job is seen as a technical and mechanistic routine. However, with this has come a demoralization of workers in social services departments and a recognition that this is not what they entered the profession to do. There is still a hankering after the 'helping' role and the desire to assist people in finding ways out of their troubles. For some social workers the only solution to the stress and burn-out this creates is to leave the profession altogether.

The turn to authoritarianism

Along with the business mentality has come a new moralistic, conformist and prescriptive agenda of both Tory and New Labour governments. For New Labour this is in the form of what is known as 'tough love' – rewards for those who conform to the government's agenda, and harsh punishment for those who prove to be difficult and troublesome. As a result the prison population in the UK is now one of the highest in the 'developed' world (Jones and Novak 1999). Not only has there been developing a preoccupation with criminalization, detection, conviction and punishment of people who have committed crimes, but new kinds of criminality are being defined such as 'anti-social behaviour', with sanctions available for children as young as ten. The boundary between 'deserving' and 'undeserving' is clear in the punishments for those who fail on the range of 'New Deal' programmes, for example, or neglect to sign up for one. The New Labour government regards work as the main route out of poverty and has invested billions of pounds in education, training and employment. However, the sanctions imposed on those who do not play by the rules include an increase in the time they receive a reduced rate of benefit, to create a 'class of citizen entirely beyond the safety net, left without any form of income whatsoever to meet even the most basic of survival needs' (Butler and Drakeford 2001, p.13). So along with the aim of *independence* as a central goal of government policy is a parallel aim of *obedience*, ensured through surveillance of various sorts. Social work and social care is targeted as one of the state functions that will support this system. Butler and Drakeford argue that the New Labour government seldom mentions social work directly, and when it does emerge in New Labour vocabulary, it is almost always associated with the government 'in social authoritarian mode' (p.14). They give the example of the modernization of mental health legislation, which has entailed draconian shifts in policy, involving the enforced treatment of patients against their will and the loss of freedom for individuals who have committed no offence to warrant detention. Social workers are seen by the government as playing a 'key role' in this new assertiveness (Butler and Drakeford 2001, p.14). These authors contend that this alignment of social work with authoritarianism is characteristic of the Government's wider thinking:

> Social work is part, not of an inclusive, but of an incorporative agenda, in which awkward, troublesome and risky individuals who do not play by the rules of their own volition, must be made to do so. The social worker appears in the open in this government's lexicon only in its often deeply conservative family policy, its shockingly reactionary approach to youth justice, its conflation of crime and disorder, or in the field of mental health in the way that we have described. The danger is that again an accommodation will be made and that the social work enterprise will accept what is on offer. (*ibid.*, p.15)

The White Paper, *Modernising Social Services* (DoH 1998), and the Care Standards Act 2000 that followed it were informed by the two objectives of independence and obedience, and introduced 'new supervisory bodies and scrutiny committees, new layers and tiers of government, and new agencies and experts, to ensure that its goals and standards are accomplished and implemented' (Jordan 2000, p.66). There are already signs that if local authorities are seen to be failing in their duties, these will be removed to other agencies, putting them under the direct control of central or regional government, as modelled by NASS (National Asylum Seeker Support).

Disciplining social work

As implied above, social work has always been deeply ambivalent about the poor, which has led to a weakening of that aspect of its response that is angry about the structures which maintain poverty and stigmatization. At the same time, there have been times when social workers have attempted to shrug off, or at least resist, the function of control placed upon them. These resistances were by no means mass rebellions. Most social workers, although aware of the depth of poverty and human suffering and of the limitations of their role to change this, have been content to continue with individualistic models of practice and ignore any attempt to change social structures. Nevertheless, in the 1970s there were rebellions, including a strike, arising out of the Community Development Project and the involvement of radical social workers (Langan 1993); there were challenges from feminism, the lesbian and gay movement and the disability movement, all of which left their mark on social work. Particularly effective was the anti-racist movement in the 1980s and early 1990s, which succeeded in achieving changes in the rules and requirements for social work education, including the statement that racism is endemic in all British institutions, and that social workers have an obligation to challenge the practices of these institutions.

This was not well received by government and some quarters of the media, and the 'political correctness' furore that resulted led to a determination to bring social work into line (and incidentally coincided with the New Right project of subjecting state services to market principles). Within two years of the notion of 'endemic racism' appearing in Paper 30, CCETSW (Central Council for Education and Training in Social Work, the then validating body for social work) was forced to remove it and dilute the 'dangerous aspects' of the policy (Webb 1996).

There followed a period of ensuring that social workers became obedient employees by introducing narrow training requirements based on 'competence' – behavioural change rather than understanding of social ills, and an increasing surveillance of practice. Now the nature of social work has two dominant strands, both of them destructive: it is run as a business on business values, and it has developed a much more explicit function as an authoritarian, policing occupation. The practice of social work and of probation has shifted decisively towards the policing of those seen as constituting or being at 'risk', and training has progressively focused on 'high risk' situations.

Butler and Drakeford (2001, p.10) observe, 'The translation of ideology into values, of critical capacity into competency and of collective struggles into an individualistic anti-oppressive practice all sit comfortably enough with the paradigm'. The anti-oppressive element is no more than tokenism. All of this is manifested in plans for the new social work degree to be introduced in 2003/2004. Although at last the Government has acknowledged that a minimum of three years' study at degree level is required for the practice of social work, the curriculum is prescribed by the Department of Health, the 'National Occupational Standards', and an *inspection* role for the newly-formed GSCC (General Social Care Council), where formerly there were 'advisers' at the level of social work education. The direction of the new degree follows the changes in social work practice towards managing, gatekeeping and controlling resources and behaviour. The dominant preoccupation of state social work is with criteria of eligibility for services. The role of knowledge from the social sciences and its importance for understanding social problems and their origins is greatly diminished, and anecdotal evidence suggests that courses attempting to preserve the academic aspects are coming under pressure from GSCC inspectors to reduce them even further. Moreover, rhetoric about oppression and anti-oppressive practice, and racism and anti-racism has virtually disappeared from the requirements, to be replaced by bland and trite references to appreciating and encouraging 'diversity'.

Disciplining the poor

Coupled with this, over recent years there has been an increasing obsession with 'assessing risk', so that the policing role now dominates over any urge to support service users. Social work has become a residual occupation, dealing with those who are defined as in need of control. The consequences of a globalized free market economy are deepening poverty and inequality, alienation, a denial of democracy and an erosion of citizenship. The use of curfews and tagging for offenders, the increased use of imprisonment ('life means life') as a tool of control, the surveillance of the poor (especially if they are poor single women with children), the draconian laws introduced to tackle the 'terrorist threat', including increasing the time suspects can be held without charge, are all indicative of the surveillance society in which we now live. This is mirrored by a willingness of others to surrender their civil rights in a world that seems increasingly frightening. Social work is one of an army of state officials that support this system. A number of the chapters in this book describe research that confirms the function of social work where internal immigration controls are concerned, and in many cases note the worrying ways social workers legitimate and justify it. Their activities are increasingly monitored and regulated by the state through the General Social Care Council (GSCC), accountable to what Jordan (2000, p.128) calls the 'Panoptican Minister' (the Secretary of State).

Both social work practice and social work research have been gathered into this mentality of efficiency, calculability and predictability to the extent that the idea of 'public services' has been degraded.

> 'Evidence-based practice', dependent on positivist and behaviourist methods to identify 'what works?' largely excludes other ways of knowing and is more concerned with changing behaviour of those refusing to or unable to conform, than it is with a critical understanding of people's circumstances. (Humphries 2003)

Part of the strategy is to bring social workers into line through regulation and surveillance. Managers are concerned with budgets, value for money and 'efficiency' at practice levels, and GSCC inspectors exist to ensure conformity.

The role of the voluntary sector

Statutory social work is not the whole of social work. The tradition of social work in the voluntary sector is a longer one than in the state sector. The possibilities for innovation, identifying gaps in services and radical approaches to practice have always been important functions of the voluntary sector. Opposition to oppressive state practices has also been an important role. However, funding is increasingly dependent on voluntary groups carrying out Government policy, and the autonomy of such groups has been dramatically reduced. The voluntary social work and social care sector is subject to inspection by GSCC. Its activities are also constrained by Government funding and the restrictions that accompany such resources.

Cohen (2002) describes the ways NASS has drawn the voluntary sector into its policing of asylum-seekers. He quotes the draft Process Manual for the Asylum Support System (Home Office 1999) that suggests the voluntary sector might encourage asylum-seekers to seek help from friends and sources other than NASS:

> In other words, voluntary sector agencies, whose role is normally to assist claimants in accessing and maximising state benefits, are now expected to actively discourage asylum-seekers from even the poor law support left to them. (p.147)

Some voluntary immigration advice groups have adopted a principle not to take central government funding, but do accept local government funding. This was effective during the period of Conservative government, where the local authority may have been governed by a Labour council which may have been only too happy to support the aims of radical voluntary groups against the Government. With the shift to a New Labour Government at Westminster, local Labour-led councils face dilemmas in supporting local groups who oppose Government policies. This has happened in the case of immigration controls, for example: before New Labour came to power, radical Labour councils willingly offered financial support and sent councillors as representatives to sit on management committees of organizations opposing Government policy on immigration and asylum. Since New Labour has continued the harsh policies of the previous Conservative Government, such local authorities are less keen to be seen to support these organizations. In many cases this has resulted in more restrictive conditions attached to grants offered to them, forcing them to look for funding elsewhere and increasing the pressure on their activities. The fracas concerning giving a national lottery grant to the NCADC (National Committee for Anti-Deportation Campaigns), which took place during 2002, illustrates the problems.

Social work and immigration controls

In a climate which has seen a narrowing of focus, a concern with value for money and an authoritarian turn, it should come as no surprise that social work is one of a number of professions charged with the task of tracking movements, checking on status, deciding on eligibility for and administering poor relief, and ultimately withdrawing relief and accommodation from those seen as 'undeserving'. These are tasks emanating from values concerned with investigation, rationing, gatekeeping and surveillance. These activities have been effectively separated from ethics, sensitivity, accountability and empathy about what *should* be the role of professional practice. In the modern, disciplinary state, this separation of practices from morals, this isolation of the activities of workers from other processes, this fragmentation of legal author-ity and political motives have led to an unreflective enforcement of inhuman policies. These practices are undertaken with scant regard for the rights, the suffering and the dignity of those affected by controls (see Humphries 2002).

But there is more to it than this, as will become clear to readers of this book, and as the first chapter has already identified. Cohen (2003) speaks of 'economic' racism and 'social' racism. This chapter has been concerned largely with the links between the construction and reconstruction of social work as a response to economic imperatives, and the ways in which state workers have been called upon to contribute to the control of the poor and to maintain unequal social relations. However, the other dimension, not divorced from poverty and exploitation but integral to it in the global marketplace, is a per-vasive, ruthless and vicious racism. I do not wish to enter here the debate about the relationship between racism and capitalism, save to say it is clear that the people who suffer most from the harsh effects of immigration controls come from backgrounds that are unlikely to be white, Christian and European. This is the case whether controls are external in defining who may enter the UK, or internal in the policing of welfare. Talk of anti-racist and anti-oppressive practice in social work is a nonsense, a self-deception and a hypocrisy, while social workers continue to accept without a murmur of protest their allocated role in the hounding, the harassment and the impover-ishment of some of the most vulnerable people on the planet. We hope this book will lead to conscientization (Friere 1972), to anger and to resistance to these oppressive practices.

The alternative voices never go away

All that has preceded this section of the chapter is rather pessimistic, but voices of resistance have never been silenced. The purpose of this part is to encourage those voices to speak out and to support others in their understand-ing, their protesting and their oppositional practice. Social work is not inevi-tably an arm of oppression. The profession has a choice to make a new moral effort, to find its anger about the plight of the poor, to engage its knowledge about the sources of inequality with a new sense of imperative and urgency. Asylum-seekers and others subject to immigration controls are a dramatic example of many regarded as undeserving, excluded, non-citizens, worthy only of derision, abysmal treatment and ultimate expulsion. We cannot be content with this culture of punishment instead of welfare, and the implica-tion in it to both statutory and voluntary workers.

There are examples in both the voluntary and statutory sectors of resistance to and defiance of the direction of Government policy (see Cohen 2002). In social work, amidst conservative and reactionary practice there is also a recurring thread of opposition to practices that exclude and condemn poor and oppressed people, and that use social work as a tool in that process. There exist groups that agitate against unequal practices in relation to disability, class, gender, 'race', sexuality and age, for example, with which some social workers are affiliated. In the field of immigration controls (which touches on all these dimensions of inequality), social workers and others have supported asylum-seekers in collective resistance through anti-deportation campaigns and trade unions. Collusion with the system is not inevitable or unavoidable. Social workers who regard themselves as anti-racist will view compliance with controls as offensive to this moral position.

It is time for a reconstruction of social work that draws on its radical historical strand and reinterprets this within a globalized and marketized context. The first step is a commitment to understanding the contemporary role of social work in this wider framework, leading to a praxis that involves action for change and the beating of a different drum. There are many who are waiting for such allies to help mobilize political forces that will seek to transform social structures. We hope this book will help in some small way towards such a goal.

References

Butler, I. and Drakeford, M. (2001) 'Which Blair Project? Communitarianism, social authoritarianism and social work.' *Journal of Social Work 1*, 1,7–19.

Clarke, J. (1993) 'The comfort of strangers: social work in context.' In J. Clarke (ed) *A Crisis in Care? Challenges to Social Work.* : London: Sage and Open University Press.

Cohen, S. (2002) 'Dining with the devil: the 1999 Immigration and Asylum Act and the voluntary sector.' In S. Cohen, B. Humphries and E. Mynott (eds) *From Immigration Controls to Welfare Controls.* London: Routledge.

Cohen, S. (2003) *No One is Illegal: Asylum and Immigration Control Past and Present.* Stoke-on-Trent: Trentham Books.

Department of Health (1998) *Modernising Social Services: promoting independence, improving protection, raising standards* (Cmd 4169). London: stationery office.

Drakeford, M. (2000) *Privatisation and Social Policy.* London: Longman

Fine, B. and Leopold, E. (1993) *The World of Consumption.* London: Routledge.

Friere, P. (1972) *Pedagogy of the Oppressed.* London: Penguin.

Harris, J. (2003) *The Social Work Business.* London: Routledge.

Home Office (1999) *Asylum-seekers' Support.* London: HMSO.

Humphries, B. (2002) 'From welfare to authoritarianism: the role of social work in immigration controls'. In S. Cohen, B. Humphries and E. Mynott (eds) *From Immigration Controls to Welfare Controls*. London: Routledge.

Humphries, B. (2003) 'What *else* counts as evidence in evidence-based social work?' *Social Work Education 22*, 1, 81–91.

Jones, C. and Novak T. (1999) *Poverty, Welfare and the Disciplinary State*. London: Routledge.

Jones, C. (2001) 'Voices from the Front Line: State Stocial Workers, and New Labour.' *British Journal of Social Work*, 31 (4), 547-562.

Jordan, B. (2000) *Social Work and the Third Way: Tough Love as Social Policy*. London: Sage.

Langan, M. (1993) 'The rise and fall of social work.' In J. Clarke (ed) *A Crisis in Care?* London, Sage and Open University.

Novak, T. (1998) *Poverty and the State: An Historical Sociology*. Milton Keynes: Open University Press.

O'Brien, M. (2000) 'Class struggle and the English Poor Laws.' In M. Lavalette and G. Mooney (eds) *Class Struggle and Social Welfare*. London: Routledge.

Powell, F. (2001) *The Politics of Social Work*. London: Sage.

Reade, E. (1987) *British Town and Country Planning*. Buckingham: Open University Press.

Webb, D. (1996) 'Regulation for Radicals: The state, CCETSW and the academy.' In N. Parton (ed) *Social Theory, Social Change and Social Work*. London: Routledge, pp.172–189.

Chapter 3

Refugees, Asylum-seekers, Welfare and Social Work

Beth Humphries

Introduction

During November 2002, Liz Timms, the Chair of the British Association of Social Workers, sent an open letter to the British Prime Minister, the First Minister of Scotland and ministers for Northern Ireland and Wales. The letter celebrated European Social Work Action Day, and was designed to celebrate the achievements of social work with children in the UK. Part of the letter read:

> Ahmed is an unaccompanied asylum-seeking child who arrived in this country traumatised and alone. This 15-year-old had become separated from all that is familiar to him and had travelled thousands of miles. He was vulnerable and at risk from exploitation. Not only was he the victim of torture and persecution, but he had seen family members killed before his eyes. His immediate needs were for our protection, and time to recover physically and psychologically from his trauma. He has been looked after by social workers in the UK. He has been given help in learning a new language, getting into school, meeting other people his own age, and been given help, support and counselling for his own unique and special experiences. To provide this total response to the needs of the young person, social workers have been trained in child protection, counselling in grief and loss. They have a sound knowledge of the law and the legal status of the young person and they have helped

him move from a troubled and scared environment to a safe and secure future. (*Professional Social Work*, December 2002, p.3)

This letter illustrates a problem that has dogged social work for many years. Although it is encouraging that so many resources have been brought into play to help this young man, sadly his experience is not a description of the services offered to refugees in general. What Liz Timms should have taken the opportunity to point out is that it is unusual for social services to accept readily that they have a responsibility for asylum-seeking children and other groups affected by immigration controls, and that there is an urgent need to include the needs of those affected by immigration controls explicitly, in strategic planning of services.

The quote is problematic because the content is individualistic and de-politicized. One example of good practice is chosen to imply that this level of support to people subject to immigration controls is typical of social workers' treatment of them. The letter ignores the social context in which such services operate – the criminalization of asylum-seekers by legislation, the Government and the media, the second-class system of welfare and housing set up to support them, and the new role carved out for social workers and other workers, in acting as agents of the Home Office through taking steps to confirm immigration status before offering a service. It also sets aside any research that has been done in this area. Such research suggests that social workers are ignorant of immigration law and its primacy over children's legislation (Jones 1998); many social workers are not even aware that unaccompanied asylum-seeking children come under the Children Act (Braybrooke 2002); services are in any case very poorly coordinated (Humphries and Mynott 2001); social workers still do not accept that the social problems faced by asylum-seekers and others subject to immigration controls are any of their business (Jordan and Jordan 2000); and local authorities have actively attempted to avoid their responsibilities under community care and national assistance legislation (Humphries 2002).

This chapter sets out to examine the evidence, and to ask what anti-racist practice has to do with this treatment from social services. It is based on on-going research taking place in northwest England, which is investigating the experiences of people subject to immigration controls (largely refugees and asylum-seekers), and the responses of social work agencies. It includes those who have been dispersed to rural as well as urban areas.

Support to refugee communities

The picture of support to refugee communities is varied and uncertain. The package of support provided by the National Asylum Support Service (NASS) includes a weekly allowance, which is valued below the poverty line at 70 per cent income support equivalent. Under the 1999 Immigration and Asylum Act, all people subject to immigration controls are denied council housing and a range of non-contributory benefits. These benefits comprise the core means-tested benefits of last resort (income support, income-based jobseeker's allowance, housing benefit, council tax benefit, a social fund payment) as well as family and disability benefits (child benefit, working families' tax credit, attendance allowance for disabled people, severe disablement allowance, invalid care allowance, disabled person's tax credit, disability living allowance). This shutting of the gate to a whole range of benefits, along with an income below the poverty line, inevitably leaves some families destitute. Research carried out by Refugee Council and Oxfam (2002) found a deeply disturbing picture:

> Often it is the most vulnerable who suffer from lack of additional support: parents worry for the health and well being of their children. Mothers who are unable to breastfeed because they are HIV+ or have other forms of ill health cannot afford to buy formula milk. Disabled asylum-seekers struggle to receive the extra help they need, or receive no additional help at all. (p.4)

Where asylum-seekers find themselves destitute they may seek help from local authorities, but again they may encounter incoherent services and confusion about responsibilities. Some local authorities have asylum-seekers teams who deal largely with families, though local authorities can claim a special grant for supporting unaccompanied asylum-seeking children (Humphries and Mynott 2001). Even where an asylum-seekers team exists, families may instead be allocated to the Social Services Department Children and Families team. The relationship between asylum teams and social work teams is far from clear. The extent to which asylum-seekers teams see social work as part of their remit is uncertain. Some deal entirely with housing matters, some do employ social workers, others would like to. With regard to social work teams, they are often not sure whether asylum-seekers and refugees are any part of their responsibility, and take the attitude that 'the asylum-seekers team will deal with them'. The possibilities for no service at all to be offered are obvious. Moreover, many social services departments have no particular policies or targets in relation to people subject to immigration controls. Families often depend on voluntary groups or local support groups who survive on piece-meal funding and whose continuing existence is, to say the least, precarious.

With regard to children, unaccompanied asylum-seeking and refugee children in England have the same legal entitlements as citizen children. This includes the right to education and health care, and the rights enshrined in the Children Act (1989) and the Human Rights Act (1998). Local authorities have responsibility for all unaccompanied children whom they define as 'in need'. Under the Children Act, they have an obligation to provide a range and level of services appropriate to each child's needs. All unaccompanied children are likely to meet the definition of 'children in need' under Section 17 and should be registered with the social services department of the local authority where they first present themselves. Local authorities with responsibility for more than one hundred unaccompanied children are able to claim a grant for each child. *Accompanied* asylum-seeking children have lesser rights than citizen children, as they are supported through the inferior NASS (described above) and do not ordinarily have access to the provisions of the Children Act or access to child welfare benefits, although they do have the right to education and health care.

Save the Children carried out research into the experiences of unaccom-panied asylum-seeking children in England (Stanley 2001) and found a pattern of chaotic, disturbing and inconsistent treatment of the young people interviewed, both on arrival and in their contact with services, including edu-cation, health and social services. Many of them had had a substantial wait for their initial asylum decision, as a result experiencing great anxiety. There was little evidence that the Home Office commitment to speed up asylum decision times has had any impact on their claims. In addition there was some evidence of inconsistent decision-making by the Home Office. This experience is con-firmed in relation to families and individuals interviewed in my current study.

In the Save the Children study, the level of care and type of support received by young separated refugees depended more on which social services department they arrived at rather than on their individual needs. There were particular concerns about 16- and 17-year-olds, who are not 'looked after' children, and many were living in poor quality and inappropriate accommo-dation, sometimes raising child protection issues where they were living with adults. The study found that some social services departments enter into con-tracts with private companies to provide care and accommodation. This arrangement leaves these young people without adequate support, and no access to a social worker or an independent complaints procedure. Although learning English was a priority for the young people interviewed, access to opportunities varied from area to area, adding to their sense of social exclusion. A substantial proportion faced bullying and harassment both inside and outside school. Many of the young separated asylum-seekers appeared to have emotional and possibly mental health problems, resulting from their experiences in their country of origin, and compounded by their experiences here. Few had accessed mental health services. The study highlighted enormous variety in the standard of care and protection, and a number of gaps in provision. Generally the treatment of these young people falls well below that required by the Children Act and the Human Rights Act.

In their contribution to the Save the Children study, Humphries and Mynott (2001) found that in Greater Manchester the care of unaccompanied asylum-seeking children relied on the efforts of individual social workers without any pre-planned procedures or specialist training. The social workers interviewed were aware of the trauma experienced by the young people and were concerned to offer what support they could. Some had spent much time following up resources. However they had not had any training in understanding the needs of this group, and had little knowledge of the relevant legislation or of the immigration status of the young people. They were vague as to the stage applications for asylum had reached. Moreover, asylum-seeking children demanded more of their time than others on their workload, and they already felt overburdened with work. The study concluded that

> the overall impression was of professionals who were caring and concerned, but unprepared for understanding or dealing with the particular needs of young separated asylum-seekers, and unsupported in material ways by their departments. (p.44)

A key contradiction for asylum-seeking children is that which exists between their immigration status on the one hand, and their status as 'children' on the other. The status of asylum-seekers carried lesser rights and often aroused antipathy or hostility. The status of 'child' brings enhanced rights as indicated above. In addition, the UK Government has reserved the right not to apply the UN Convention on the Rights of the Child (1998) to asylum-seeking and other non-citizen children (Martin 1998). Humphries and Mynott discovered some cases of discrimination where children were treated as 'illegal immigrants' and denied a place in school. There are other examples of legislation concerning children conflicting with legislation to ensure immigration control. When these conflicts have been tested legally, the need for immigration control has been accepted as paramount over the rights and welfare of children (Jones 1998). In a variety of ways there is clearly discrimination against asylum-seeking and refugee children, who need and should enjoy the same protection and the same promotion of their welfare as other children. Indeed their traumatic experiences in their country of origin and their flight to the UK, as the research confirms, may be compounded by separation, loss and social dislocation in this country, making them especially vulnerable.

More generally, a major source of support for families and individual adult asylum-seekers comes from refugee support groups, some of which have been set up to offer a service to particular communities, and others that offer a broader service. In some rural areas no other services are available, other than a single support group with very uncertain funding, a situation that creates a constant fear that projects will be closed down at short notice. Yet social services, health, the police, the Benefits Agency and so on, depend on them to support refugee communities. A project I visited received financial support (reassessed annually) from the local authority, yet the authority refused to allocate a budget to it. The project leader commented, 'They won't give us a budget, because a budget means commitment'. These projects are particularly important in rural towns where refugee communities are small and other supports are not available. One support worker was told by the local social services that if her project folded, refugee families would be at the end of a long list of other families, and if they needed support they'd wait in a queue the same as everybody else.

It has been reported to me that many local people in small towns, in Cumbria for example, have welcomed refugees and have worked very hard to make them comfortable and accepted. Alongside this goes a covert racism that only emerges when there is publicity about initiatives designed to improve services, and that leads to protests and letters to the newspapers. Some support agencies are reluctant to advertise the location of their office because of fear that it may be attacked. Workers have been threatened because of the work they are doing. Some rural and urban schools have responded to refugee children with sensitivity, support and enthusiasm (see also Humphries and Mynott 2001), and have dealt quickly and firmly with bullying or harassment. So the picture is mixed, with a willingness to welcome running alongside currents of racism and hostility.

Sensitivity is an important aspect of dealing with refugees. Support services, anxious to help, sometimes bombard new arrivals with advice,

English lessons and other help, but their good intentions are frustrated when they meet resistance. Often people who are disorientated, traumatized, unwell or missing their families, need time to settle before they are ready to take on new challenges. Yet the issue of 'settling' is not a straightforward one. People without refugee status may find themselves in a state of uncertainty for years before they know whether they have permission to stay in the UK, and find it difficult to devote themselves to the business of putting down roots, or less permanent than that, whether to buy a television for example. They desperately desire a positive decision and fear what will happen to them if it is not granted. One support worker in my research said:

> It's horrendous watching people in a state of limbo, and that's what worries me about this team not being able to continue (because of finances), because we know every single one of them, every detail of what's happening, and we can judge now what the decision might be, so we can get prepared for it and do some preventative stuff, whereas if they were passed to the social services...you can imagine them coming in and saying 'I've just got this decision, what am I going to do about it?' Social services take six months to get round to it, and they've lost their appeal date.

The reality of this scenario is that when the last point of appeal is reached and refugee status is not granted, asylum teams and by implication some social workers, are in the position of having to remove families from NASS support, including their accommodation. As the effects of the 1999 Act are worked through the system, the pretence is shattered that asylum teams and social work teams are in place to offer help and support to asylum-seekers. As an arm of the Home Office they exist also to evict and to play a part in their expulsion and deportation.

If refugee status *is* granted to families, another dilemma arises – do they really *want* to settle here, or return to their country of origin when it is possible to do so? The family may be divided as to whether they should stay or return, and the burden of choice after not having any, may lead to a need for sympathetic support to help them work through to the best decision for them.

One cannot underestimate the contribution that is made by refugee support groups and other centres supporting specific minority ethnic communities where refugees are welcomed. In some of the projects I visited, refugees had no contact with social services, and were entirely dependent on the support offered by the support groups who were likely to have intimate knowledge of their situation. I was told that if social services can evade their statutory responsibilities, that is just what they will do. Where an application for asylum has failed, families may lose their source of income and may be at risk of eviction. Social services have in some cases had to be reminded by a solicitor of their legal duty to keep families together, and that asylum-seeking families are part of the local community, before they have been prepared to accept their role. Yet that role is a contradictory one. An obligation to keep families together does not appear to apply when the family is an asylum-seeking one. In this case social workers are likely to have an active role in contributing to their breaking up.

In situations of crisis voluntary organization support workers ask, 'What would have happened if we had not been here? They keep telling us it's not their business.' Many families would have been destitute, without support groups intervening with NASS or the Benefits Agency, or the housing authority. Yet those projects that battle on their behalf are often at permanent risk of having their resources cut or withdrawn. The workers themselves are often unsupported emotionally and intellectually, and in one project a representative of the local authority finance department responsible for their funding responded to a telephone call from them with 'Oh, are you still there?'

However support projects have similar political problems to social services departments in dealing with immigration officials. Elsewhere I have written about the ways the Home Office has sought cooperation and partnership with public services, particularly health, welfare, education and housing, in the checking of documentation and the general policing of provision (Humphries 2002). The leader of one of the support projects I visited had tried to work with the Home Office, and indeed had accepted that there was a need for rules. He was in favour of checking claims for asylum, and of expulsion where a claim was refused. He had approached a Home Office representative about problems of bureaucracy and frustration in his attempts to get information that would help families. The Home Office representative said she would be willing to try to facilitate easier access to her department. The quid pro quo asked for was that the project would let the Home Office know if asylum-seekers who had been refused refugee status were likely to abscond before deportation could be arranged. The project leader replied that absconding was most unlikely because in his experience, if families are told to leave the UK they will go: 'If they have to go back, they want to go back with dignity; all they need is a week to get their finances in order and say goodbye to friends.' He even offered to ensure they got to the airport. The Home Office official rang back a few days later saying, 'Sorry, we can't agree to extra time nor can we accept your undertaking to ensure people get to the airport. Where people do not leave by the due date, we will come and lift the father, take him to a detention centre, and come back for the mother and children.' The project leader was appalled that his offer to make life easier for immigration officials had been rejected, and that the attempt to work together had to be entirely on the terms set by the Home Office.

This worker betrays a naïve view of the asylum system and of the risks of cooperation with immigration officials. The commonsense acceptance of immigration controls as necessary, and by implication, of the process of assessing applications as fair, is ill-informed and not in the interests of asylum-seekers. Immigration controls can never be 'fair' and decisions about individual cases are arbitrary and whimsical (see Cohen, Humphries and Mynott 2002). The worker's actions came from good intentions, but, because they were ill-informed and lacking in political astuteness, could have devastating consequences for the people he was trying to help. His actions are also an example of the ways workers in both statutory and voluntary sectors are not outside the system but part of its all-encompassing grip.

Mental health services

The Government has made mental health one of its top three health priorities, alongside coronary heart disease and cancer. It has published a number of documents pledging to improve services in the community (e.g. DoH 1998, 1999, 2000, 2001, 2002). The 1998 White Paper, *Modernising Mental Health Services*, made a number of promises: services will be *safe*, to protect patients and provide effective care for those with mental illness at the time they need it; *sound*, ensuring that service users have access to the full range of services which they need; and *supportive*, working with service users and their families and carers, to build healthier communities. The ten guiding principles set out in the White Paper include that services 'will be well suited to those who use them and be non-discriminatory'. A key aspect of the care to be offered is the role of the community mental health team (CMHT), a multidisciplinary team, consisting of community psychiatric nurses (CPNs), social workers including approved social workers (ASWs), occupational therapists (OTs) and clinical psychologists. Their responsibility is to offer a service to adults of working age. The implementation guide (DoH 2002) identifies two groups of people in particular:

Most patients treated by the CMHT will have limited disorders and be referred back to their GPs after a period of weeks or months (an average of 5–6 contacts), when their condition has improved.

A substantial minority however, will remain with the team for ongoing treatment, care and monitoring for periods of several years. (p.4)

The main functions of CMHTs are to work closely with primary care teams, to carry out an assessment of everyone who is referred to them (both in terms of mental illness and social needs), to assign a care coordinator to ensure appropriate assessment, care and regular review, and risk assessment as a 'routine, recorded component' (DoH 2002, p.9). Teams are also expected to provide support in the basics of daily living, help in accessing work opportunities and family and carer support and help.

The National Service Framework, NSF (DoH 1999, 2001), provides seven standards, that service users can expect:

1.   the promotion of mental health for all, combating of discrimination against people with mental health problems, and promotion of their social inclusion

2.   assessment and identification of their mental health needs, and the offer of effective treatments

3.   availability of workers to service users 'round the clock'

4.   care which optimises engagement of service users, anticipates a crisis and reduces risk; a written care plan which is reviewed regularly

5.   access to a hospital bed if necessary, close to home and within the least constrictive environment consistent with their and the public's safety; a written care plan on discharge

6.   assessment of the needs of carers, and provision of a written care plan for them

7.   reduction of the risk of suicide through supporting local prison staff, ensuring that such staff are competent to assess risk, and develop systems for suicide audit, to learn lessons and take any necessary action.

People with refugee status are entitled to all these services. The NSF summary document (DoH 2001) concedes that 'for far too long the needs of people from minority communities have not been adequately met by mainstream mental health services' (p.15). Elsewhere (DoH 1999, p.14), the NSF includes the statement: 'Some black and minority ethnic groups are diagnosed as having higher rates of mental disorder than the general population; *refugees are especially vulnerable*' (my emphasis), and again: 'Refugees and asylum-seekers are a particularly vulnerable group. Post traumatic stress disorder is the most common problem, and the risk of suicide is raised in the long term' (p.17); 'All services should be sensitive to cultural needs, including the needs of people from black and minority ethnic communities' (p.29)

> Depression in people from the African-Caribbean, Asian, refugees and asylum-seekers communities is frequently overlooked, although the rate has been found to be 60% higher than in the white population, with the difference being twice as great for men. People from black and minorities ethnic communities are much less likely to be referred to psychological therapies. (p.32)

> Mental health services need to develop and demonstrate cultural competence, with staff having the knowledge and the skills to work effectively with diverse communities. An interpreter, or in the last resort a family member, will be necessary when language is a barrier between service user and practitioner. But recruitment from, and representation of, local communities is the most effective longer-term strategy to build cultural competence. (p.44)

The policy in practice

In the interviews I carried out with members of CMHTs and primary care teams, mental health was identified as an urgent issue for refugees. A number of suicides amongst asylum-seekers was reported, often linked to their receiving a letter from the Home office refusing their application for refugee status or whilst they were awaiting deportation.

The key agencies for identifying people at risk seem to be housing providers and GP surgeries. Housing providers' support workers are often the first to identify mental health problems, and are also instrumental in helping refugees and asylum-seekers to register with a GP. There were examples of good practice from housing providers (including some in the private sector) whose workers were well informed, providing support and advice, and going beyond only the provision of accommodation. This is an important service where workers have direct contact with people who are under enormous stress, and where suicide and attempted suicide are not uncommon after, for example, the receipt of refusal letters from the Home Office.

Some refugees were reported turning up at surgeries with needs such as housing, finance, food, areas that GPs do not see themselves as dealing with, nor do they want such people coming to their surgeries. Many get turned away by receptionists, without an opportunity to see the doctor. In one instance a concerned nurse from a health centre approached the community mental health team asking for their cooperation and help in such situations. She left without any satisfaction, and with the prospect of continuing to attempt to help people where other services could not cope. In spite of the obligation to make an assessment of social needs as well as mental health needs, the CMHTs said there was little they could do. The main problem was one of interpreters. Not only were interpreters difficult to find and expensive, but also there were no extra resources for them. There was an insistence too that they be 'psychologically trained', so that they could convey accurately the problems being related. This was emphasized repeatedly as a fundamental difficulty. Indeed the perception of the importance of psychological training led to reluctance within teams to refer people elsewhere for counselling, because many of the prospective counsellors did not have appropriate training.

Community mental health workers conveyed both a sense of helplessness regarding what they could offer, and a sense of resistance to accepting responsibility for refugees and asylum-seekers or seeking help for them elsewhere. Under NSF Standard 7 they are obliged to carry out a risk assessment of the needs of all people who are referred, and to attempt to reduce suicide (see above). Yet a very vulnerable group is perceived as peripheral to whatever and whomever the CMHTs see as their main responsibility.

Moreover, the interpretation by CMHTs of the Government's implementation guide (DoH 2002) has also resulted in a very limited service being offered. For example, one team saw their role as only offering short-term help, and ignoring that part of the guidelines that also envisaged that some people will need longer-term help. This attitude is legitimized by the argument that there is no point in offering *any* help to people suffering from post-traumatic stress disorder and thus raising unrealistic expectations, because what such people need is a much longer-term service. Some workers confessed that they do not have expertise and skills in post-trauma work, another reason they are reluctant to offer help.

In some areas refugees do receive six weeks' counselling through their GP surgery, but this is seen to be the upper time limit for the service since there are likely to be others waiting for help. Refugees also reported feeling a burden and 'in the way'. Some are put on to a list for help from NHS community mental health facilities where they may eventually receive counselling or the services of a psychologist for as long as a year. Sometimes the effects of experiencing war, torture and displacement may not become apparent for several years after arrival in the UK and can be easily missed by professionals, or not recognized as linked to events in the past. Health authorities may have planned for an increase in demand in the first months after arrival of asylum-seekers, but are taken unawares when what might appear to be a settled community begins to seek psychological help further down the line. Meanwhile refugee support workers (some of whom are dealing with their own experiences of trauma) are being pushed into the role of counselling for which they feel unprepared and as a result of which they feel drained and often helpless. I met one rural worker working with Kosovan refugees, who was attending a counselling skills course and another on teaching English as a foreign language because she saw these were needed, but there was no one else to do it.

Mental health teams and members of refugee support teams also made the point that for some cultures, treatment from a psychiatrist or other mental health worker is an alien concept, and problems are dealt with in other ways, such as in the family or with workers with whom they have a close familiarity. Anne Fadiman's haunting study, *The Spirit Catches You And You Fall Down* (Fadiman 1997), tells the story of the tragedy of an ill child in an immigrant family, against the background of the family's adherence to the beliefs of their ancestors, and the rigidities and arrogance of a Western medical tradition. The clash of cultures sets in motion a chain of events that ends in death and disillusionment. This and many similar stories, instead of leading to reluctance to deal with such communities, should teach us of the urgent need to understand and to engage with the diverse ways of seeing that characterize our shrinking world.

The theme of depression arose over and over again in my research. This was related not only to worries about Home Office decisions, and post-traumatic stress, but also emerged in interviews of refugees and asylum-seekers with permission to work who could not find a job. It is estimated that between 75 and 90 per cent of refugees are unemployed or underemployed (AET 1998; Ahipeaud 1998; Sargeant and Forna 2001). The effort of seeking and applying for jobs where they are told they will be contacted but nothing further happens, or being told they must get or upgrade their qualifications, or that their English is not good enough, leads to despair and loss of confidence, and eventually people may stop trying. This is particularly the case with young men – from Turkey, Iraq, Afghanistan, Angola, Somalia, Kosova and other parts of eastern Europe – who become bored and isolated, especially when they are dispersed to rural areas where they do not want to be.

On the other hand, some people refuse to stop trying. I interviewed a 37-year-old Somali woman with a high standard of English who had already trained as a classroom assistant, but could not find a job in an area of work where there is a shortage. She is now doing a foundation course for university and hopes to train as a teacher (but with the prospect of facing high fees and other costs). She is left asking: 'What is the reason I am unable to get a job? Is it because of the clothes I wear, or when I telephone, is it my name?' She is well aware of the racism she meets, but is determined not to let it get her down. After she qualifies as a teacher, will she be told she has to acquire further qualifications (as have others who are pushed to collect more and more) and still find themselves with the 'wrong' ones? Contrary to stereotypes of asylum-seekers, many who arrive in Britain are educated to university level, and have training and qualifications which are in demand in this country. Indeed one of the aims of the Nationality, Immigration and Asylum Act 2002 was to expand the possibilities for recruitment of workers from abroad, in order to fill vacancies in professions such as medicine, nursing, social work, teaching, and for unskilled workers generally. Yet, as noted above, between 75 and 90 per cent of refugees and others with permission to work are unemployed or underemployed (AET 1998; Ahipeaud 1998).

Overall the position of women asylum-seekers and refugees is particularly worrying. A consistent theme of my research is that they are very often at home, are not able to access services and are not afforded the opportunity of learning English. Assumptions are often made that refugee women have no interest in the wider society, or are confined at home by their husbands (Shields and Wheatley Price 2003). It is difficult to know to what extent this is the case. At a women's centre in an urban conurbation I found a group of Somali women of all ages gathering regularly to learn English with a view to finding work and with a willingness to tackle a wide range of jobs. I interviewed workers elsewhere, with a particular concern to reach women and identify their needs, and again, learning English emerged as a priority for them. The particular issues faced by women were also highlighted by

Aldridge and Waddington (2001), who commented: 'The position of women asylum-seekers who are in the minority and often housed in mainly male environments, is one of vulnerability' (p.23). Victoria Brittain has written about women's experiences in war (Brittain 2003). She has travelled and met women in many countries affected by conflict, and has commented:

> What is common to all…is a kind of circle of negative factors all reinforcing each other, creating a downward spiral in people's lives. At whatever point you enter the spiral, it is always moving on and down. I identify five elements in this spiral, constantly reacting on each other and forcing it further and further down. They are: *displacement, psycho-social health and HIV/AIDS, economic impoverishment, the destruction of education and sexual violence.* For many reasons, of which the most important is women's low status in every society we studied, the impact on women caught up in this spiral is particularly acute. (p.43, emphasis in the original)

Some asylum-seeking women arrive in the UK with needs arising from these experiences that are unacknowledged and not addressed because they are not seen as a priority, and because their nature is such that they are not easy to discuss. There is clearly a need for more attention than currently exists, for women's issues to be addressed specifically. This point was made by research carried out in Glasgow, which highlighted women's mental health needs and the inappropriate services offered (Ferguson and Barclay 2002). Incidentally, Ferguson and Barclay emphasized that women's mental health needs were not only related to their experiences before coming to Britain, but also to the racism, poverty and despair they encounter after their arrival. There seems little hope that social services teams or mental health services will be prepared or able to offer help. The dedicated services of informal and voluntary groups – often willing to take on this kind of support, and as often untrained for such intricate work – may fill the gap yet again. They deserve more financial security than they currently receive.

Conclusion

The picture of the obstacles, burdens and inadequate services faced by asylum-seekers and refugees is a depressing one indeed. At one level, their experiences before coming to the UK make it astonishing that their resolve and resilience has led them across continents to arrive in what they hope is a place of safety. At another level, the repressive policy and legislation – Section 55 of the Nationality, Immigration and Asylum Act 2002 which risks making them destitute, an inferior system of welfare benefits in any case, a Government commitment to halve their numbers, the threat of sending them on to 'protection zones', segregation in 'reception centres', separate education for children, increasing restrictions on whether they may work, the general climate of hostility and stigma, compounded by a threat of withdrawal of citizenship (if this is granted) – can make life here miserable and unfulfilled. At yet another level, the reality of a piecemeal, chaotic and incompetent system of official social work support can at the extreme result in exclusion, exploitation, illness and death. The evidence is building up daily of ways local authorities are avoiding their statutory duties, apparently without restraint.

Asylum-seekers and refugees are individuals, many of whom have skills and qualifications this country needs, yet who live on the margins, in what Bill Morris calls in another context, 'ante-rooms for the dispossessed' (*The Observer*, 6 April 2003). And the government's preference seems to be to seek workers from abroad, rather than use the skills they have available to them. It is no wonder many communities have organized their own welfare systems to offer advice, training and English language teaching in ways that are culturally appropriate. These support groups are often appallingly poorly resourced. The policy context of short-term targets, meagre funding, a myopic vision of the future and a mean and distorted perception of those who come seeking refuge, results in a model of social work that betrays its beliefs about itself as empowering and humanitarian. It results too in an inward-looking and small-minded society.

References

African Educational Trust (AET) (1998) *Refugee Education Training and Development in Inner London: A Base Line Study.* Focus Central London: AET.

Ahipeaud, M. J. (1998) *Employment Training for Refugees in London: A Survey Analysis.* London: Pan London Refugee and Training Network.

Aldridge, F. and Waddington, S. (2001) *Asylum-seekers Skills and Qualifications Audit Pilot Project.* NIACE.

Braybrooke, M. (2002) 'That community feeling', reported in *Professional Social Work*, December 2002, 8.

Brittain, V. (2003) 'The impact of war on women.' *Race and Class 44*, 4, 41–51.

Cohen, S., Humphries, B. And Mynott, E. (eds) (2002) *From Immigration Controls to Welfare Controls.* London: Routledge.

Department of Health (1998) *Modernising Mental Health Services.* White Paper. London: Department of Health.

Department of Health (1999) *National Service Framework for Mental Health: Modern Standards and Service Models.* London: Department of Health.

Department of Health (2000) *The NHS Plan*. London: Department of Health.

Department of Health (2001) *The Journey to Recovery: The Government's Vision for Mental Health Care*. London: Department of Health.

Department of Health (2002) *Mental Health Policy Implementation Guide: Community Mental Health Teams*. London: Department of Health.

Fadiman, A. (1997) *The Spirit Catches You and You Fall Down: A Hmong Child, her American Doctors and the Collision of Two Cultures*. New York: Farrar, Straus and Giroux.

Ferguson, I. and Barclay, A. (2002) *Seeking Peace of Mind: The Mental Health Needs of Asylum-seekers in Glasgow*. Stirling: University of Stirling.

Humphries, B. (2002) 'From welfare to authoritarianism: the role of social work in immigration controls.' In S. Cohen, B. Humphries and E. Mynott (eds) *From Immigration Controls to Welfare Controls*. London: Routledge.

Humphries, B. and Mynott, E. (2001) *Young Separated Refugees in Greater Manchester*. London: Save the Children.

Jones, A. (1998) *The Child Welfare Implications of UK Immigration and Asylum Policy*. Manchester: Manchester Metropolitan University.

Jordon, B. and Jordan, C. (2000) *Social Work and the Third Way*. London: Sage.

Martin, G. (1998) *The Effects of the UK's Reservation on Asylum and Immigration to the UN Convention on the Rights of the Child: A Report*. London: UK Committee for UNICEF.

Refugee Council and Oxfam (2002) *Poverty and Asylum in the UK*. London: Oxfam and Refugee Council.

Sargeant, G. and Forna, A. (2001) *A Poor Reception: Refugees and Asylum-seekers: Welfare or Work?* London: The Industrial Society.

Shields, M.A. and Wheatley Price, S. (2003) *The Labour Market Outcomes and Psychological Well-being of Ethnic Minority Migrants in Britain: Home Office: Online Report July 2003*.

Stanley, K. (2001) *Cold Comfort: Young Separated Refugees in England*. London: Save the Children.

Chapter 4

Dilemmas of Care and Control: The Work of an Asylum Team in a London Borough

Rosemary Sales and Rachel Hek

Introduction

Tensions between care and control are endemic to social work (Jones 1998; Jordan 1997; Parton 1997; Thompson 2000). Developments in immigration policy during the 1990s heightened these tensions and created them in new forms. This chapter discusses the conflicts this has produced for social workers working with asylum-seekers, as they have been required increasingly to take on the role of 'gatekeepers' to services and to separate 'deserving' clients from the 'undeserving'.

The chapter draws on a research project carried out with a specialist asylum team in a London borough (Dutton *et al.* 2000)[1]. The team – like others established in London following the Immigration and Asylum Act 1996 – was set up in 1997 to provide emergency support to newly-arrived asylum-seekers, and involved assessing eligibility in relation to immigration status as well as need. Our research focused on the views of the team about their work, their feelings about their role and relations with clients. We also interviewed representatives from some refugee community groups about their experiences of the team when representing their members. Our original aims included a broader examination of the work of social workers with refugees (including recognized refugees and asylum-seekers) in supporting them in the process of settlement. Other research has suggested that many creative ideas are being put into practice in direct work with asylum-seekers. This is particularly true in relation to work with young people being carried out by social workers (Ayotte 1998; Kohli and Mather 2003; Williamson 1998) as well as other professionals such as teachers and support workers (Hek 2002; Richman 1998). We were also interested in the extent to which social workers are able to coordinate the response to the needs of refugees with other service providers.

In the event, our focus became narrower as it emerged that, in the borough in which we worked, these longer-term strategies had largely been subordinated to the work of the asylum team. This team had limited regular working involvement with other services and its role was limited mainly to emergency provision rather than longer-term care. This chapter discusses the strategies that front-line social workers used in their dealings with clients in a situation where they were forced to decide on eligibility based on immigration status. While this requirement was not new (Cohen 2003), this function was at the centre of the work of the asylum teams, and thus the tensions between the professional values of providing for those in need and the requirement to exclude people from services on other grounds were ever present. Our work, like that of Duvell and Jordan (2001), which also examined the work of asylum teams in London, suggests that this imperative represented a substantial barrier to good professional practice.

Subsequent legislation has changed the circumstances in which the asylum teams operate. They were, however, 'pioneers' (Humphries 2002, p.131) in the policy approach which brought social workers into the role of gatekeepers to subsistence, and their experience is relevant to social workers and other professionals who are being forced to operate in an environment of ever greater scrutiny of immigration status.

Care and control in social work

State intervention into individual and family life has always served a dual function. On the one hand, intervention has meant providing for the destitute and needy, or those deemed to be 'deserving' of help; on the other, intervention has also meant controlling the behaviour of the 'deviant' or attempting to reform the behaviour of the 'undeserving' poor. Social work has always been at the heart of these contradictory pressures. Banks (2001, p.16) recognises the ambivalent role that social workers play in society, both as 'expressing society's altruism (care) and enforcing societal norms (control)'. This double-edged role is enacted in all areas of social work and has been particularly apparent in relation to child protection and mental health.

This tension has grown over time, particularly as the role of social workers was reshaped during the 1980s, making them increasingly gatekeepers to resources. Parton points out that a growing preoccupation with the concept of risk has contributed to social workers' involvement in auditing and budgetary control, as well as to shaping their role in individual casework practice. He argues that as need increases, and inequalities become wider: '(r)isk has become the key criterion for targeting scarce resources, protecting the most vulnerable, and making professionals and agencies accountable' (Parton 1996, p.104). Manthorpe and Bradley (2002, p.281) also point to the dilemma created by social workers' role in means testing when 'they act within local authorities, many of which, simultaneously, have placed poverty on their corporate agenda'. This twin role of defining need while controlling resources is an important aspect of balancing care and control functions as the majority of users of social services are poor, have low social status and lack power or agency over their situations (Becker and McPherson 1988). These relations therefore take on an element of coercion. As Payne (1997, p.19) puts it, clients are involuntary if 'they feel disadvantaged or oppressed in a relationship, even though they retain it because they get something out of it'.

The social work task has been recognized as a balancing act by those responsible for its regulation and for social work training. The Central Council for the Education and Training of Social Workers (CCETSW 1996, p.16) stated that a major element of social workers' role is to 'balance the needs, rights, responsibilities and resources of people with those of the wider community, and provide appropriate levels of support, advocacy, care, protection and control'. The Codes of Practice (GSCC 2002) and the Subject Benchmark Statement in Social Work (QAA 2000) also recognize the dilemmas of respecting individuals' rights whilst at the same time ensuring that their behaviour is not harmful to themselves or others, and balancing resources and need. Thompson (2000, p.5), commenting on the complex nature of the social work task, suggests that '(f)ormula responses do not equip social workers for dealing with the complexities of being caught in the middle'.

The problems for social workers in balancing the caring and controlling aspects of their role has been highlighted in the debate around intervention and support which followed a number of child death enquiries in the late 1970s and 1980s (Farmer 1997; Hayden *et al.* 1999; Parton 1991, 1997), and the Cleveland enquiry and debate around sexual abuse. The media, public and Government response to social work was both 'too little too late, too much too soon'. Most recently, the 'too little, too late' issue has been to the fore in relation to the outcome of the Climbié Enquiry (Laming 2003). The report noted that a number of key agencies had come into contact with Victoria Climbié and her great aunt, Marie-Thérèse Kouao, but that although each agency had identified concerns about Victoria, none had acted to protect her. Chand (2003) points out that the fact that Victoria was African was a factor in this failure to respond adequately and that issues of race and ethnicity often impact on the balance between care and control. Assumptions about childcare practices, and levels and types of need can lead to both a reluctance to intervene and inappropriate interventions.

In relation to refugees and asylum-seekers, the split between care and control is presented in an extreme fashion by the Government and the media in the alleged division between 'genuine' refugees and 'bogus' asylum-seekers. Those working in the social care professions, who are required both to define need and to judge eligibility, are not, of course, themselves immune to this discourse. Asylum-seekers arriving in the UK without means of support are forced to negotiate with social workers from a position of severe disadvantage. They are often unfamiliar with the social work role which does not exist in many refugee-producing countries. This compounds the problems of communication which arise from language difficulties and reinforces the authority of the social work professional in the relationship. These pressures tend to strengthen the control rather than the caring aspects of the relationship.

The background to the establishment of asylum teams

The exclusion of 'undesirable aliens' from welfare and the barring of immigrants from 'recourse to public funds' have been at the heart of the welfare state from its inception (Cohen 2003; Humphries 2002). A series of policy measures in the 1990s, however, shifted welfare to the centre of the asylum debate as they reduced entitlement to support and made benefits more tightly related to immigration status (Sales 2002). In 1993, the Government initiated an 'efficiency scrutiny' to ensure greater cooperation between service providers, including social services, and the Home Office in detecting 'illegal immigration' (Cohen 2003, p.143).

The ostensible reasons for the heightened profile of the asylum issue during the 1990s lie in the increased flows of asylum-seekers and delays in processing cases, which increased the cost of supporting asylum claimants (Audit Commission 2001, p.5). The terms of the mainstream political debate have been predicated on the notion that the majority of asylum-seekers are 'bogus' and therefore not entitled to enter Britain or to receive social support when they arrive. The increased visibility of asylum-seekers was also, however, itself an artefact of policy. Successive legislation has increasingly separated asylum-seekers from mainstream social support, making them identifiable and thus making it easier to portray them as a 'burden'.

The Immigration and Asylum Act 1996 removed the right to welfare benefits from asylum-seekers who made applications in-country rather than at the port of entry. A subsequent court decision ruled that, under the National Assistance Act 1948, local authorities had a duty to provide basic subsistence to those deemed 'destitute', including asylum-seekers. This support had to be 'in kind' rather than cash, and asylum-seekers were provided with basic accommodation and issued with vouchers, which they had to exchange in designated supermarkets for goods. The voucher scheme marked asylum-seekers as different, frequently exposing them to racist abuse from other customers and from supermarket staff who were required to check eligibility. This new structure also shifted the cost of supporting asylum-seekers from national benefits to local authority budgets. The costs were not recouped in full and were concentrated in a small number of boroughs, most of which had high levels of deprivation (Audit Commission 2000). The majority of asylum-seekers entering Britain during the 1990s were based in London (Carey-Wood et al. 1995; Audit Commission 2000), largely because of the networks of support which the communities had developed.

The London boroughs with large populations of refugees and asylum-seekers, as well as being poorer, were generally those with a more positive attitude towards their reception and had developed a range of support structures to support them (for example, refugee support teachers) outside the framework of statutory provision. While opposing the new legislation, these boroughs took on the role of implementing the new support structure resulting from it. A joint report by the Association of London Government and the Refugee Council committed them to providing for the needs of these groups within the constraints of the legislation, and to consulting with refugee community organizations (Association of London Government/Refugee Council 1996).

Asylum teams were established in a number of boroughs in response to this new situation. Most were based in social work departments but also involved other services. Social services departments thus became the main agents for the provision of subsistence and for making decisions about who was eligible. Those leading and working with these teams were often professionals with a long-standing commitment to working with refugees and asylum-seekers. The constraints of the new role were, however, acute (Cohen 2003). Asylum teams experienced a growing demand for the service as a result of new arrivals in a period of budget constraint and their work tended to be dominated by assessing eligibility and providing for immediate needs, rather than a broader social work role.

The Immigration and Asylum Act 1999 removed the direct responsibility of local authorities for the social support of asylum-seekers, replacing it with a new directorate, the National Asylum Support Service (NASS) within the Home Office, and introduced compulsory dispersal of asylum-seekers to areas outside London. Part of the justification for the new policy was the perceived 'burden' on London authorities (Audit Commission 2000), a burden that was itself largely a creation of the 1996 Act. London boroughs have largely retained their existing teams and NASS has devolved responsibility to them for provision of direct services.

The asylum team

The asylum team in the borough with which we worked was based in social work but also involved housing. It was, however, located outside the mainstream structures of social work within the borough. The team had a high turnover, and was heavily dependent on a temporary staff, with the majority employed by agencies. Many had been employed in the authority for less than a year and some stated that they were planning to leave in the immediate future. A manager spoke of the problems caused by the high turnover:

> You're continually trying to induct someone, train someone and just as you think someone's got the experience and the knowledge and skills in dealing with the particular issues…you're replacing someone and you're going through the recruitment period again. It's quite exhausting and demoralising in that it's not recognised that there should be a permanent team so there's consistency for the client group.

While the team was diverse in terms of national and ethnic background and professional experience, the team members could broadly be divided into two groups: those who had chosen to work in this area and those for whom it was largely accidental. Of the former, many had a long-standing commitment to work with refugees either in a professional or voluntary capacity. They included some from refugee and other migrant communities who felt that this enabled them to empathize with the experience of clients. Others were more transient both in their relation to the team and to the borough. Some were on working holidays and others were working temporarily in Britain. Most had little knowledge of the specific issues concerning refugees or of the services available to them, particularly in relation to community groups.

> I had no idea about where most of our clients come from; I had no idea where it was or that sort of thing...

> The client knows the system better than you do, particularly when you begin.

Induction, training and professional support was limited and largely informal. An induction pack providing information on legislation and entitlements of asylum-seekers was not regularly updated, while training was also seen to be restricted due to resource constraints.

> Being such a transient team there hasn't been the opportunity to maybe get in and get some really good training done...we haven't been a team that's been consistent for long enough and also being a temporary team within the council there's a reluctance to place those resources into it.

Most staff also talked of limited formal supervision and felt that this impacted on the consistency of their practice. This was particularly problematic in dealing with the conflicts within their role. Several team members spoke of an erosion of their skills, particularly therapeutic skills, in a service focused on meeting immediate needs rather than developing long-term work with clients.

Although many had not chosen this kind of work, all expressed commitment to the client group and to the team. This was in sharp contrast to a widespread feeling of isolation from other services within the borough and to a perception that they were under-valued and under-resourced. The team itself was seen as an emergency response to a crisis, rather than as a planned response to the client group's needs, and there was a perceived reluctance by management to invest in it. Several suggested that other departments were reluctant to take on asylum-seeking clients because in a situation of financial targets and budgetary constraints they were not confident that the service would be paid for.

The feeling of isolation from other social service departments was reflected in the generally poor reports of working relations with other teams, particularly within social services. This was linked to a feeling that workers from other services and teams agreed with the generally negative stereotypes about asylum-seekers promoted in the media. This isolation led to a strong loyalty to the team in relation to the outside world. There was a widespread belief that other professionals did not see refugees or asylum-seekers as part of their client group. It was felt that rather than taking referrals and responding to the needs which the team had identified, they would tend to 'dump' all work relating to refugees and asylum-seekers onto them. Towards the end of our work with the team an internal section was set up to deal with the needs of unaccompanied children. Whilst it is recognised that specialist input can be beneficial (Stanley 2001; Stone 2000), there is also clearly a need and a responsibility for 'mainstream' social services teams to be involved to ensure a holistic assessment of need and provision of a full range of services.

Many mentioned the poor environment in which they worked as evidence that they and the client group were under-valued. The building was dirty and depressing: no children's toys or books were provided in the reception area, and no pictures or posters displayed as is usual in mainstream local authority services across London. Interview rooms were noisy and lacked privacy. This gave the impression that there had been little thought about the needs of the client group.

The work of the team

The main focus of the work was on providing basic needs for those deemed eligible. The team's offices were open to the public every weekday and asylum-seekers attended on a drop-in basis. Staff carried out initial screening of clients to ensure eligibility (based on proof of a connection with the borough, and 'destitution') and made assessments of their entitlement to social support and of other needs. The interviews revealed considerable confusion within the team about their working arrangements, and individual staff appeared to be interpreting the process differently. Clients were referred by the team to other services (both statutory and voluntary) for support with longer-term issues. The range of services and organizations with which regularly working relationships had been established was limited, and very few front-line staff referred clients to community groups for support.

After this process, it was rare to see clients again and the files were generally dormant. Many spoke of the high volume of work, and said that the result of this was that 'we can't do what we want to do' to support asylum-seekers, and that the work was 'quantitative rather than qualitative'. The work was focused on responding to emergencies rather than meeting long-term needs. This meant that other, deeper, problems were often neglected. Many pointed to their frustration at not being able to follow up cases and develop on-going relations with clients. As some pointed out, some of the problems faced by asylum-seekers, particularly those resulting from trauma, do not surface until later, and the focus on immediate needs means that these are often neglected.

Another impact of the workload was stress, or what one described as 'burn-out'. This was a particular problem for longer-term staff who had made a greater professional investment in the work.

Relations with clients

Relations with clients were fraught with conflicting pressures and feelings. All expressed strong commitment to the client group and most recounted examples suggesting that they carried out work beyond the minimum required. Many spoke about the way in which recent Government policy had eroded asylum-seekers' rights, arguing that asylum-seekers should have basic citizenship rights and not be treated as second-class citizens. There was also recognition of their clients' specific needs, both in relation to dealing with trauma and longer term settlement. The structures in which they worked, however, forced them into more complex and sometimes conflictual relations with clients.

Some mentioned the atmosphere of the reception area and offices as hostile and unwelcoming to clients. Security guards questioned service users as they entered the premises, which team members described as potentially intimidating, particularly for those who had suffered persecution at the hands of state officials. The presence of security guards was, however, a response to the demands of staff themselves for protection. This followed incidents where people became upset in the reception area if they had been refused a service or had had to wait a long time, sometimes leading to violence breaking out. While recognizing the reasons for client anger, staff also viewed some clients as potentially dangerous and felt the need for protection from them.

Some described their own role as 'inquisitors' and as 'immigration offi-cers'. They recognised that their role could be seen as hostile especially for people who have experienced torture and persecution. One talked repeatedly about the 'intrusion into people's lives' they were forced to carry out:

> It's like a mirroring of what has happened to a lot of asylum-seekers…they have had to tell lies to use their wits to survive, to get out of the situation that they have been in and come to this country. Then the social services department continues the interrogation…that is the underlying dynamics that's going on.

Many felt they were being forced into roles which were inappropriate for social workers, since they had to make sometimes apparently arbitrary decisions which were not based on need. The requirement to establish entitlement led to a focus on establishing the credibility of the client's claim and thus to a relationship built on suspicion rather than trust. They exercised power over clients, but this was ambivalent and often unwelcome, since it involved implementing policies with which they were uncomfortable. Many spoke of clients who, though not meeting the eligibility criteria, nevertheless had serious financial or other needs which ought to be met. The power over clients was not matched by feelings of power within the broader organization, in which they felt isolated, or by a sense of control over their working lives.

All the interviewees expressed these conflicts and often expressed apparently contradictory views. Several criticized their own role as 'police officers', but also cited examples of situations where they had – rightly they felt – refused support when they had found what they believed was evidence of fraud or misrepresentation. These conflicting feelings were also expressed in relation to refugee community associations. Some, particularly the more senior and longer-term staff, recognized them as a resource, as potential mediators between their own community and the services. Others saw them as outsiders who disrupted the work of the team and raised false hopes in their clients. One suggested that they encouraged people to tell lies and to adjust their stories in order to 'milk the system'. Although staff talked about the conflicts in their roles and expressed commitment to individual clients, some tended to reproduce stereotypical views about asylum-seekers in relation to the community as a whole.

Community group representatives also felt this suspicion, particularly those from countries where social work is unfamiliar. Social workers were seen as representatives of the state, interrogators from whom asylum-seekers attempt to conceal information, rather than people to be trusted. In spite of this initial suspicion, working relations had been established with the more senior managers within social services. Several drew a distinction between the management of the service and the front-line team.

My reaction to the work of the Team is divided into two. I am happy with the work of those at the top, but not happy with those on the front line. Refugees are interviewed as if by immigration officers or police officers. If you have a gold ring, they tell you you are not destitute. The staff members don't want to treat people properly. We have good relations with those at the top, but not with those at the bottom. If there is a problem, we go to the top; the front-line staff would not listen to us.

All gave a generally negative view of the front-line service by the asylum team. Typical responses were:

They ask all sorts of unnecessary questions.

There is a bad reception for almost all refugees... From day one there is a negative image.

They feel interrogated like criminals.

One incident, described to us both by a social worker and a member of a community group, demonstrated the hostility of some front-line workers towards these groups. This concerned a young single refugee who had been sent out of the borough as part of their own dispersal strategy. He had become ill with depression and his request to be returned to London was refused. The community group took up the case, employing a lawyer. The social worker described the group as 'screaming blue murder' and she described her own role as 'holding the line' against what she considered an unreasonable demand.

Strategies for dealing with tensions in the work

A constant theme expressed by team members was the tension between ways of working which emphasized qualities such as empathy and others, which emphasized detachment in order to establish entitlement to support. Many felt uncomfortable with the inquisitorial role they were required to adopt, which one described as 'gatekeeping' rather than social work. All were forced to negotiate between this role of controlling access to support and that of providing care. People drew lines in different ways and developed different strategies for dealing with feelings of guilt about leaving clients with what they felt was insufficient support. The tensions and conflicts implicit in this work and the relationship with clients had a number of dimensions and were felt differently depending on their own position within the team, their own experiences and background and their personal beliefs. They were generally more acute for people with a stronger commitment to the work particularly those who had come to the job with high expectations of being able to provide support and those who had a personal commitment to refugee communities, especially those from a refugee or migrant background themselves.

These strategies involved making a series of distinctions between individual clients and broader social groups or processes, separations that allowed team members to carry out the job. These fell into four broad groups:

1. *Differentiation between the response to individual clients and broader political issues over which the team had no control.*

Senior staff and those in a management position tended to emphasize the broader aims of the service and the borough, citing a commitment to equal opportunities and multicultural policies. They were aware of the budget constraints in which they operated. Within this context they were able to feel comfortable with the need to strike a balance between suspicion of clients in order to assess eligibility and the need to develop trust. This balance was difficult to maintain for front-line staff facing hostility and sometimes aggression from clients who were refused support, and who sometimes felt unsupported by the organization in dealing with these issues. A front-line worker attempted to distance herself from the constraints in which she was required to operate by being 'up front' with clients, explaining the interview situation and staff's role. This was an attempt to establish trust and to clarify in advance the limitations of the support on offer so that expectations would not be raised. It also aimed to shift the focus of hostility from individual social workers to the system in which they operated.

Another front-line staff member managed to disengage himself from concern with individual clients. He spoke of the global inequalities, which created refugee flows, but did not see them as having implications for the power relations within which he carried out his own role. He felt fairly comfortable with the service provided to asylum-seekers, suggesting that the support provided was relatively generous in relation to the income available in asylum-seekers' home countries.

2. *Making a distinction between the needs of individual clients and broader issues of rights.*

Several team members talked of individual clients, with whom they would attempt to develop a relationship and go beyond the 'call of duty' while rejecting a more general notion of rights to services. Some expressed the attitude that clients should be grateful for what they were given rather than raising issues of entitlements or rights and making further demands. They were particularly critical of community organiszations, which are the main vehicles for expressing collective claims and rights. Relations between refugee community groups and front-line staff were characterized by a lack of trust on both sides. The groups were seen as demanding and disruptive or unhelpful to the work of the team rather than as raising legitimate claims and as potential collaborators

More senior and long-term staff tended to see their role as a positive way of enhancing the potential resources available and of bridging the gap between clients and the service. The developing collaboration between community groups and senior staff and management has not filtered down to the rest of the team.

3. Differentiation of the 'deserving' and 'undeserving'.
Most staff talked of feeling uncomfortable with the role of gatekeeper and they accommodated it in different ways. One staff member talked at length of individual cases where she had invested time and been able to achieve some success, and of the gratitude of clients. At the same time, she spoke disparagingly of individuals who were not destitute, and therefore in her view undeserving, and of groups which she described as 'typically very demanding, very aggressive'. Another mentioned a client who she believed could not be regarded as destitute because he smoked cigarettes. This statement echoes the moral surveillance over the lives of asylum-seekers contained in the ban on the use of the vouchers for buying cigarettes.

Some, particularly the more senior staff, had begun to pride themselves on their ability to make 'hard' decisions. They felt that they were able to get the balance right between suspicion and support.

4. Avoiding decisions on eligibility.
Some preferred to pass on decisions to others, which was an option available to junior staff. One team member, who was herself from a refugee community, spoke of 'doing a bit more' than the minimum for clients. This involved, for example, photocopying information sheets, spending more time on referrals, and listening to clients. This was, however, an individual strategy and she received complaints from other staff members that she was not getting through her workload. Some staff suggested that they would prefer to work in the voluntary sector where there would not be a conflict of interest since they would be working directly for the client group.

All of these strategies represented individual solutions to the tensions inherent in their role, and were only partially successful in relieving stress. These strategies allowed the social workers to evade issues of personal power and responsibility in their work. No one suggested the possibility of any collective voice, which could make an impact on changing the basic structures in which they worked. Staff tended to look inwards and develop their own solutions based on an accommodation with their own value system and sense of identification or distance with the client group.

Conclusions

Many people are attracted to working with refugees out of a strong commitment to their rights. This was true of the members of the asylum team whom we interviewed, who all expressed an awareness of the limitations of the services which they were providing, and an interest in enhancing the rights of asylum-seekers and their access to services. Interviewees expressed concern at the implications for asylum-seekers' rights of the Immigration and Asylum Act, 1999, which was being debated at the time of the research. They acknowledged that the support system established under the National Assistance Act was extremely limited and most felt that the scrutiny which claimants were required to undergo was humiliating. The need to establish eligibility shifted the balance of their work from care to control, and social workers increasingly found themselves in the role of gatekeepers to resources and forced to play an investigative role in relation to clients' immigration status.

The research showed that individuals developed a range of strategies for dealing with the dilemmas posed by working in this environment. Some involved attempting to 'get round' the system by providing more – mainly in terms of their own time – than the strict entitlement. Thus they attempted to evade the problems of establishing eligibility. Others managed to disengage themselves from individuals while expressing a general commitment to the group. Some adopted a more punitive role, making sharp distinctions between those they deemed deserving and others. Those in management positions were able to draw on notions of their responsibility to the wider goals of the local authority in order to make decisions. What was missing was any collective response to these dilemmas. Individuals remained isolated within the team, while the team members – rather than attempting to seek common cause with others – felt themselves isolated both from other council staff and from the communities, which they were attempting to serve. As Duvell and Jordan (2001) suggest, staff become 'immersed in the day-to-day routines of such tasks, ethical reflection and long-term planning become luxuries that cannot be afforded' (ibid., p.203).

The members of the asylum team felt marginalized within the council services, reflecting what they saw as a lack of value for their work. The impermanence of the team and the transitory nature of many staff were each part of this marginalization. It also presented obstacles to developing good practice and to joint working with other service providers. A striking feature of many of the responses was the hostility displayed by front-line workers to the self activity of refugee community groups. Rather than being seen as potential allies in resistance to inadequate provision, the advocacy role of these groups on behalf of their members was seen as obstacles to the smooth running of the service. Managers, on the other hand, saw these groups as potential partners in providing services. This reflects a general trend toward the involvement of the voluntary sector in the provision of services, which has been developing in relation to asylum-seekers and refugees (Duvell and Jordan 2001; Zetter and Pearl 2000).

The specific role carried out by the asylum team has been removed with the development of the National Asylum Support System (NASS). Nevertheless, specialist social work teams are still involved in working with asylum-seekers, often in partnership with NASS. Similar tensions are likely to continue within these teams, exacerbated by the political hostility towards asylum-seekers. The dilemmas of this group represent in extreme form those of social workers attempting to balance their duties of care and control. As Duvell and Jordan (2001, p.201) argue, the asylum teams represented an opportunity for the introduction of new principles into the area of welfare provision, and thus their importance lies not merely in the specific circumstances but in the questions they pose about the future of social work practice in what they describe as 'intentionally deterrent facilities' (ibid., p.202).

In the report of our research, we suggested a range of strategies for improving practice within the asylum team (see Dutton et al. 2000). Some of these involved relatively few resources, for example, improving the environment of the offices to make them feel more welcoming and safe for clients, and the provision of information in community languages. Others were more resource intensive, including adequate training and induction for staff, and professional support for their practice. Progress in these areas would necessitate a reduction in the reliance on temporary staff. Another set of recommendations, on the development of improved inter-agency working and partnerships with other groups, would involve a more fundamental restructuring of the work. The building of partnerships with refugee communities would involve a change in the perception of these communities from a problem to a resource. This potential role was welcomed by the leaders of community groups whom we interviewed, who expressed a desire to work more closely with service providers in relation to such issues as training, translation and mediation. This role, however, raises tensions in relation to the role of the refugee committee organizations, which are increasingly being drawn away from political campaigning into becoming providers of services (Kofman, Lloyd and Sales 2002). As the policies framework in which these services are offered becomes more punitive, this raises the danger that these organizations become coopted themselves into the process of making judgements about eligibility for support of members of their own communities.

These strategies, however, while they may improve practice, would not tackle the basic contradiction within the work of the team. The culture of suspicion – both of groups and individuals – which is endemic to this work is not the basis for developing good social work practice. The dilemmas of this group represent in extreme form those of social workers attempting to balance their duties of care and control. While the specific role carried out by the asylum team no longer exists, these tensions are likely to continue within specialist teams working in this area, exacerbated by the political hostility towards asylum-seekers. Constructive work with asylum-seekers, like that cited above, depends on the building up of long-term relations of trust, which is only possible in a situation where the element of scrutiny of immigration status is removed.

Notes

1   We are grateful for the support of Middlesex University, which funded this project

References

Association of London Government/Refugee Council (1996) *No Place to Call Home.* London: ALG/Refugee Council.

Audit Commission (2000) *A New City: Supporting Asylum-seekers and Refugees in London.* London: Audit Commission.

Audit Commission (2001) *Halfway Home: An Analysis of the Variation in the Cost of Supporting Asylum-seekers.* London: Audit Commission.

Ayotte, W. (1998) *Supporting Unaccompanied Children in the Asylum Process.* London: Save the Children.

Banks, S. (2001) *Ethics and Values in Social Work* (2nd ed) London: Palgrave.

Becker, S. and McPherson, S. (1988) *Public Issues, Private Pain: Poverty, Social Work and Social Policy.* London: Social Services Insight.

Carey-Wood, J., Duke, K. Karn, V., and Marshall, T. (1995) *The Settlement of Refugees in Britain.* London: HMSO.

CCETSW (1996) *Assuring Quality in the Diploma in Social Work – 1: Rules and Requirements for the DipSW.* London: CCETSW.

Children Act (1989) London: HMSO.

Cohen, S. (2003) *No One is Illegal: Asylum and Immigration Control Past and Present.* Stoke-on-Trent: Trentham Books.

Dutton, J., Hek, R., Hoggart, L., Kohli, R. and Sales, R. (2000) *Supporting Refugees in the Inner City: An Examination of the Work of Social Services in Meeting the Settlement Needs of Refugees.* Unpublished report, Middlesex University.

Duvell, F. and Jordan, B. (2001) '"How low can you go?" Dilemmas of social work with asylum-seekers in London.' *Journal of Social Work Research and Evaluation 2,* 2.

Farmer, E. (1997) 'Protection and child welfare: Striking the balance.' In N. Parton (ed) *Child Protection and Family Support: Tensions, Contradictions and Possibilities.* London: Routledge.

General Social Care Council (2002) *Codes of Practice: For Social Care Workers and Employers.* London: GSCC.

Hayden, C., Goddard, J., Gorin, S., and Van Derspek, N. (1999) *State Child Care: Looking After Children.* London: Jessica Kingsley Publishers.

Hek, R. (2002) 'Integration not separation: Young refugees in British school.' *Forced Migration Review 15.*

Humphries, D. (2002) 'From welfare to authoritarianism: The role of social work in immigration controls.' In S. Cohen, B. Humphries and E. Mynott (eds) (2002) *From Immigration Controls to Welfare Controls.* London: Routledge.

Immigration and Asylum Act (1996) London: HMSO.

Immigration and Asylum Act (1999) London: HMSO.

Jones, C. (1998) 'Social work and society.' In R. Adams, L. Dominelli and M. Payne (eds) (1998) *Social Work: Themes, Issues and Critical Debates.* London: Palgrave.

Jordan, B. (1997) 'Social work and society.' In M. Davies (ed) (1997) *The Blackwell Companion to Social Work.* Oxford: Blackwell.

Kofman, E., Lloyd, C. and Sales, R. (2002) *Civic Stratification, Exclusion and Migratory Trajectories in Three European Cities – London, Paris and Rome.* Final Report to the Economic and Social Research Council.

Kohli, R. and Mather, R. (2003) 'Promoting psychosocial well-being in unaccompanied asylum-seeking young people in the United Kingdom.' *Child and Family Social Work 8,* 3.

Kohli, R. (2000) 'Breaking the silence.' *Professional Social Work.* June 2002, 6–9.

Lord Laming (2003) *The Victoria Climbie Inquiry.* London: HMSO.

Manthorpe, J. and Bradley, G. (2002) 'Managing finances.' In R. Adams, L. Dominelli and M. Payne (eds) *Critical Practice in Social Work.* London: Palgrave.

National Assistance Act (1948) London: HMSO.

Parton, N. (1991) *Governing the Family: Child Care, Child Protection and the State.* Basingstoke: Macmillan.

Parton, N. (ed) (1997) *Child Protection and Family Support. Tensions, Contradictions and Possibilities.* London: Routledge.

Parton, N. (ed) (1996) *Social Theory, Social Change and Social Work.* London: Routledge.

Payne, M. (1997) *Modern Social Work Theory* (2nd ed). Basingstoke: Macmillan.

Quality Assurance Agency (2000) *Subject Benchmark Statement for Social Work.* London: QAA.

Richman, N. (1998) *In the Midst of a Whirlwind.* Stoke-on-Trent: Trentham.

Sales, R. (2002) 'The deserving and the undeserving: Refugees, asylum-seekers and welfare in Britain.' *Critical Social Policy 22,* 1.

Stanley, K. (2001) *Cold Comfort: Young Separated Refugees in England.* London: Save the Children.

Stone, R. (2000) *Children First and Foremost; Meeting the Needs of Unaccompanied Asylum-seeking Children.* London: Barnardo's.

Thompson, N. (2000) *Understanding Social Work: Preparing for Practice.* London: Palgrave.

Williamson, L. (1998) 'Unaccompanied – but not unsupported.' In J. Rutter and C. Jones (eds) *Refugee Education: Mapping the Field.* Stoke-on-Trent: Trentham.

Zetter, R. and Pearl, M. (2000) 'The minority within the minority: Refugee community-based organisations in the UK and the impact of restrictionism on asylum-seekers.' *Journal of Ethnic and Migration Studies 26,* 4.

Chapter 5

Immigration is a Social Work Issue

John Collett

Introduction

I am writing this chapter from two perspectives: first, I am a newly-qualified social worker who attained the DipSW before the Nationality, Immigration and Asylum Act 2002 got final royal assent and second, I am the Operations Manager of a local authority asylum team contracted to the National Asylum Support Service (NASS). I therefore have direct experience of some of the welfare issues that arise for people subject to immigration controls.

This chapter focuses on asylum-seekers, and why they should be seen as a legitimate social work client group. It will examine their experiences of oppression, and will discuss social work and the place of immigration within it, with a reflection on anti-racist practice and the implications of social work involvement. It is based on my own experience and on discussions with people in various teams about social work and asylum.

Asylum is an issue that impacts on all social and political strata. It is seen by some as a site of danger to national identity, security and wealth. Others see it as part of the process for enriching the cultural life of Britain. The most powerful voices see asylum as a threat. By describing asylum-seekers as bogus and criminal, their ill-treatment can be legitimized, and a group can be objectified based on perceived characteristics. As a result the human rights of masses of people can be overlooked. In defending what is 'ours' we deny the human situations of the 'other'.

Asylum-seekers – from there to ignominy

An asylum-seeker can be legitimately defined as: 'a person who has applied for asylum in the UK' (Chatwin *et al*. 2001, p.49). This definition tells us very little about popular perceptions of asylum-seekers. As Cohen (2001, p.117) points out:

> Issues of asylum do not exist independent of immigration controls. Without controls, asylum laws would be unnecessary... To justify controls a distinction is made between 'genuine refugees' and 'economic migrants'. This fails to explain why 'economic migrants' should be excluded. The line between political and economic refugees is itself blurred.

What is implied here is that the genuine is the political, and the bogus is the economic. We arrive at the idea of economic migrant, or bogus asylum-seeker via various means, including the media, which becomes a 'key political actor' by employing negative terminology to describe this group (Bloch and Schuster 2002, p.406). Also, asylum-seekers are the scapegoats of societies in turbulent economic and social phases (Taylor 2001). Yet access to Europe as a refugee becomes more difficult with each passing year. Restrictions on legitimate routes ensure that people who need to escape persecution have to make their way to the border of a country to have even the remotest chance of being afforded protection.

There are doubtless economic attractors for people wanting to start a new life in the UK, but most of the access points to them are not available until they have been officially allowed to enter. The poverty people are escaping is often tied in with the political and social malaise a country is experiencing:

> by suggesting that there are 'genuine' people that are forced out of their homes by persecution and war, on the one hand, and those who simply seek a better life, on the other, the simplistic and unhelpful dichotomy between an asylum-seeker and an economic migrant...is perpetuated... It has been noted that leading migration scholars have argued that asylum-seekers and economic migrants arise out of the same situation of societal transformations and crisis linked to war, poverty, and nation-state formation... In this context, to question whether people leave out of desperation or aspiration is irrelevant. They seek to escape from social, economic and/or political insecurity to a more secure future. (Khan 2000, p.121)

People come to Britain because 'refugee migration is forced' (Bloch 2000, p.82) and thus you go to where you can. Bloch's research showed that 20 per cent came because of family connection, whereas 68 per cent came because they had no choice of destination. Other pull factors to a specific country are to do with colonial ties. This point is reiterated in other research (Stalker 2002) and is seen as the 'most important single factor' (Bloch and Schuster 2002, p.403). However, we are not being 'swamped' by asylum-seekers:

> Estimates are that, in 2002, just 5 per cent of refugees came to the European Union, of which less than 0.04 per cent came to Britain. The total number of asylum-seekers in Britain is just 0.3 per cent of the total UK population. (Kundnani 2001, pp.43–44)

This relatively small number of people has been transformed from humans into criminals, terrorists and scroungers by politicians and the media, and they suffer discrimination through UK immigration and social welfare processes.

People with needs – the illegal has landed

As social work clients, asylum-seekers need a viable identity. In this first part of the chapter, I focus on the experiences of women and on mental health issues, particularly post-traumatic stress disorder (PTSD), in order to highlight particular discriminations and the need for professional intervention from social workers. These issues affect people arriving, being processed, and ultimately obtaining a decision on their 'status'.

Asylum-seekers are people. But they are people in very unsettled situations. The trauma of leaving home, the trials and tribulations of escape and the treatment received via immigration processes operate in conjunction with the same social divisions experienced by the most marginalized groups in British society. These divisions will be familiar to everyone, located as they are around age, gender, culture, religion, 'race', sexuality, ability, political belief and affiliation, health, poverty, employment, education, housing, participation in society, marriage, family life, social networks and identity.

Those divisions are sharply felt by asylum-seekers and impact on the treatment and access to services and support they may require whilst in the UK, but there are additional gender and mental health issues added to the asylum situation. For example, women are at greater risk than men of discriminatory treatment through the asylum process: a woman claiming asylum with her husband is more likely to be added as a dependent than treated as a main applicant. Previously, when permission to work was afforded to some seeking asylum, it was offered to the man and not the woman (Bloch and Schuster 2002). This reflects where we, as a nation, think men and women should be between the hours of nine and five. For women, it reinforces the social isolation they often experience.

The position in which women find themselves in society as asylum-seekers is one of vulnerability: they are open to physical assault, sexual harassment and rape. Something less obvious to the observer is that women, as a result of the claim process within which men are the dominant claimants, will have to shoulder a greater burden in relation to the family: 'Divorce and serial marriage are common in communities living under pressure, which may leave women with sole responsibility for the children and with overwhelming domestic responsibilities' (Burnett and Peel 2001, p.322).

The Labour Government made concessions to women suffering domestic violence back in 1999. Women in violent situations would be allowed settlement but would have the burden of proof on them to get the concession, such as conviction in court of their partner, non-molestation orders or an injunction (Cohen 2001). However, if women are seen as dependents, moving out of the family home will result in their isolation. Some women will stay in an abusive relationship rather than cope with asylum on their own (Bloch and Schuster 2002). The effects of asylum processes lock people into situations where coping with daily life is very difficult, and can lead to:

> a high incidence of domestic violence both in asylum-seeking families and in those where one parent is subject to immigration controls, having been admitted to the UK as a 'spouse' with limited leave to remain. (Fitzpatrick 2002, p.1)

Thus there needs to be a greater recognition of the impact of sexual and physical trauma on women seeking asylum (Parker 2000). Historically, immigration control is based on gender roles and stereotypes, particularly around the view that women are looked after by men. Linked to this, there have also been fears that women will produce male children who will eventually become a threat to the indigenous workforce (Cohen 2001). Debates promoting the nuclear family as the ideal unit in society took place in parliament during the discussion of what became the Children Act 1989. There were discussions on how families are the foundation of our society, and that a particular kind of family is the best environment in which children can prosper. A paper for the Institute of Economic Affairs Health and Welfare Unit puts the idea of family in ideological terms:

> our free and reasonably successful society will be able to remain free and stable only when each generation moves into maturity and its civic responsibilities when it has effectively internalized those values which make for freedom and stability. The only institution which can provide the time, the attention, the love and the care for doing that is not just 'the family', but a stable two parent mutually complementary nuclear family. (Davies 1993, p.7 in Jones 2002, pp.83–84)

This results in locking women into dangerous environments. However, the irony of this concept is that immigration procedures serve to *break up* two-parent families by rejecting or refusing entry to one of the parents (Jones 2002). This cannot promote the health and well-being of children. It will certainly cause distress, separation and feelings of loss. Immigration also serves to force our cultural view of what a marriage is on others, in an attempt to invalidate cultures that differ from our own:

> One of the clearest forms of institutional racism is the way in which British immigration laws do not recognize Asian 'arranged marriages' and hence often prevent Asian families in the UK from bringing brides or grooms into the country to marry their sons or daughters. (Bernardes 1997, p.135)

Women suffer discrimination as producers of children, as dependents of male partners, as carers in families, as an assumed collection of stereotypical female behaviour. These are all sites of discrimination that serve to increase the vulnerability of the female asylum-seeker.

> Women are at special risk both during flight and in asylum because of the dependency of children and the sick and disabled on them, and because of their vulnerability to sexual exploitation. (Muecke 1992, pp.517–518)

The discriminatory asylum process is added to by assumptions made about the culture a woman has departed, and how she will behave in Britain. Instead of the media-suggested hordes of economic, bogus asylum-seekers, we have a small, highly visible and vulnerable minority. This leads to fear and often to subsequent mental health problems. People are often unsure of approaching immigration services to state their case. In 1998 it was noted that many people delay making asylum applications because:

> Highly traumatised, often having experienced torture, asylum-seekers are known to avoid officials on arrival in fear of being imprisoned or sent back to their home country, often waiting many weeks or months before making a claim for asylum. (Khan 2000, p.124, discussing research by Morrison 1998)

Section 55 of the NIA Act 2002, which establishes the need to apply for asylum 'as soon as reasonably practicable after the person's arrival in the United Kingdom' (HMSO 2002, p.31) ignores the causal factors for migrating:

> There are a number of reasons why asylum-seekers might not claim asylum immediately on arrival to Britain. Some arrive in a confused and frightened state, some fear officialdom, some fear deportation and some have language difficulties that might present barriers at the port. (Bloch 2000, pp.78–79, discussing research by the Refugee Council 1998)

It is these factors that need to be considered when looking at what is 'reasonably practicable'. People are far less likely to go through immigration processes whilst in Britain if the upshot is a spell in a removal centre. The idea of approaching services is one that causes anxiety and fear. A major factor relating to this fear of the immigration processes is post-traumatic stress disorder (PTSD). There is a lot of evidence to suggest that 'being' an asylum-seeker is detrimental to health:

> In getting to asylum, refugees may have to dodge military or guerrilla surveillance, sea pirates, or land mines: survive on wild foods while travelling through unfamiliar terrain at night to escape detection... That fraction who manage to attain recognition as refugees in asylum thereby win...a life style of dependency on their hosts. (Muecke 1992, pp.517–518)

PTSD can be brought about by cultural bereavement – departing what is familiar for the unknown (Bhugra and Jones 2001). Poor social support in the receiving country has been raised as a closer link to PTSD in some cases, even compared to previous torture (Mentality 2002). And once asylum-seekers are in the safe country, there is: 'the negative impact of factors such as fears of being sent home, interviews with immigration officials, separation from a spouse, threats to family, poverty and discrimination on mental health' (Watters 2001, p.1711).

Whilst research is ongoing and conclusions are tentative (ibid.), the psychological aspect of migration and reception into the host country is undeniable:

> Salient ongoing stressors identified across several studies include delays in the processing of refugee applications, conflict with immigration officials, being denied a work permit, unemployment, separation from family, and loneliness and boredom. (Silove, Steel and Watters 2000, p.5)

PTSD is a factor affecting the lives of asylum-seekers in our country. Added to this is the effect PTSD can have on performance. Immigration interviews require evidence for the right to stay in the country. Once an asylum-seeker has given evidence, he or she may be required to give further evidence at another interview reinforcing the claim. This stirs up memories and can cause distress. It can also lead to inconsistencies in the story, which may jeopardize the claim. The experiences an asylum-seeker has gone through may be difficult to relate to someone in authority:

> Post-traumatic stress disorder may impede memory, leading to inconsistent testimony. Lack of trust of officials may lead to evasiveness. Sensitive material such as a history of rape or sexual trauma may be suppressed. Yet discrepancies in histories often are used as the key reason for rejecting refugee claims. (*ibid.* p.3)

These prior experiences lead to people becoming asylum-seekers. The traumas and violations undergone in the home country are brought with them to our shores. They have a legitimate claim on support and therapeutic services, yet the response is often an excessive concern over cost, and a suspicion about the economic motives for the movement of people. The examples given of gender, and of mental health, demonstrate the isolation and lack of understanding experienced on coming to the UK. This is compounded by perceptions of asylum-seekers as feckless itinerants breaking into the land of milk and honey. Seeking asylum is a frightening experience.

The social work response

The main professional group in a position to address issues of oppression and discrimination on a day-to-day basis is that of social workers, yet the involvement of social workers is too little and too reluctant. Emphasis on the health and welfare of children allows social workers to become focused on specific issues, such as safe case transfer of 'unaccompanied asylum-seeking children'

(UASCs) whilst not focusing on the needs of adult asylum-seekers. PTSD, for example, requires strong advocacy within systems to ensure that people access the support they need. Whilst people in local authority teams do provide support, they do it in a context that demands a strong focus on housing management. This is because of the local authority's contractual relationship with NASS and the possibility of incurring financial penalties if properties are not ready for use when NASS want to disperse people. Also, housing stock is often poor quality because properties that are 'hard to let' are used to house asylum-seekers. This reduces tension with local people, who cannot really claim an interest in the properties used for dispersal, but also means that properties are often in a poor state of repair, at least initially, and repair work is constant and on-going. This does not leave a great deal of time to wrestle with systems on behalf of the client.

A certain level of support is, and must continue to be, provided by local authority asylum teams and other providers, but a recognition of the complexity of the issues facing the client brings with it a need for longer-term involvement. Once an adult client has been 'processed' for asylum purposes, and has moved through the NASS system in one way or another, virtually all contact with the asylum team will cease. There may be exceptions to this, particularly with children and young people, but for adults there is little continuity of care through the process unless the individual's needs are addressed whilst in the NASS system. Thus, a group of people who are vulnerable can drift out of potential helping systems. Social work involvement with asylum- seekers could serve to stop this drift, and could enable clients to succeed in developing a new life in Britain.

Yet asylum-seekers are still not regarded as significant enough to be a focus of social work training. It is not seen to be a social work issue; but 'Social work appears where archaic community begins to break down, and it aims to restore inclusion and cooperation' (Jordan 1997, p.20). Asylum-seekers are clearly an excluded group with limited access to adequate supports. The range of issues, backgrounds, stories, and events in people's lives requires a range of services, from basic day-to-day support in dealing with health services, immigration appointments and settlement, to professional input where advocacy and detailed support are necessary.

However, social workers are poorly trained in issues of immigration. They are not encouraged to view asylum-seekers as clients, and instead are being increasingly drawn into issues of gatekeeping and informing on behalf of the immigration services:

> Social Services are increasingly perceived by asylum-seekers as the coercive arm of the state in that social workers are compelled to inform immigration authorities of illegal – 'bogus' – asylum-seekers and have the unenviable responsibility of having to make unpopular decisions of who is and who is not eligible for social service assistance. (Khan 2000, p.126)

Social workers are not expected to work with this client group unless absolutely necessary, but are expected to report to immigration anyone they suspect as bogus. My training in social work came before the NIA Act 2002. Whilst I was being trained, the new law introduced a requirement on local authorities to report to the immigration services anyone subject to immigration controls suspected of misusing services. This was not made explicit in the training, because of the perception of immigration as a side issue. The opportunity was missed to examine the process of labelling this group as bogus, dangerous and criminal. Anti-oppressive practice is one of the 'sacred cows' of social work (Wilson and Beresford 2000, p.553), yet the contradiction between our role as social workers and our role as pseudo immigration officials needs to be highlighted and the ethical implications grasped. Social work is an anti-discriminatory practice, but immigration is an area where discrimination is allowed because of the illegitimacy ascribed to the client group. Not to offer a critique of this in training creates professionals who are unaware of their collusion: '…a social work that is unaware of its potential for discrimination and oppression is a dangerous social work' (Thompson 1997, p.70). Successful social work interventions with asylum-seekers do occur, but this is often down to individual examples of good practice. Greater success in local authorities has been based on the strategic approach of councils to involve social workers directly. This entails trading on personal knowledge of systems and the people who operate them – thus, if someone has been in an authority for some time as a worker, they may be better able to access support for the client. At the same time, some local authority asylum teams may feel that it is better to leave the social work aspect to the experts (i.e. social workers), whilst they maintain their housing role. An argument against that position acknowledges that many asylum-seekers will not, or may not be able to, access services without support. The most contact individuals and families will have with a service will be with the local authority team. Placement of social workers on those teams would help reduce the workload of support workers who also have to deal with housing issues, and would place a professional in a setting familiar to the client. This can then help in clients developing trust, and asking for support. Teams that have been noted nationally for the quality of their support have integrated social work and support work teams. Where provision is limited, as it is for asylum-seekers, I argue that there is greater need for highly trained advocates to access that provision wherever possible on behalf of the client.

It would be unacceptable for racism to be quietly ignored in any other area of social work, yet it is a barrier to effective working faced by many in the field. My discussions within local authority teams suggest that some council services and employees, when approached for support for asylum-seekers, show discriminatory attitudes towards them. Yet the ethics and values of social work, as expounded by the British Association of Social Workers (BASW), state that social work is about challenging and respecting the rights of everybody.

> The social work profession promotes social change, problem solving in human relationships and the empowerment and liberation of people to enhance well-being... Principles of human rights and social justice are fundamental to social work. (BASW 2001, in BASW 2003 pp.1–2)

The five basic values of social work are: human dignity and worth, social justice, service to humanity, integrity and competence. We are working with human beings and:

> Every human being has intrinsic value. All persons have a right to well-being, to self-fulfilment and to as much control over their own lives as is consistent with the rights of others. (*ibid.*, p.2).

The asylum process does not interfere with the rights of others – it merely restricts the rights of the person subject to immigration control. Thus, if we are to follow the code of ethics, we should challenge these systems, and work with the asylum-seeker. However, the current framework of policy does not allow social workers to do this effectively. Within social work, the idea of challenge, though emphasized in ethics, does not necessarily translate to the workplace: 'being political is synonymous with being "unprofessional" in public sector services where professional detachment and its function in maintaining power relations are accepted uncritically' (Husband 1991, p.66 in Ford 2000, p.18). This causes problems for those wishing to work in an anti-racist manner. There is recognition that social work is a middle-class, white preserve (Dominelli 1997); working alongside immigration systems demonstrates the implications of this:

> Immigration policy has been the major public arena in which the politics of 'race' which impinge on social work practice have been officially played out. This process has shifted immigration policy from being a matter of concern to immigration officials at the point of entry, to a key mechanism for internal control. (*ibid.*, p.27)

Thus, a white-dominated profession is being drawn into the restriction of the 'other'. This is completely at odds with anti-racist practice (ARP), which aims to raise awareness of how white people are taught to perceive diversity as a negative factor, and to challenge the notion that our largely white country does not have a racism problem. This is particularly relevant when considering local authorities charged with the responsibility of placing asylum-seekers in their area. A small and silent black population does not mean an absence of racism in an area. Indeed, the opposite is more likely to be true (Dominelli 1992). Therefore, ARP is required in practice to encourage social workers towards genuine acceptance of other cultural activity and experience as of equal worth and merit to that of the white Western way of doing things (Duncan 1988):

> White social workers adopting an anti-racist position have a conscious-ness raising role to play in enabling white people to perceive racism as a social issue. Their day-to-day interactions with black people living in decaying urban areas, resisting poverty and coming to grips with hardship provides them with information for countering racist claims that black people are responsible for creating their own problems. White practitioners can challenge such allegations by using their practice expe-rience to demonstrate the resilience of black people in overcoming adver-sity. This also gives social workers an edge in participating in public debates about policy, its social causes, its debilitating effects on individ-ual personalities, and its destructive impact on black-white relationships. Also, they can use knowledge so gained to argue for the transformation of social work practice in accordance with egalitarian anti-racist princi-ples. (Dominelli 1997, p.41)

Whilst this definition is rigid in its application of colour, for the most part the removal of the phrase 'black people', and the insertion of 'asylum-seeker' in its place, makes a more inclusive definition, where asylum-seekers include white people, and are discriminated against because of their belonging to a particular social group.

Anti-racist practice serves to raise awareness of everyday racism, and nowhere is racism more explicit than in immigration systems. If we do not acknowledge this position, we leave ourselves open to the acceptance of 'new racist' ideas such as the immutability of culture – a stance that allows for us to make sense of our behaviours by discounting the cultural and behavioural differences of others (Barker 1981 in Ford 2000; Husband 1991, 1992 in Ford 2000). This in turn plays into the concept of familism, where families that do not fit into the white Western norm can be categorized as deviant (Dalley 1996). Such approaches are demonstrated in terms of the lack of acceptance of arranged marriages (Bernardes 1997) or polygamous ones (Cohen 2001) through immigration systems. They are also located in the vague concepts of ethnicity as found in some social work texts, where an ethnic background is identified by its difference from the mainstream culture; its visible differences a process of reducing people to a set of external identifiers (Fook 2001). Without an active challenge to racist systems, social workers are in a position where they may perpetuate such notions. The diversity that should be celebrated becomes an inconvenience because it does not fit with service provision.

Without operating in an anti-racist manner, social workers are increasingly drawn into the dirty work of social policy, where we reinforce the oppressions that we should be challenging. Thus, social work becomes an

> activity that in the recent past has been extraordinarily explicit in its stand on anti–racist…practice, but which has been at times rather naïve about its contradictory positioning, and which latterly has been increasingly drawn into a disciplinary and surveillance role in policing the poor, to the extent of having now been 'tamed'. (Humphries 2002, p.126)

Anti-racist practice (ARP) is fundamental to effective social work. The problem lies in the fact that we are using this approach in an environment of institutionalised racism. Those who seek to defend the rights of asylum-seekers are working in conflict with Government policy, increasingly framed around removal. In effect, social workers are forced out of ethical pursuits and challenging systems, because the very make-up of the asylum process, with its separate form of provision under the auspices of NASS, excludes, for the most part, social work activity. A result of this separation is that asylum-seekers, no longer able to provide for themselves, become 'welfarised' (Thompson 1998). The irony is that the main criticisms against the client group come from the fact that they enjoy our benefits, when the reality is that they have no choice to do otherwise.

Some may feel that ARP does not allow for a focus on a range of oppressions that asylum-seekers endure. A focus on blackness per se can lead to a reduced view of difference. What is helpful with ARP is that it allows for attention to be paid to a form of oppression, which in turn highlights other oppressions. A conception of racism that focuses on skin colour does not allow for differences within 'blackness' – such as in those who are from Asian and Chinese populations (Ford 2000). It also obscures those who are white asylum-seekers, those from eastern Europe, for example. This is where an ethnocentric point of view interplays with new racism. Immigration rules, laws and practices are formed around the notion that Britain has a certain way of life. The assumption is that people from outside act differently from those within Britain. White and black asylum-seekers are corrupt, and culturally different. They must be legislated against. In terms of anti-racist practice around immigration, white is the new black. The construction and treatment of asylum-seekers is a hybrid of ethnocentrism, and new racism. Since the discrimination of the immigration system does not take account of colour per se, ARP becomes more important as a tool of resistance because immigration laws are created in environments of racist assumption against all asylum-seekers.

Whilst the ethics of social work and the realities of practice are in conflict, social workers themselves are called upon to be unofficial immigration officers:

> where the Secretary of State reasonably suspects that a person has committed a specific offence under the 1971 Act and is, or has been resident in a local authority area, the Secretary of State may require that local authority to provide information for the purpose of locating that person. It further provides that local authorities must comply with such a requirement. (HMSO 2002a, p.53)

One of the reasons local authorities can be asked to provide information is if the Secretary of State believes someone has broken immigration rules (including illegal entry, without which some would never gain entry). As a social worker in such a circumstance, I would be obliged to help the Government in tracking a person down. Without the awareness gained by opting to learn about immigration controls, I may remain ignorant of the surveillance role allocated to me. Yet, regardless of the latest legislation, local authorities have been providing information to the Home Office on an informal basis since 1996 (Cohen 2003). The reality is that in order to carry out their function, the immigration services require a transformation of the role of other professions in the process. It should be a matter of some resentment amongst social workers that, having gone into a substantial amount of debt to study and eventually enter a profession of choice, the role of their work is not what it is taught to be. And this is not solely a social work issue. It affects all welfare provision (Cohen 2001; Hayes 2002).

Social workers are not generally trained in immigration issues, yet it is the site of massive institutional discrimination, and an area of work in which they are increasingly expected to participate. Those social workers who want to work positively with asylum issues are doing so in a context of suspicion. They are also doing it with little training and with few resources.

> There is some evidence, both anecdotal and those derived from national, and local newspapers and social work newssheets, that SSDs are struggling to provide services to recently arrived asylum-seekers and that social workers are increasingly feeling embattled in the face of limited resources, increasing volumes of work arising from asylum case assessments, as well as lack of experience, and specialist training in working with asylum-seekers. (Khan 2000, p.124)

Successive attacks on the universality of welfare, in accordance with New Right philosophies, have always singled out 'undesirable' elements within society. This leads to the labelling and separation from society of those perceived as unworthy, with particular reference to asylum-seekers: '"Popular racism" – which has already defined them as "illegals" and "scroungers" – gives European governments the mandate to exclude them from social provision altogether' (Feketi 1997, p.11, in Hayes 2000, p.64).

There would be greater benefit in the acknowledgement of the validity of asylum-seekers as a client group, than there is in promoting negative stereotypes or restrictive policies that can then be adopted by extremist political groups for their own gain. These people are future citizens, not temporary inconveniences to be pushed from pillar to post. Even if their claim for asylum is rejected, or clients are only offered temporary status in the form of humanitarian protection, their human rights need protecting as much as anyone else's. Instead of equipping social workers for understanding and working with the diversity of the society around them:

> We deprive social work students, whatever their ethnic identity might be, of knowledge about the wide range of ethnic groups in this country, many of whom they will meet during the helping process. (Fook 2001, pp.39–40)

As is evidenced above, social work training has some way to go. The development of the Diploma in Social Work has been along lines of anti-oppressive, anti-racist and anti-discriminatory practices, but still has some ground to cover in terms of developing a worker base that is competent in working with diversity. The social worker, as restrictions tighten, will be operating within and through the personal, cultural and structural levels of discrimination faced by clients. Though the politics of our country have been shifting to the right,

> Social work has preserved its commitment to anti-oppressive practice, however, and as part of this there is a need to highlight oppressive and damaging practice and to promote the rights of disadvantaged and stigmatized groups. It is perhaps especially important for social workers to utilize specific knowledge in their assessment and provision of services to meet needs and to advocate strongly within communities for the rights of groups who have already experienced distress and trauma. (Parker 2000, p.67)

Even if the asylum-seeker does not attain status that allows him/her to remain in the UK, our profession ought, in line with its ethics and values, to be engaged in providing a professional service that respects human rights. The perspective, as mentioned before, is of future citizen, not current problem.

Onslaughts on one client group can easily be transposed onto another. Allowing the framing of asylum-seekers as bogus is a backdoor assault on welfare in general. By allowing ourselves as social workers to be silent partners in this ideological discussion, we pave the way for further restrictions on people who are actually allowed to be resident in our country. This may result in social workers buying into the marginalization of people who are 'less' than ourselves:

> To complain of the 'burden' of asylum-seekers in this way is also to attack, implicitly, the principle of welfare and the moral idea of care beyond the measure of market values. For the New Right, asylum-seekers, the long-term unemployed, anyone forced to survive by the welfare state, all stand side by side, all are 'scroungers'. And at a time

when the welfare state is enjoying a partial revival in support, the asylum issue is a way in which the welfare principle can once again be driven back, just as 'dole cheats' was the cry in the 1980s. Bill Morris, leader of the Transport and General Workers' Union, was right to warn that if today the state can force the voucher system on asylum-seekers, then tomorrow it can force it on the unemployed as well. (Kundnani 2001, p.54)

Debates within social work often focus on the position it wants to attain in society. Do we maintain the status quo or do we challenge it (Shardlow 1998)? Can we do both? Do we subscribe to the systems or do we act around them, individually, finding ever more protracted ways of providing support for people who need it? Do we rely on solicitors defending the human rights of asylum-seekers, or do we do it ourselves? Many would say these arguments are not located within reality. But the reality is happening. People whose claims fail have limited options: voluntary return, destitution, or going underground.

Conclusions

Asylum-seekers are not allowed to work. They live on lower than subsistence levels of income. They would like to work but they cannot. They want to be independent but our systems have the opposite effect. Many would like to be at home with their families, but that is not possible. Instead, they want to participate in the immigration processes, but have a fear of being rejected. They would rather be in society than on the fringes, but we demonize, illegalize and marginalize them to the point where they cannot participate.

When asylum-seeker claims are refused, financial and accommodation support stop. An asylum-seeker may not be removed for many months after a failed claim, thus being left in destitution. Some local authority workers find that being forced to place someone in destitution is more than they are prepared to accept in their job. People who care about the clients may leave rather than put another individual in such a situation. Personal experience of local authority work has demonstrated to me that people will threaten their own lives rather than face the streets. Those clients prepared to go to extremes will get services, usually based around an assessment of their mental health. Those who accept their situation simply disappear from view.

The role of social workers would be as advocate and negotiator. Social workers can better access services and support the client through the process.

Individuals and families are under great pressure in the asylum process and feel suspicious of people in institutions. With all the other exclusion suffered by this client group, advocacy and awareness of the issue are crucial. Without social work intervention, many would not access supports they need.

The different agencies that social workers are part of and engage with need to change also. Access to services needs to be increased, or social workers will eventually find themselves hitting the same barriers an unsupported client would do. In the meantime, however, social workers can protect the interests of the client group up to the point our laws currently allow. Just as services should be provided to adults and children in Britain, so they could be provided to asylum-seekers. If the Government is inefficient in removing people, it seems unfair to place people in destitution until departments catch up with their workload. This is not a call for more efficient removal of asylum-seekers – merely more humane treatment whilst they undergo the asylum process.

As a final point, immigration is in fact an issue that affects all areas of society and all people. It is not with any arrogance that I assert social work's position in the field. Racism and its policy manifestations affect all workers, and all people, in the UK. As such, we are all subject to immigration control. I focus on social work as something I am proud to be a part of. Unfortunately it is being increasingly drawn into the provision of immigration services. That is not what I became a social worker for.

References

Bernardes, J. (1997) *Family Studies – an Introduction*. London: Routledge.

Bloch, A. (2000) 'Refugee settlement in Britain: The impact of policy on participation.' *Journal of Ethnic and Migration Studies 26* (2000), 1, 75–88.

Bloch, A., and Schuster, L. (2002) 'Asylum and welfare: Contemporary debates.' *Critical Social Policy 22*, (2002), 3, 393–414.

Bhugra, D. and Jones, P. (2001), 'Migration and mental illness.' *Advances in Psychiatric Treatment 7*, (2001), 216–223.

British Association of Social Workers, (2003) *The Code of Ethics for Social Work*. Located via website: www.basw.co.uk/pages/info/ethics.htm

Burnett, A. and Peel, M. (2001), 'Asylum-seekers and refugees in Britain – health needs of asylum-seekers and refugees.' *British Medical Journal 322*, (2001), 544–547.

Chatwin, M., Coker, J., Crockett, T., Finch, N., Lukes, S. and Stanley, A. (2001) *Asylum-seekers: A Guide to Recent Legislation*. London: Resource Information Service (RIS), and Immigration Law Practitioners' Association (ILPA).

Cohen, S. (2001) *Immigration Controls, the Family and the Welfare State*. London: Jessica Kingsley Publishers.

Cohen, S. (2003) *No-one is Illegal – Asylum and Immigration Control Past and Present.* Stoke-on-Trent: Trentham Books.

Cohen, S., Humphries, B. and Mynott, E. (eds) (2002) *From Immigration to Welfare Controls.* London: Jessica Kingsley Publishers.

Dalley, G. (1996) *Ideologies of Caring – Second Edition.* London: MacMillan.

Davies, M. (ed) (1997) *The Blackwell Companion to Social Work.* Oxford: Blackwell.

Dominelli, L. (1992) *Anti-racist Perspective.* MBA Video Productions.

Dominelli, L. (1997) *Anti-racist Social Work – Second Edition.* London: MacMillan.

Duncan, C. (1988) *Pastoral Care: An Anti-racist/Multicultural Perspective.* Oxford: Blackwell.

Fitzpatrick, P. (2002) 'Hostile reception.' Located via website, www.communitycare.co.uk/article

Fook, J. (2001) 'Emerging ethnicities as a theoretical framework for social work.' In L. Dominelli, W. Lorenz and H. Soydan (2001) *Beyond Racial Divides: Ethnicities in Social Work Practice.* Aldershot: Ashgate Publishing.

Ford, D. (2000) 'The commitment to anti-racist practice.' In P. Stepney and D. Ford (eds) (2000) *Social Work Models, Methods and Theories: A Framework for Practice.* Lyme Regis: Russell House.

Hayes, D. (2000) 'Outsiders within: The role of welfare in the internal control of immigration.' In J. Batsleer and B. Humphries (eds) (2000) *Welfare, Exclusion and Political Agency.* London: Routledge.

Hayes, D. (2002) 'From aliens to asylum-seekers: A history of immigration controls and welfare in Britain.' In S. Cohen, B. Humphries and E. Mynott (eds) (2002) *From Immigration to Welfare Controls.* London: Jessica Kingsley Publishers.

Nationality, Immigration and Asylum Act (2002) London: HMSO.

HMSO (2002a) *Explanatory Notes – Nationality, Immigration and Asylum Act 2002.* London: HMSO.

Humphries, B. (2002) 'From welfare to authoritarianism: The role of social work in immigration controls.' In S. Cohen, B. Humphries and E. Mynott (eds) (2002) *From Immigration to Welfare Controls.* London: Jessica Kingsley Publishers.

Jones, A. (2002) 'Family life and the pursuit of immigration controls.' In S. Cohen, B. Humphries and E. Mynott (eds) (2002) *From Immigration to Welfare Controls.* London: Jessica Kingsley Publishers.

Jordan, B. (1997) 'Social work and society.' In M. Davies (ed) (1997) *The Blackwell Companion to Social Work.* Oxford: Blackwell.

Khan, P. (2000) 'Asylum-seekers in the UK: Implications for social service involvement.' *Social Work and Social Sciences Review 8* (2000), 2, 116–129.

Kundnani, A. (2001) 'In a foreign land: The new popular racism.' *Race and Class 43* (2001), 2, 41–60.

Mentality (2002) 'Mental health promotion with black and minority ethnic groups.' A Briefing Paper for the Black and Minority Ethnic Forum Meeting, 25 April 2002.

Muecke, M. (1992) 'New paradigms for refugee health problems.' *Social Sciences and Medicine* (1992), 35 4, 515–523.

Parker, J. (2000) 'Social work with refugees and asylum-seekers: A rationale for developing practice.' *Practice* (2000), 12 3, 61–76.

Shardlow, S. (1998) 'Values, ethics, and social work.' In R. Adams, L. Dominelli and M. Payne (eds) (1998) *Social Work – Themes, Issues and Critical Debates.* Basingstoke: Palgrave.

Silove, D., Steel, Z. and Watters, C. (2000) 'Policies of deterrence and the mental health of asylum-seekers.' *Journal of the American Medical Association* (2000), 284 5, 604–611.

Stalker, P. (2002) 'Migration trends and migration policy in Europe'. *International Migration* (2002), Vol. 40 2, 151–176.

Taylor, A. (2001) 'Our Land of the free?' *Community Care*, 13th September 2001, via website: www.communitycare.co.uk/article

Thompson, N. (1997) *Anti-Discriminatory Practice – Second Edition.* London: MacMillan.

Thompson, N. (1998) *Promoting Equality – Challenging Discrimination and Oppression in the Human Services.* London: MacMillan.

Watters, C. (2001) 'Emerging paradigms in the mental health care of refugees.' *Social Science and Medicine 52* (2001), 1709–1718.

Wilson, A. and Beresford, P. (2000) 'Anti-oppressive practice: Emancipation or appropriation?' *British Journal of Social Work 30* (2000), 553–573.

Chapter 6

Social Work Intervention: The Deconstruction of Individuals as a Means of Gaining a Legislative Perspective to Remain in the United Kingdom

Chris Brown

Introduction

This chapter will evaluate and provide an analysis of the dichotomy between the social work process and the ensuing deconstruction of an individual or individuals, in order to provide sufficient rationale to the Home Office that there is real and necessary reason why they should remain within the UK. I intend to present an argument that, under current policy, refugees and those applying for asylum are forced to undergo a critical examination of their circumstances which magnifies and creates a pathology of their difficulties. Under other circumstances this would be perceived as oppressive and an act undermining their human rights.

An increasing number of legal practitioners are asking for social work reports to evaluate a person's social circumstance. Whilst certain pieces of legislation provide a framework for this investigative process, e.g. the Children Act 1989, there is no specific pro forma for the undertaking of such pieces of work. In order to gain a perspective of need or necessity, practitioners have to create an index of difficulties that in other social spheres would not require such emphasis. As a result of such intense dissection, individuals become the focus of increased stigmatization and labelling as a paradoxical means of gaining liberty and the opportunity to continue to live in a 'democratic' Western society.

It is, I feel, necessary to examine the ethics of this process when taken against a background of individuals requesting to remain for humanitarian reasons – be they fear of persecution or the need to care for a dependent family member. From desperate circumstances, individuals have little choice other than to be portrayed in an often negative and dehumanizing manner.

When I initially became drawn to this area of practice, I was a field social worker undertaking primarily child protection work. I subsequently moved to a health care setting before recognizing that, in order to work in a manner which I felt appropriate to proactive intervention, I would be better placed working independently without the constraints set by local authority policy and protocol.

Background

> They arrived in Midwinter, with almost no winter clothes. In the airport building the children clung around her, restless in their insecurity, as they shuffled with the slowly moving queue to the desk marked ALL OTHER COUNTRIES. When finally it was their turn she found it difficult to speak, to answer the questions of the man with the impassive face. His fingers twitched in silent irritation round the rubber stamp in which was invested the power to let them in or turn them away. Back. Once they were through she felt momentarily at a loss. All her energies had been concentrated on getting past that point. She became aware of one of the children tugging at her hand, pulling her towards the baggage collection point where the suitcases lurched out through rubber flaps to flop heavily on the conveyor belt and begin circling slowly round. (Molteno 1992, p.3)

Ms Molteno (above) was born in Zambia and came to the UK in 1977. For me this passage evoked and conveyed the dread and uncertainty of those entering the UK from a country offering no security and that indeed for many had engendered absolute fear and terror, to a receiving country which was both alien and formidable. Many of those attempting to enter the UK had witnessed and experienced horror and loss on a scale unimaginable to those of us who have been brought up in Western culture and society. We have as a society become complacent in our attitude towards those for whom persecution is an everyday occurrence.

Elizabeth Little (1997, pp.10–11) describes her experiences as a social work manager working with orphaned unaccompanied refugee children. She states:

> Until recently, children were treated the same as adults in the asylum application process. Although children can now make a claim in writing within a month rather than being required to respond verbally on arrival, and these claims are dealt with by a separate Home Office section, they are still responsible for recounting clearly how and why they came to be here. They are also expected to provide acceptable evidence, despite being empty-handed, traumatised, bewildered and bereaved... Revelations about starvation, imprisonment and torture are completely alien to Western culture. One girl watched a TV news item in her country in which her father was shot dead. One boy constantly relives the day when his grandfather saved his life by moving to take the bullet directed at him.

Little goes on to give further harrowing examples, the point being that the majority of those entering the UK do so because they are simply desperate and have little choice other than to flee. For many this is a choice which they would not have made were it not for circumstance. Current media portrayal, and the diatribe against asylum-seekers pouring into the UK because state benefits and accommodation are easily available to them, is wildly inaccurate. Asylum-seekers and refugees leave behind families, friends, social networks and value systems which are integral to them as individuals. The xenophobic viewpoint of an increasing number of westerners, that asylum-seekers are simply 'scroungers', is an extremely disturbing one with more than a nodding acquaintance to the growth of fascism in pre-war Germany. It is therefore within this context that individuals and families have to provide sufficient rationale to the Home Office that there is a real and necessary reason why they should remain in the UK. These individuals and families, who may have already experienced unimaginable trauma, have to begin the process under current Home Office policy of undergoing a critical examination of their circumstances which, given their extraordinary personal situations, magnifies and creates a pathology of their already profound difficulties.

My own awareness of the oppressive and dichotomous nature of social work practices with regard to asylum-seekers and refugees began to develop long before the current crisis. Society has seen a return to the moral panic and hysteria witnessed in the 50s and 60s about a youth culture analysed in detail by Stanley Cohen (1980). It is necessary to illustrate how society creates a deviant 'underclass' on which is focused all of its ills and bigotry. More contemporary argument of this theme is put forward by Jock Young (1999), which links the issue of asylum-seekers to the creation of the 'other'. A person seeking asylum is one somehow separate from society as a whole and in effect becomes demonized. History is littered with such societal bullying: the Spanish Inquisition, the plight of Jews in pre-war Germany and the ethnic explosions in eastern Europe during the 1990s, which have led to an increase in the numbers of individuals who need to seek asylum through no fault of their own.

The fleeing/arriving connection

In June 1989 I was invited to and travelled to Somalia. Civil war had begun, particularly around Hargeisa, the main city in the north of the country. The fighting had yet to reach Mogadishu but was only a matter of months away. There was a peculiar sense of normality, of people going about their everyday activities unsure if and when the fighting would escalate and come to the middle and southern regions of the country. In Mogadishu itself there were many who had fled or been airlifted from the conflict. The wealthier Somalis were able to find accommodation in the few hotels dotted throughout the city. For others it meant imposing on relatives or living in makeshift plastic tents which would form small estates of misery. Travelling further south I found a real sense of anxiety, exacerbated by the tribal differences existing around the area of Baraawe. The poverty in which people lived was simply shocking. There were numerous street children who appeared to be homeless, some as young as five years old.

In the squalid local hospital lay corpses awaiting collection, wrapped in blankets covered in flies. Next to these was a young boy, his lower body eaten away by tuberculosis, his mother desperate for some hope. This hope took the form of a German woman who had moved temporarily to Somalia to be with her partner. She was a nurse who went daily to visit the boy to give him some physiotherapy. The nurse knew her input gave little more than a focus to the boy's day and she felt totally inadequate when faced with such overwhelming misery within the facility, donated by the Italians who had occupied the region prior to World War II. There was no basic sanitation and what drugs were available were rudimentary and useless against the degree of disease and infection.

Shortly after my return from Somalia the war, as anticipated, escalated. There were many casualties, the country was decimated and a huge influx of refugees fled to the UK. Many were dispersed to the north west. At this time I was working in a childcare setting whilst undertaking an MA in Social Work. The focus for my dissertation was a social policy study to examine how adequately and impartially social agencies attempted to meet and understand the needs of the then Somali refugees entering the UK from an area of civil war and conflict. This was 1992/3. I conducted my research by using an ethnographic approach, employing qualitative methodology. In doing so I undertook a comparative study of a group of Somalis who were generally established in Liverpool 8 and had been for some time prior to the fighting. All knew of people or had family members involved in the conflict but they appeared to have an established structure of support. However, my other study group consisted of recently arrived Somalis, mostly women with young families who had arrived without their husbands. One woman with a very young family recounted how she had attempted to travel to Mogadishu to find her husband but she had passed him on the road to Baraawe. He had been caught up in the fighting and was shot and killed. The woman was clearly traumatized and desperate with grief. To add to her difficulties, the dialect of Baarawen-speaking Somalis is different from the language spoken throughout the rest of the country. She was more isolated and marginalized than many others fleeing from the country, as the authorities in the north west had at the time very few Baarawen-speaking interpreters. Also, many refugees who had come to the UK had done so via camps in Ethiopia, Kenya, Yemen and Djibouti. Those who had left family in Somalia were unsure due to displacement whether or not relatives had escaped the conflict, been returned to Somalia or been killed. What became apparent whilst conducting the research was how little provision had been made available to this particular group of refugees and how little understanding there was of their needs. There were pockets of expertise but on the whole, other than standard social work practices and services to meet the needs of children and families, there was no specialist provision for the victims of war – particularly those services offering psycho-social or therapeutic input.

Services which were available were open to arbitrary allocation and a system of duality which one hopes could not operate in today's climate. I was aware that in the welfare rights sector of a large local authority, colleagues were told in a memo to prioritize their work in favour of the refugees coming to the UK from the then disintegrating Yugoslavia. Their need was perceived as the greatest, but by whose criteria? The welfare rights teams refused to implement the directive, perceiving it to be racist and not in any sense indicative of their practice. The aforementioned directive was withdrawn. Some practitioners felt it to have been issued because individuals coming from the former Yugoslavia were white and therefore of greater significance than black refugees whose image was a frequent visitor to our media screens. This process created a resentment that 'white' refugees were important whilst black and Asian asylum-seekers were deemed somehow used to their situation and more able to deal with the effects of displacement. Neither viewpoint was clearly justifiable or accurate and only served to undermine all individuals seeking asylum; the reality was that the eastern European asylum-seekers received much the same indifferent and alienating response as any other refugees.

> Social workers are accustomed to advocating for access to services for children in need. However, with young asylum seekers they encounter greater difficulties accessing mainstream education, health, housing, benefits and police, which are not geared up to their particular needs... The emotional impact of work with young asylum seekers can be devastating on staff. Social work training and experience do not prepare them for stories of large scale inhumanity: whole communities being wiped out; parents and siblings murdered; the expectation that 'any child who can carry a gun must go in the army'; school friends blown up; children forced to walk into minefields; slavery and executions; routine rapes in refugee camps.' (Little 1997, pp.10–11)

This strays some way from media presentations and is evidenced by the Africa Watch Report 1990, which lists some of those killed in conflicts throughout the northern region of Somalia and the manner of their deaths. What is so poignant is the very normality of their lives and occupations even whilst the conflict was on-going. The report notes amongst others who died a nurse, a poet, a shopkeeper, the captain of Hargeisa football team, a student, a police officer and a housewife. The report also takes account of numerous individuals who died of war-related diseases whilst fleeing or in the camps. Many died of insufficient medical treatment readily available in the west: jaundice, diabetes, blood loss, complications related to childbirth and malaria.

Access to care

Having traced the somewhat precarious progress of those Somalis who had entered the UK following the conflict of the late 80s and early 90s and having completed my research, I felt unsure what to do with it. Throughout the 90s many groups and local authorities initiated policies aimed at supporting asylum-seekers and refugees. However, a particular watershed occurred in 1999. Whilst working within a health setting, I was asked by a senior legal adviser working in Manchester to undertake a community care assessment. This was on behalf of a patient who required an urgent assessment of need as outlined in the Community Care Act 1990. The asylum team who had been working with this individual was unable to continue as the application for asylum had been rejected by the Home Office. The team manager was more than a little concerned for the welfare of this man who had severe health needs and, as a result, care needs. Due to a change in Government policy, people who had asylum applications rejected had no immediate recourse to state benefits, including accommodation and so were at risk of homelessness if they could not meet their rent obligations. Some asylum-seekers are 'overstayers', e.g. those who arrived with visas then failed for whatever reason either to apply for asylum or to lodge an appeal once a refusal was issued. Some individuals have been in the UK for a number of years and have families, homes and jobs without realizing the implications of their status. Once this is noted and recorded by the authorities, state benefits are withheld. The onus is then placed on other processes to secure food and accommodation whilst a further application is made for those individuals to remain in the UK. The team manager felt that responsibility for them should be met by social service and health provision under the Community Care Act.

What I found shocking as a practitioner was that the welfare of this individual was not paramount but rather the question of who would pay if his status was insecure. In this instance, the assessment, which I undertook, was put in place and a significant package of care was undertaken, but not without a battle. What this scenario illustrated, I believe, was a lack of practitioners in a position to undertake social work reports to evaluate a person's social circumstances, particularly since the introduction of the care management system (DoH 1991). This can be seen in the prescriptive nature of care assessments which allow little margin for individual needs. Local authority practitioners, whilst more than capable of undertaking such assessments, are prevented from doing so by agency policy practices which focus more readily on cost- effective case management rather than the needs of potential and existing service users. This is particularly so with recent policy changes in care management, where a certain quota of community care assessments must be undertaken in a given timescale in order to meet the demands of Best Value.

Assessment models for undertaking social work reports within an immigration context

In the case of the individual described above, his need for both medical treatment and a package of care to support those needs was urgent and eventually granted after some debate regarding funding. Within this there was no financial package offered which would have made for a test case of this sort of provision being offered to asylum-seekers and refugees. This was averted. For others, many of whom are equally vulnerable, the process to ascertain need and risk and to identify a purpose to remain within the UK is less easy to establish. Shortly after completing this initial assessment I was approached by a number of legal advisers specializing in the area of immigration to assess and report on individuals and families who were at risk if refused leave to remain in the UK.

There was no model of assessment immediately available in which to develop these evaluations other than the prescriptive format of a community care assessment. It is also important to note that most immigration legislation takes precedence over existing legislative frameworks established to identify risk and implement strategies of protection, in particular with regard to the Children Act 1989. Therefore, whilst in other areas of childcare law and practices the welfare of the child is paramount and enshrined within the principles of the Children Act 1989, this is not always so for the children of refugees and asylum-seekers. This is in contrast to and in violation of the UN Convention on the Rights of the Child (2003 p.4). This internationally recognized treaty was ratified by the UK in 1991. By accepting the points of the treaty the Government agreed to make 'all its laws, policy and practice compatible with the UN Convention on the Rights of the Child'. Article 4 of the treaty states that 'Governments who sign up for the treaty must fully implement it.' The broad aims of the treaty are to 'give children and young people a set of comprehensive rights to express and have their views taken into account on all matters that affect them, the right to play, rest and leisure and the right to be free from all forms of violence' (p.1). However, the Convention does not enable children and young persons to access the courts to claim their rights. In respect of asylum-seekers and refugees of all ages and with a diverse range of needs, the Human Rights Act 1998 outlines in its schedules a number of fundamental human rights, some rights being absolute, others qualified.

Because the majority of the applications made by legal representatives are based upon arguments taken from specific areas of the Human Rights Act 1998 and the UN Convention on the Rights of the Child, this gave me the basis to develop an evaluation of a person's circumstances and then to apply it to a given piece of legislation. Whilst not strictly enforceable in law, it does enable the courts and tribunals to focus on particular aspects of a person's circumstances which may highlight a given area of risk from a social work perspective. This is imposed upon a recognized tool of assessment, primarily the *Framework for Assessment of Children in Need and Their Families* (2000) alongside, where applicable, the community care assessment pro forma. The aforementioned *Framework* does in fact reflect the principles contained within the UN Convention on the Rights of the Child. The *Framework* is not so prescriptive; rather it allows for adaptation to suit individual circumstances.

It is also important to take into consideration that requests for family circumstance/human rights reports are often in addition to work already being undertaken by social service, health and education departments. The focus of the report is to aid, and indeed persuade in certain instances, the Home Office or an independent immigration appellant body, to agree that a person or persons should remain within the UK, and that not to do so would potentially place those persons at risk. The practitioner working in this area is faced with the dilemma of having to create an index of difficulties which in other provinces of the social care system would not require such emphasis. In doing so the practitioner, by employing such intense dissection, colludes with the legal process in placing a person in a position of increased stigmatization and labelling as a paradoxical means of facilitating their liberty and the opportunity to remain living in a western democratic society such as the UK.

Case studies

A large eastern European family have fled to the UK from an area of conflict, a result of ethnic tensions. Several of the male family members have been involved in political activities aimed at undermining their government. The family had younger members threatened with torture while numerous friends and acquaintances were killed. The children had witnessed at gunpoint young men being shot and killed. Were the family to return to their country of origin, their personal safety could not be ensured. Since their arrival in the UK, it was found that two of the adult family members had health needs which would not be addressed in their own country due to lack of medical supplies and the ad hoc nature of treatment currently available. Two of the children have specific medical needs, which require constant attendance at a large teaching hospital some distance away from where they have been dispersed. One child in particular has had several operations with considerable periods of recuperation. He has limited mobility and is now leaving the toddler stage so his parents have to carry him up and down stairs. Another sibling has a condition whereby she requires assistance every two hours during the night or her health would also be compromised. The parents are frightened and fearful for the future. Another child displays behavioural diffi-culties, which could be indicative of a learning disability but may also be the direct response to having witnessed traumatic events at an early stage in his life; he cannot communicate easily.

There are several elements to this case study. The family is a large and mutually inclusive unit, which is the cultural norm within the country of origin, each family member having a specific role to play. The family came to the UK as a traumatized but cohesive group. They spoke little or no English between them. The parents of the two children with serious health issues are highly dependent upon a younger unmarried relative who relieves them of much of the pressure of caring for children who have so many diverse needs. The mother has had to spend many days away from two of her children to care for her third whilst they receive hospital treatment. The father cannot cope alone whilst his wife is away. The children have a well-founded fear of strang-ers and so the younger family member can provide consistent and culturally appropriate care for the two remaining children in order to support his brother and sister-in-law. The third child possibly witnessed the killing of a young man during the conflict; he has certainly been exposed to the horror of seeing dead and mutilated bodies outside the makeshift apartments in which the family had to hide.

The argument which could be put forward in this case might be as follows. Due to the still erratic and volatile nature of the country of origin, it would place all family members in a position of risk were they to return. The health services could not meet the needs of specific family members. The two adult family members suffer from routine health problems, which in the UK would be treated effectively and swiftly. However, in a country which still had rudimentary health care provision as a direct result of the war, a return would jeopardise their continued well-being.

A return for younger family members could prove catastrophic. There would not be the skill and knowledge available to treat the particular illnesses suffered by two of the children, and they would lack ancillary services provided by physiotherapists, dieticians, community nurses and health visitors. Both children would be at direct risk of significant harm were they to return. The infrastructure within the country remained fragile and regardless of country profiles issued by the Home Office stating the contrary, opponents of their government, as this family was, remained targets for recriminations and acts of terror. This information provided by the family has to be measured against the background information stated in these independent profiles. So far this is a routine establishment and presentation of facts gathered via the assessment process. Pathology of presenting difficulties begins to emerge where you have an individual or groups whose particular situation becomes highlighted as a means of critical examination greater than perhaps would be the norm. For instance, the third child, referred to as Albie, presented with a number of difficulties. The dilemma is in the deconstruction of those difficulties to make an argument as to why Albie's interests are best met by remaining in the UK.

For each individual who requests asylum or refugee status their legal team will have access to a *Country Information Policy Unit Report* (CIPU 2002), which is issued by the Home Office. The CIPU will cover in detail all major aspects of a country, for instance, political history, parties and allegiances, religion, geography, economic factors and how well the overall infrastructure is operating at a given time. These reports are updated on a regular basis. They are complemented by other reports issued by Amnesty International, Human Rights Watch and US state departments. For the purpose of making an assessment for a social circumstance/human rights report, these documents also cover human rights, medical services, education, women's rights and include sections on children, disability and mental health. The reports are sourced by independent watchers who travel to the country and make detailed informed assessments about how a country is functioning. This has a direct and vital impact upon the formation of the argument put forward by a social work practitioner wishing to gain evidence to support a claim for asylum whilst still maintaining an impartial stance. A CIPU and other relevant country profiles, i.e. those compiled by Amnesty International and Human Rights Watch, are given considerable weight by the tribunal adjudicators in their consideration of any matter.

In Albie's case, he was exhibiting vague and distant patterns of behaviour. This may have been due to learning difficulties yet to be assessed. It may also have been as a result of trauma. Because the country of origin has recognized education facilities which would meet the needs of the majority of children, the case must then be made as to why it would not meet the needs of this particular child. Other children who are UK residents would perhaps be monitored for some time before a decision as to how to proceed would be taken, in conjunction with the parents. In this instance, evidence has to be gathered quickly in order to establish grounds for the child remaining in the UK. For Albie, this meant close scrutiny by a child psychologist, an educational psychologist and a consultant paediatric psychiatrist, all within a very short space of time. The far reaching implications in later life of such an assessment can be detrimental to the individual under examination. Perhaps Albie was feeling alienated and alarmed at the swift removal from his country of origin; in time, maybe symptomatic behaviours would stabilize. But children and adults seeking asylum do not have the luxury of time to explore options available to them. The response must be almost immediate and this allows for misjudgement and an intensified process of labelling and stigmatization to take place.

This is not an unfair observation to make. Professionals whom I have encountered in these situations have been anxious and willing thoroughly to evaluate a given situation. However, it is always from the viewpoint that should that individual fail to gain asylum then they return to a place of risk. This becomes particularly emotive in the case of children and vulnerable adults, whom any reasonable society would seek to protect. Albie's needs were seen as wanting further immediate investigation, i.e. that he required the services of an educational psychologist and a paediatric consultant pychiatrist. It is possible that Albie would have required input from one or both services had he been born in the UK but the argument for intervention intensifies when there is the additional perspective of an asylum application.

The ethical debate is complex. Albie spoke little or no English. It is very unlikely that he understood the process of assessment he had been subject to and would continue to be for the foreseeable future. For Albie's parents, their foremost priority was and remained their children's continued well-being. As I outlined at the start of this chapter, individuals and families fleeing trauma and persecution do so out of desperation and by this act of necessity find that their human rights have been suppressed. Parents in this position are more likely perhaps to overemphasize a child's difficulties/disability when the issue of returning to an oppressive regime is the alternative. This is a double-edged sword. If the child or individual returns to his or her country of origin there is every likelihood that they will suffer as a result. For those granted leave to remain, they are then placed in a position of entering the institutionalized process of assessment and diagnosis. Do parents and carers then continue to emphasize negative aspects of an individual in order to maintain equilibrium in their lives? Additionally, there is the question of whether or not, faced with such overwhelming circumstances, informed consent to the process can be truly given. Even if this were possible, would it in all reality garner a more anti-oppressive response from families and carers?

Problems and dilemmas

The *Framework for the Assessment of Children in Need and their Families* (DOH/DEE 2000) may offer a blueprint as to what should be addressed when accounting for and evaluating the needs of vulnerable children. But, it fails to address and present the position of children who are seeking asylum. If the criteria of the assessment document were to be applied to any given child in this position, they would almost invariably meet the benchmark criteria. Not, I hasten to add, because of the inadequacies of the parenting that they receive but because they come from a place where everyday health, educational, emotional and behavioural development, identity, family and social relationships, stability and safety are compromised. Little wonder that immigration legislation takes precedence over most childcare law and that professionals and asylum-seekers themselves inadvertently collude in some respects to present a picture which overemphasizes the global.

With current political debate so firmly focused against those seeking asylum, the tension between ethics and politics is ever greater. Immigration legislation is prescriptive and not open to interpretation in perhaps the same way as childcare law. There are also tensions within the organizations established to meet the needs of asylum-seekers. So, for example, the National Asylum Support Service (NASS) is felt by many social work practitioners in the immigration field to be overly punitive and that it undermines the human rights of those requesting asylum. Practitioners in asylum teams are often at odds with the prescriptive dictates issued to them by what is in effect their governing body. Whilst this remains the case, there is little room for practitioners working for a local authority to extend their role and make a more comprehensive assessment. Little (1997, pp.10–11) notes scepticism even in her own department and a constant questioning of 'genuineness'.

Conclusion

Somewhat paradoxically, it is my experience that tribunals do take note of and are influenced by social enquiry/human rights reports which portray a more traditional picture of individuals being in need or at risk, regardless of immigration legislation. So, where it can be argued that a child or young person is at risk from abuse or harm in a more conventional sense, then there is greater scope to present a potential for significant harm. I am thinking of children and young persons who may not come from established danger and/or war zones, but from the Caribbean, areas of Africa and Europe. If these young people or children can be shown to be at significant risk from sexual and physical abuse or particular cultural practices such as female genital mutilation if they were to return home to family members, the tribunals appear more readily to take note of the welfare checklist. However, tribunals can also be quick to state that social work reports have no bearing on proceedings and I have on occasion been told that my assessment has no relevance to the legislative framework for immigration and asylum matters. Nonetheless, this has been rare and, on the whole, the provision of these reports has had a satisfactory outcome.

In terms of the position of neutrality that must be maintained by a social work practitioner, I have not as yet come across any circumstances in which I have felt the appropriate recommendation to be that there was no basis for someone to remain in the UK. But it is important to remember that this form of assessment is not part of a partisan process whereby it is assumed that those making an application for asylum have exceptional reasons to remain in the UK. Moreover, the practitioner can easily become caught up in the system of campaigning which some cases attract. This is a very important and necessary service in order to preserve the human rights of those involved. By the same token, it may compromise value free practice and so should be seriously considered. This is important in order to walk the fine line between pathology and need, otherwise the process of assessment and recommendation becomes worthless and the immigration appellant bodies will be quick to recognize this. Whilst the role of the social worker/report writer must remain at all times neutral, others within the organizational machinery may focus on campaigning. That is not to say that the social work practitioner does not maintain a keen and effective eye upon any such developments. Rather, the social work practitioner has a specific role to fulfil, which must not appear to become clouded by emotive issues. This is still a relatively new area of practice. But it is one in which practitioners can 'borrow' the tools of assessment and protocol from more established working patterns. I offer these observations in the hope that, as a profession, we can develop effective assessment tools and report-writing practices for those seeking asylum and others subject to immigration control.

References

Africa Watch Report (1990) *Somalia, a government at war with its people: Testimonies about the killing and the conflict in the north.* New York: 485 Fifth Avenue NY 10017 Publishers.

Cohen, S. (1980) *Folk devils and moral panics: The creation of the Mods and Rockers.* Oxford: Martin Robertson (first published 1972 by MacGibbon and Kee Ltd).

Country Information and Policy Unit (April 2000) *Country Information Policy Report (Children) Federation of Yugoslavia.* HMSO.

Department of Health, Department of Education and Employment (2000) *Framework for the Assessment of Children in Need and their Families.* London: HMSO.

Department of Health, Social Services Inspectorate (1991) *Care Management and Assessment: Practitioners' Guide.* Norwich: HMSO.

Little, E. (1997) 'Building trust again in the victims of man's dark heart.' *Professional Social Work* November 1997. Birmingham: British Association of Social Workers.

Molteno, M. (1992) *A Shield of Coolest Air.* London: Shola Books.

Human Rights Act (1998) London: HMSO.

The United Nations (1989) *United Nations Convention on the Rights of the Child.* New York: United Nations.

Young, J. (1999) *The Exclusive Society: Social Exclusion, Crime and Differences in Late Modernity.* London: Sage.

Chapter 7

And Now it has Started to Rain: Support and Advocacy with Adult Asylum-seekers in the Voluntary Sector

Peter Fell

Soft blue seats

They are soft blue seats. It's unusual to find upholstered seats in an agency which is visited by those who have to wait a long time to be processed by state bureaucracies and who might take out their frustration on the furniture. Perhaps that risk has been pre-empted here by the security search at reception and the airport-style metal detector which visitors have to pass through. So soft blue seats it is, three or four rows, fixed to the floor, of course, facing three windows. We are visiting the UK Immigration Service, in fact the office of its Enforcement Unit in Salford. It is here that many asylum-seekers have to come to report weekly or monthly in accordance with the terms of their temporary admission to the UK, which they are given whilst their claim for asylum is being processed. It's also here that you come to get your ARC, your Applicant Registration Card with your personal details, photograph and fingerprints. I wait. Every few minutes, new people arrive and take a seat until their allocated number appears on a screen.

Patrice was waiting here yesterday. He came to sign on, but when he went to the window, they told him to sit down again. He got scared. He thought the only thought that many asylum-seekers think when they come to this place: 'They are going to detain me.' So Patrice did a runner. His friend brought him to my office yesterday, and that's why I'm now waiting for him. I assured him that it would be okay, that there might be trouble if he didn't go, that I would go with him.

So Patrice and I came and the same thing happened as yesterday. We both waited on the soft blue seats and then Patrice was called away. The officers wouldn't let me go with him as I didn't have legal connections. Patrice's problem is to do with the law. The Home Office haven't received the appeal that his solicitor said he lodged six months ago. They think that he is a failed asylum-seeker.

I start to wonder if I will see Patrice again. Although I have explained the situation to the officers, sitting in a place like this gets to you. What am I doing here? Am I likely to be detained? Do the other people sitting here know that I'm not an asylum-seeker? Or am I an asylum seeker? Does it matter? Do I care? If Patrice is detained, I'm free to leave, after all. I can just walk out and get into the car.

An officer enters the waiting room and beckons me over. 'I don't know what his lawyer's been telling him, but if we don't get a copy of his appeal, then he's on his way out.'

'Okay,' I say, and think something about 'docile bodies' and 'the disciplinary state.'

'Oh, what about my NASS?' says Patrice as we are about to leave.

'We don't deal with that here,' says the security officer.

I take Patrice back to the office.

In many ways, this scene encapsulates the conditions facing asylum-seekers in the UK in 2003, those persons who arrive here because they have, in the terms of the UN Convention on Refugees of 1951: 'A well-founded fear of being persecuted for reasons of race, religion, nationality, membership of a particular social group, or political opinion.' There is the climate of control, fear, uncertainty and anxiety engendered by the role of the state in assessing their applications for asylum; the pervasive role played by the law in the lives of asylum-seekers and their need for effective legal representation; the linking and continuation of state subsistence allowances and shelter to immigration controls; and the marginalization, social exclusion and effective denial of citizenship.

Many of these issues have already received detailed comment from authors such as Cohen (2001 and 2002) and the contributors to Cohen, Humphries and Mynott (2002). In particular, the effects of the 1999 Immigration and Asylum Act in the creation of the National Asylum Support Service (NASS), the forced dispersal of asylum-seekers away from London and the south east of England to the various urban regions of the UK, and the subsequent separation of the welfare and community care needs of asylum-seekers from mainstream statutory social services have all received critical analysis both from these authors and others such as Sales (2002) and Pierson (2002).

My aim in this chapter is not therefore to attempt a further critique of the current position of asylum-seekers in the UK from the perspective of welfare policies and politics, although such issues inevitably frame all social work with asylum-seekers. Rather, I will attempt to give a report from the 'front line' about my experience of the first year of managing a small voluntary agency providing advocacy and support services to asylum-seekers and refugees in Salford, in north west England. I will mainly limit my discussion to work with asylum-seekers, as I will argue that their position as persons subject to strict immigration controls and whose lives are constrained by a tight legalistic framework poses many issues for reflexive social work practice. Work with any marginalized group inevitably poses questions concerning the social worker's understanding of self and his/her practice in that issues of power/powerlessness, inclusion/exclusion, and freedom/constraint are constantly raised in work with such service users. Work with asylum-seekers also poses the question of the extent to which effective action may be limited by all-pervasive legalistic procedures in which constraint is exerted upon this group of service users in a way that is fundamentally different from the application of the law *by* social workers in the protection of their service users, as, for example, in the working of the Children or Community Care Acts.

Revive

At the end of 2002, the City of Salford had approximately 1500 asylum-seekers (Home Office 2003), mainly from the Czech Republic, Iraq, Afghanistan and various African countries such as Zimbabwe and the Democratic Republic of Congo.

Revive started work in January 2002 and was set up by Ann-Marie Fell and myself as voluntary outreach worker and paid manager respectively. It was established both as a direct response to the dispersal of asylum-seekers which commenced in May 2000 and to continue work which had been done on a voluntary basis by one of its originators since that time. We offer support and advocacy to all asylum-seekers in the immediate geographical area and also beyond who wish to use our services. Since its inception Revive has provided either long-term support or work requiring immediate action because of the stage of an asylum applicant's case to approximately 200 people from most of the Salford communities just mentioned, but in particular to the French-speaking communities from west and central Africa, and also women from Zimbabwe and other parts of Africa which have a heritage of British colonial hegemony.

We were funded initially by the English Province of the Congregation of the Holy Spirit, a missionary order of the Catholic Church whose priests and lay members work with the poor and marginalized throughout the world. In 2003, the RC Diocese of Salford agreed to provide additional funding to 2006. Revive has since been identified by the Congregation as a significant project of its European mission which it will continue to support as a matter of priority.

Models

I qualified as a social worker in 2001 and have drawn on two models of social work practice encountered on practice placement as a model for work in Revive.

The first was the work done by Manchester City Council in the reception of Kosovan refugees in 1999. As a student involved in a community social work placement in north Manchester, I was able to visit the support team that had been set up to cater for the Kosovans who were accommodated in several tower blocks in the area. Their support workers acted as an interface between the Kosovans and the 'host' society, facilitating all necessary contacts with legal representatives, schools, the health service and so on, whilst gently encouraging a degree of self-sufficiency in their service users as their length of stay increased.

I was impressed by the work undertaken with these refugees (or technically 'asylum-seekers'), in a climate then relatively free from moral panic on asylum issues. Were the Kosovans constructed as 'white' and 'European' by the state and media and therefore deemed to deserve protection by 'us'? Is it possible that the forced dispersal system has led to an increased racist and pejorative discourse surrounding applicants for refugee status? Is the arrival since May 2000 of large numbers of asylum-seekers from African and Asian ethnic groups into areas such as Salford, which were previously predominantly white, working class and economically deprived, fuelled the need for a scapegoating strategy to 'explain' increasing inequalities in British society?

After this initial contact with the Kosovans, I then spent an extended period of time on placement as a family support worker with a local Family Service Unit, undertaking both support with children and their families, and parenting assessments, work which was contracted to the FSU by a local authority.

Both models served as a template for the work with asylum-seekers which is now undertaken by Revive. On the one hand, it seemed that a group which is marginalized on many counts such as language, faces media hostility and whose lives are subject to legalistic and repressive immigration controls, is quite simply entitled to supportive social work which might not generally be offered by mainstream services on account of the divorcing of the care of asylum-seekers away from these services under the 1999 Asylum and Immigration Act. On the other hand, it was evident that existing forms of support could be modified and applied to service users who were not to be recipients of such support through some kind of failure to conform to collectively sanctioned patterns of, say, parenting or social behaviour but whose 'problems' are that of a culture of disbelief when they are represented either as 'bogus' by the media or 'lacking in credibility' by the Home Office when it comes to the assessment of their asylum claims; who exist at a level of subsistence well below that of benefit levels available to the 'host' population; and who are forbidden to work (Dummett 2001; JCWI 2001; Pierson 2002; Sales 2002). To adopt the terminology of Martiniello (1994, p.42), quoted in Castles and Davidson (2000, pp.95–6), asylum-seekers can be described as 'margizens', quasi-citizens: 'truly living on the margins of prosperous western societies' (Castles and Davidson 2000, p.96).

I also felt that a professional social work approach to work with asylum-seekers could bring the benefits described by England (1986, pp.33–4):

> Social work will...never have any genuinely exclusive knowledge, nor its practitioners any exclusive competence; there will always be people who have an unusually developed yet untrained ability to understand others and to act upon that understanding. Social work can only be distinct because of the *reliability* with which its workers master such an unusually developed understanding. (Emphasis in original)

In this way, support could also be offered to existing individuals and groups who had befriended asylum-seekers. The recognition that trained social workers do not have a monopoly of understanding or compassion paves the way for the training of volunteers, who can undertake work with the agency under the supervision of workers who are able consistently and, to use England's term, reliably to use a structured approach to social work intervention.

Finally, as Christians, we could not ignore Christ's exhortation to 'feed the hungry, clothe the naked, care for the sick and those who are in prison, welcome the stranger' (Gospel of Matthew, c.25), radically elaborated by the liberation theologians of South America and elsewhere into an 'option for the poor':

> The people who have been marginalized should be empowered to speak and act on their own behalf, so as to overcome their sense of helplessness. This means that those who have opted to be in solidarity with them often have to 'hold back'. And when they do intervene it should be to encourage or to facilitate the disadvantaged people themselves in articulating their known experience and planning realistic action. (Dorr 2000, p.156)

Power and professional identity

From the outset, therefore, I was keen that the work of Revive should not simply replicate an earlier concept of missionary activity (and social work) whereby white workers evangelize the deserving poor. From a postmodernist perspective, liberation theology might also be criticized because its notions of 'empowerment' embody a binary notion in which power is a commodity to be transmitted by those who possess it to those who are apparently without that power and whom we choose to label 'oppressed'. This concept of power as 'possessed' rather than 'exercised' is inadequate to an understanding of support to asylum-seekers since, as Fook (2002, p.51) comments:

> The experience of being given power may not be experienced as empowering, but in fact may have disempowering effects. Despite the best intentions, our empowerment theory does not always translate well into practice. Sometimes in the attempt to empower, a disempowering climate and culture is set up.

Foucault's definition of 'power' in the first volume of his *History of Sexuality* implies that the use of power is subtler than the exercising of force by politically dominant groups:

> It seems to me that by power we must take into account the multiple relationships of force which are immanent to the domain in which they take place and which are inherent in their organisation. (Foucault 1975, pp.121–2)

In other words, power relations pervade all forms of social relations, including those practised by organizations which seek to 'help' marginalized sectors of the population who are 'marginalized' precisely because they are decentred from and are the object of certain types of regulatory power arrangements which seek to discipline and create 'docile bodies' (Foucault 1975). However, in a Foucauldian perspective, power flows in every direction, not just from the dominant to the subordinated.

Concerning work with asylum-seekers, the state's prerogative on who is permitted to belong to the 'in' groups of acceptable migrants through the various forms of immigration controls is the visible framework that controls the lives of our service users. On another plane, workers could be seen as using power by framing their work through a particular set of theories and social arrangements (their availability determined by appointments, length of time devoted to discrete tasks, attendance at drop-ins, and so on). A third plane could consist of the power exerted by our service users: they could decide either to use us or to use another service or community resource, or regroup in ways which could bypass the need for our services as a form of disdain for the in/out dichotomy which must, at least initially, characterize relations between white professionals and asylum-seekers who are predominantly black or Asian in a society dominated by 'white' values.

Such considerations as these have led me to think reflectively and reflexively about my work with asylum-seekers with the following conclusions:

I am a citizen of my country, enjoying the rights and privileges which my citizenship confers.

I am a white male from a working-class background.

I have had access to higher education and chosen to pursue a career in social work. I have thus been assimilated into the dominant professional groups in the society in which I live and continue to choose to live.

I have decided not to do social work in the statutory sector, believing that I will be freer to practise my preferred mode of social work in a voluntary setting.

I have been fortunate enough to have been entrusted with the setting up and management of my own project.

I work with people, asylum-seekers, who are marginalized quasi-citizens of 'my' country who are here because they have fled persecution.

In order to continue to do my job, it is necessary that there continue to be such marginalized and oppressed people.

> I have certain skills of advocacy and communication which I choose to use with asylum-seekers in order that they may feel less marginalized and 'helped' towards a sense of inclusion.

> My perceptions of self-esteem and self-worth are enhanced when I have 'helped' asylum-seekers.

> I am paid approximately one hundred times more per week than a single asylum-seeker receives in NASS support.

> Although there are some aspects of the society in which I live which cause me revulsion, I am able to participate in that society to a far greater extent than the people with whom I work.

> I believe that I am justified in concluding that there exists an imbalance of power and social participation between myself and the asylum-seekers with whom I work.

Now this list is not intended to be an exercise in hand-wringing or self-flagellation, but rather a first step in recognizing the vast structural gulf, the inclusion/exclusion divide, which separates me from the asylum-seeking service user. It is also an attempt to construct a form of professional identity and practice from the ground upwards, as it were. Students who undertake practice placements with Revive usually say that they find it difficult to relate what they are asked to do to the various accepted social work theories. I reply by suggesting that this is a good thing and that they are being led to form theory and identity from their practice, rather than reaching up to the theory shelf and seeing if one of them 'fits'.

> In the mainstream literature on professions and professionalization it tends to be assumed that professional identity is something which is acquired outside of and prior to the encounter with the service user through the medium of training and regulatory procedures. (Taylor and White 2000, p.100)

For social workers whose work engages them with asylum-seekers, the construction of such an identity 'from the ground upwards' would have to encompass reflexivity at a fairly fundamental level, including such elements as those in the list above. However, as Taylor and White suggest, the encounter with service users is crucial.

To meet an African social worker who has been arbitrarily arrested because he was exposing a racket in the distribution of foreign aid; to meet a woman who was subjected to multiple rape and beaten by soldiers because she happened to be at home when they came looking for her husband; to meet a man who was a prominent local politician in his home country and who had to stand by and watch a colleague murdered for insolence to a police chief; to meet a man who is despairing because his children are stranded in a refugee camp a thousand miles away: these encounters change things. They change the way one reflects upon one's own identity as a member of a society where there is, indeed, the freedom to reflect, which is the particular privilege of the insider who has accumulated a certain amount of cultural and economic capital through education, the conscious acquisition of professional status and other wise moves.

An encounter with the people I have just mentioned must necessitate a shedding of any assumptions about our abilities to help, to be of any use to those whose stories we hear. Only by doing this, I feel, can we start to construct a practice which empowers those who are marginalized in an oppressive system which reproduces, in a sense, previous repressions of the most nefarious kind. We must forget who we are or were and how we have come to this point where we meet those who have suffered more than we may ever have to. As outsiders to the stories we hear, we must also seek our own asylum in the experiences which are related to us and learn from the resilience of those we meet. And empowerment will be mutual; we will learn how to hold in a perfect dialectical balance our status as permanent insiders/outsiders and from that position be ready to attempt a critical theorizing of our work as 'relationally embedded' to borrow Gergan's term (Gergan 1999, p.133). Gergan continues: 'One's performances are essentially constituents of relationship; they are inhabited not only by a history of relationships but as well by the relationships into which they are directed.' Our fully-achieved 'performance' as workers with those seeking the protection of the state cannot do other than be grounded in learning from them what it means to be told, in the context of applying for asylum, and especially of being refused, that they are nowhere and no one.

If one accepts that one's work with asylum-seekers is relationally 'embedded' and directed as Gergan proposes, then our theoretical base must take account of this orientation. We have found that a psychosocial model, such as that elaborated by Woods and Hollis (2000), provides a holistic model of working with those whose lives have been disrupted once by the events which have led them to flee their country of origin and once again by the inimical conditions encountered whilst seeking the protection of another country.

> When I was in Africa, we looked towards Europe as providing a model of the upholding of human rights. But since I've been here, I'm not so sure. When I went to the court for my appeal, it was the first time I had been in court in my life, and I felt as if I was being treated as a criminal who had to prove his innocence. (Nathaniel, an asylum seeker.)

Howe (1998, p.173) argues that:

> Social work *is* psychosocial work if by psychosocial we mean that area of human experience which is created by the interplay between the individual's psychological condition and the social environment. (Emphasis in original)

Revive attempts to address the needs which our service users identify to us and which present themselves on a continuum of individual fears, sense of loss and rootlessness, combined with concerns deriving from socio-political elements such as the progress of individual cases and bureaucratic muddle. Therefore, our work encompasses tasks such as assistance with practical problems connected with NASS support and housing; help in finding appropriate legal representation; accompaniment to legal appointments and appeal hearings and virtually any other issue which asylum-seekers may encounter. It also entails signposting to other appropriate organizations, and above all a stable point of call, of attachment even, for those whose lives have been disrupted by conflict, trauma and loss of many kinds (Burnett and Peel 2001b; Howe 1995). Both of our main workers are also French speaking, and being able to communicate confidently with those service users who speak this language is, we feel, a major asset for our project.

Although he was not describing the work of Revive, the list of strategies proposed by Pierson for work with asylum-seekers and refugees closely matches the direction in which our work is evolving: 'communication, assessment, resource finding, advocacy, mediation, support and counselling' (Pierson 2002, p.207). In discussing the health needs of asylum-seekers and refugees, Burnett and Peel (2001b, p.545) suggest that:

> It is important for refugees to develop ongoing links and friendships with people in the host community as well as making contact with people from their own countries, and the best mental health outcomes may be achieved in this way.

As white British workers, we feel that it is indeed vital that asylum-seekers come into contact with members of the dominant racial group in Britain who fulfil a role other than that of control and repression and offer a face that is not hostile, but one which is available, ready to listen and accepting of the world view of our service users as a valid expression of their culture and a basis for future work (Graham 2002). We are nevertheless aware that it is important for members of the asylum-seeking communities themselves to develop their own support networks and organizations. In some cases these are well-developed, but the removal of asylum-seekers' right to employment in July 2002 means that such networks can only exist on a voluntary and often precarious basis. We have assisted the paralegal training of two refugee volunteer workers who will then be able to undertake advice and signposting work within their own communities using Revive as a model.

The role of the voluntary sector

As I have already mentioned, the regulatory procedures applicable in voluntary agency work, and those on which I now wish to concentrate, are those imposed *upon* the service user by the state through the mechanisms of the asylum-seeking process and not by any formal regulatory mechanisms imposed by the agency. It would be reasonable to propose, I believe, that one of the strengths of voluntary agency social work with asylum-seekers is that it is comparatively (but in no sense *entirely*) free from the procedural and legal constraints now inherent in many statutory agencies, and that this freedom permits workers to act creatively in their advocacy against a similarly bureaucratized system of state legal and quasi-welfare controls.

> The proliferation of street-level, outreach, project and support workers...keeps alive many of the more positive traditions of practice from the expansionist era of the 1970s... On the other hand, it signifies a vacuum, filled by the voluntary and community sectors, because public sector social work has become locked into a style of practice that is legalistic, formal, procedural and arm's length... (Jordan 2001, p.537)

However, there are many constraints on the operation of small voluntary projects which can prove to be ephemeral if long-term funding is not available and no recourse is available to money provided by Government departments, such as the Home Office, who are themselves the source of the problem where asylum-seekers are concerned.

As an example of an area where statutory provision is undoubtedly rigid, local authority asylum teams have no option but to end all support to asylum-seekers when they are informed by NASS that an asylum claim is 'fully determined', in other words, when that claim fails. This can lead to an asylum-seeker being made destitute and homeless (Fell 2002). A network of well-organized and well-funded voluntary agencies situated in the dispersal areas where asylum-seekers live could be a potent agent of change and welfare provision, insinuating itself into the gaps left by bureaucracies such as NASS and the legal profession. There is perhaps even more scope for the provision of resettlement programmes to those who have obtained refugee status where none exists under Government backing.

Meeting the legal gaze

Nevertheless, any project supporting asylum-seekers is circumscribed by the same constraints that asylum-seekers themselves face. The manner in which this is done has been characterized aptly as follows:

> a kind of authoritarian Panopticon state within the welfare state, a Poor Law style of provision aimed at deterrence rather than respect for the rights and dignities of those fleeing political oppression. (Jordan and Jordan 2000, p.139)

This Benthamite/Foucauldian metaphor of the ideal penitentiary whose inmates are disposed around the building in such a manner that all can be visible from a central point of surveillance is apposite in any discussion of the processing of asylum-seekers by the British state. These processes could, indeed, be understood as a means of 'disciplining' the asylum-seeking subject, and may also have the inevitable effect of subjecting social workers to an analogous 'disciplinary' mode of being.

As advocates, empowerers or otherwise facilitating members of the society to which an asylum-seeker aspires to belong, we should seek to be truly alongside our service users in their vital encounters with state legislation. Foucault characterizes 'disciplinary' processes as taking place within 'a linear time whose moments blend into each other and which lead towards a stable, terminal point' (Foucault 1975, p.188). If we imagine this point to be the moment when the desired disciplining of the subject is fully achieved, the worker's 'time' must be similarly dependant on the temporal experience and the substantive issues encountered by the asylum-seeker as his/her case proceeds. Worker and asylum-seeker must keep in step if even a minimal amount of resistance is to be achieved.

Paradoxically, this 'stable point' of achieved 'discipline' could occur *either* by a refusal *or* by the granting of asylum by means of indefinite leave to remain, in which latter case the asylum-seeker is inducted *de facto* into a new set of disciplinary procedures – signing on, paying rent and so on – being reframed by the state as somewhat more 'deserving' rather than the opposite.

I would suggest that for an asylum-seeker, the need to prove that he/she has a case to be recognised as a refugee under the 1951 UN Convention is the concern which generally takes precedence over all others. It is the strong need to move from exclusion to relative inclusion; the desire to move from the non-citizenship of asylum-seeker to the fuller – although not complete – citizenship of someone allowed to settle in the UK. At every stage of this process, the disciplinary mechanisms of the state are present to remind the asylum-seeker of the responsibility to prove to its satisfaction that he/she is indeed fleeing from persecution and requires the protection of the state, which protection is then handed down graciously in the form of indefinite leave to remain (or limited leave to remain on compassionate grounds) or is refused.

What are the individual moments of the linear, disciplinary process of asylum-seeking?

- Application for asylum, either at a port of entry or later and application for NASS support. The provisions of Section 55 of the Nationality, Immigration and Asylum Act of 2002, denying NASS support to those who do not claim asylum at a 'reasonable time' after entering the country will have to be modified or abandoned following judicial challenge (Sale 2003; Travis 2003a).

- A screening interview at the Immigration Service, at which the asylum-seeker needs to prove his/her identity and at which biometric information, such as fingerprinting, will be obtained.

- A substantive interview, during which a Home Office official will conduct a lengthy interview about the individual's reasons for claiming asylum.

- Either the granting of asylum at this stage, or a refusal, (in approximately 90 per cent of cases) (Home Office 2003).

- If a case is refused, the applicant has an automatic right of appeal.

- An appeal heard before an independent adjudicator of the Immigration Appellate Authority (I have to report that, from personal experience, some adjudicators appear to be more 'independent' than others in their apparent willingness to accept the Home Office version of events leading up to an individual's asylum claim).

- The appeal is either lost or won by the appellant. If the appeal is refused, most appellants will have a right to apply for leave to appeal to the Immigration Appeal Tribunal. Such leave may or may not be granted. The Home Office may also seek leave to appeal against cases allowed in the appellant's favour. If leave is not granted to an appellant, this is usually the effective end of their case, as many legal representatives are unwilling to apply for further community legal funding to pursue a case at this stage. There is also the possibility of seeking judicial review of failure to grant leave to appeal, but for the same reasons, this happens comparatively rarely.

Other means of disciplinary surveillance used by the state are:

- the linking of NASS financial support to an accommodation address. Failure to live at a specified address will cause support to end

- regular attendance at a post office to exchange NASS subsistence vouchers for cash. Again, failure to do this regularly will result in support being curtailed and an explanation being demanded from the asylum-seeker

- in many cases, regular reporting, either weekly or monthly, at either a police station or an Immigration Service reporting centre

- the carrying of an ARC, or Applicant Registration Card, bearing a photograph of the asylum-seeker and biometric data. This card is also due to become the means by which asylum-seekers will access their cash allowances.

In Revive our work consists of accompanying, supporting and advocating for asylum-seekers at every stage of the process outlined above, and which I have described as 'disciplinary' because it is imposed upon the asylum-seeker in order to subjugate the process of asylum application to the needs of a regulatory state rather than to the needs of people who may well have been

caught up arbitrarily in civil wars…detained and tortured for their political beliefs (or) by criminal gangs for the purpose of extortion… The asylum process is lengthy, complicated and intrinsically stressful, with the continual fear for the asylum seeker, until the process is complete, of being sent back to the original country. (Burnett and Peel 2001a, p. 486)

It is quite possible, of course, that the process may be 'completed' by the denial of asylum.

When an asylum-seeker presents him/herself when his/her case has been refused and NASS support has been withdrawn; when, to use Derrida's terms (1994, p.51), a legal decision has not shown the requisite balancing characteristics of *conservation* and *destruction* of the law by which a *just* judgement is produced; when, in fact, the law has not been applied creatively and compassionately, the worker has little to fall back upon, apart from appeals to members of Parliament, anti-deportation groups and the willingness to hear and empathize which it is hoped that he/she will have demonstrated through his/her work with the asylum-seeker up to this point.

What is to be done?

The story which follows is typical of the long-term support which Revive has offered to asylum-seekers and refugees since the project began. There is no doubt that even in the space of a year, conditions for our service users have become harsher and more repressive. The imposition of Section 55 of the 2002 Act, may be in abeyance, as previously mentioned. However, we are seeing increased numbers of asylum-seekers whose case has 'failed' and who are being informed by NASS that their support will be discontinued and that they should leave their homes. The Home Office, for its part, simply expects failed asylum-seekers to leave the UK voluntarily.

It is up to projects such as Revive to try to provide as much support as possible, even in these difficult situations, although we have to recognize that, ultimately, we can do little to advance the claims of those who find themselves rejected in this way. We increasingly find ourselves up against the shortcomings of a legal system which is itself constrained by the strictures of community legal funding which, as mentioned above, will not entertain supporting applications for judicial reviews which might uncover mistakes and anomalies in the deciding of cases.

However, we remain available for those who need us and we will continue to do what is possible in terms of advocacy and support. We have found that the ability to describe ourselves as 'social workers' often turns keys in doors (such as applications for community care assessments) that might otherwise remain closed and this can only benefit our service users! At the other, more positive end of the spectrum, we continue to provide assistance in resettlement for those who are given refugee status.

At the time of writing, in mid-2003, the problematizing of asylum-seekers continued with the publication of an all-party House of Commons Select Committee Report which contained warnings of serious social unrest if the level of asylum applications was allowed to continue unchecked (Travis 2003b). We must remain flexible and vigilant to changing times. Our funding seems to be assured for the near future; we know that our services are needed and we hope that we can make some difference to the lives of our service users. I am certain only of one thing: that our service users have made a difference to us in the resilience, courage and determination which they show in the face of the opposition which greets them at every turn. Makemba's story, told below, is one example of this.

Makemba's story

> In general, there is no medical treatment or care available in hospitals and clinics for people suffering from AIDS in the Democratic Republic of Congo. There are no specialised hospitals or centres for the treatment of AIDS but some hospitals in Kinshasa admit AIDS sufferers for the treatment of secondary infections. Despite the lack of medical care for AIDS sufferers in hospitals and clinics, drugs imported from Europe can be bought from private individuals. The treatment is based on the tri-therapy of the combination of three of the following anti-retroviral drugs: Retrivir, AZT, DDI, Zerit and Stavidine. (Home Office 2002)

Makemba is a young woman from the Democratic Republic of Congo. When we first meet her she is in hospital, suffering from what is described as a 'serious infection'. She is visited by a French-speaking worker who discovers that she is an asylum-seeker who has recently entered the UK. The week that she is in hospital coincides with her substantive interview at the Home Office in Croydon.

Makemba's legal representatives are in London, and our first task is to contact them in order that they can arrange an alternative interview date with the Home Office. After this has been done, we learn that Makemba has been transferred to another local hospital and has received a confirmed diagnosis of HIV. Although she is now receiving appropriate treatment, she is still very ill.

Some weeks later, Makemba contacts us. She is in London, about to be interviewed at the Home Office. Should she tell them that she has HIV, as she had not known this when she claimed asylum? Our advice is that it is not necessary to tell the Home Office about her medical condition at this stage, but that she is free to tell them if she so wishes. Makemba replies that she is ashamed about her illness and does not wish to tell them. (When I later see the transcript of her interview, it is recorded that she had told the interviewing officer that she had caught an 'infection of the blood', but had not said any more on the subject).

Makemba asks us whether she should change solicitors to a local firm. We usually advise asylum-seekers that this is a preferable step: going to London to see a legal representative is usually impractical in terms both of time and cost. Fortunately, there are many specialist legal firms offering representation in asylum cases in our area. Unfortunately, they are all extremely busy. We suggest that Makemba should wait until she has had a reply from the Home Office about her asylum claim. The reply arrives in about two weeks. She has been refused.

The Secretary of State does not accept...
The Secretary of State believes that...
Although you maintain that...

(Many legal representatives believe that these 'refusal letters' are simply produced on a 'cut and paste' basis with the Home Office information about a particular country applied in a generalized fashion to individual asylum claims.)

It is at this point that I arrange to accompany Makemba to an asylum advice surgery. She is allocated a caseworker, Paula, who reads her refusal letter, agrees to represent her at her appeal, and takes some basic personal details. I interpret for her from English to French and vice versa. Makemba insists that she will allow only me to interpret as she wishes her HIV status to be kept confidential and known to as few people as possible.

Once Makemba has received a date for her appeal hearing there follows a series of visits to Paula, each lasting about two hours, where Makemba's witness statement is prepared. This is the evidence that she will rely upon at her appeal hearing. Makemba is encouraged to give a detailed chronological account of the events which led up to her fleeing her country and arriving in the UK. The appeal hearing will expect this and I wonder how reasonable it is to expect someone under pressure to give such a precise rendering of her story.

During all this time, Makemba frequently contacts our office about other matters:

- She is finding her accommodation too far away from the hospital where she has to go for consultations. I contact the local authority asylum team, as she lives in one of their NASS-contracted properties, to see if anything can be done. They are sympathetic, but are bound by NASS regulations and do not think that NASS will consider this a sufficient reason to re-house Makemba. She is never, in fact, re-housed.

- She asks me to apply on her behalf for the £50 'single additional payment' which NASS grants to its supported asylum-seekers every six months.

- A local charity supporting people with HIV and AIDS makes a small grant to Makemba to help with her living costs.

During the course of her interviews with Paula, it appears that Makemba's case to be recognized as a refugee under the 1951 UN Convention is relatively weak. However, she is assured that the UK has a duty to continue her treatment as it would not be available in her home country if she was to be returned there. There are several supporting letters to this effect from her consultant.

Eventually, the day of the hearing arrives. I collect Makemba from her flat and we drive, mostly silently, to the court. We have to wait a long time whilst other cases are heard, during which we meet with Paula who makes some last minute notes and clarifications.

It is at last our turn, and we enter the hearing room. There are just Makemba, Paula and the Home Office presenting officer, who will argue why Makemba should not be granted asylum, an interpreter, the adjudicator and me. When she learns the name of the adjudicator, Paula tells me that we might be in for a difficult time. I don't convey this information to Makemba in exactly these terms.

Paula is right. The information that Makemba provides to the hearing about the reasons why she fears persecution seems to contradict that provided by the Home Office, the US Department of State and contemporaneous BBC news bulletins. However, Makemba holds her ground. 'I was there,' she maintains. This is certainly true. What right, essentially, do any of the others in that room have to deny the subjective experience and fears of someone who genuinely believed that they would suffer if they remained in that place, that 'there', where none of us could have been and none of us would ever wish to be?

When it comes to the question of Makemba's illness, the Home Office argues, using the information which I have reproduced at the beginning of this section, that contrary to the position of Makemba's specialist, her health would not suffer if she were returned to her own country.

There *are* drugs available in the DRC for the treatment of HIV and AIDS.

But they are only available for sale from private individuals. There is no guarantee about the quality of these drugs or where they come from. There are also no facilities for the monitoring of people with HIV in that country.

But a recent decision in the Court of Appeal makes it quite clear that the UK is not a refuge for anyone seeking medical treatment here. This would open the floodgates for anyone to come here and claim asylum because they really wanted medical treatment at the expense of the UK. (This last remark from the 'independent' adjudicator.)

On that note, and after a spirited argument from Paula which my summary could not hope to capture, the hearing ends. I go back to the waiting room with Makemba and we wait for Paula. She comes in after a few moments. Makemba looks out of the window: 'and now it has started to rain.'

Shortly after starting work on this chapter, I receive a call from Paula. Makemba's asylum claim has been refused, as has her claim under the European Convention on Human Rights in regard to the continuation of her medical treatment. However, because of the partial and erroneous nature of the adjudicator's decision, her representative is going to apply for leave to appeal to the Immigration Appeals Tribunal. If leave is granted, there is a possibility that the case could be heard again, before a different adjudicator.

It could be argued that the consistent support which we were able to offer Makemba should be the right of every asylum-seeker. It is to be hoped that more examples of collective action against immigration controls and the organization of anti-deportation campaigns might arise from within asylum-seeking communities with appropriate aid from the legal and social care professions.

Such campaigns often use a simple but effective rhetorical device as a slogan, such as 'X will stay'. It is the formation of a discourse whereby the desired future action or state of affairs is presented as an achieved reality. It is an urgent collective voice expressing resistance to repression.

I have attempted to give some idea, in this chapter, of the possible scope of professional social work with asylum-seekers within the framework of a voluntary agency. I would hope that all work in supporting those who have a claim to be refugees can be understood as a form of resistance to a harsh, highly legalized and 'disciplinary' framework by which those who are 'margizens', barely subsisting in a supposedly civilized, humanitarian society, are coerced into proving that they have a right to come 'inside' and benefit from the protection which the UK has an obligation to provide to those fleeing persecution.

Makemba will stay.

Note: Although based on actual events, the names of all persons mentioned in cases have been changed.

References

All references to Acts of Parliament, the UN Convention on Refugees, the European Convention on Human Rights and appeals procedures have been taken from:

MacDonald I.A. and Webber F. (2001) *Immigration Law and Practice in the United Kingdom (5th edition)*. London: Butterworths.

Burnett, A. and Peel, M. (2001a) 'What brings asylum-seekers to the United Kingdom?' *British Medical Journal 322*, 24 February, 485–488.

Burnett, A. and Peel, M. (2001b) 'Health needs of asylum-seekers and refugees.' *British Medical Journal 322*, 3 March, 544–547.

Castles, S. and Davidson, A. (2000) *Citizenship and Migration: Globalization and the Politics of Belonging*. Basingstoke: Palgrave.

Cohen, S. (2001) *Immigration Controls, the Family and the Welfare State*. London: Jessica Kingsley Publishers.

Cohen, S. (2002) 'The local state of immigration controls.' *Critical Social Policy 22*, 3, 518–543.

Cohen, S., Humphries, B. and Mynott, E. (eds) (2002) *From Immigration Controls to Welfare Controls*. London: Routledge.

Derrida, J. (1994) *Force de Loi*. Paris: Gallilée.

Dorr, D. (2000) *Mission in Today's World*. Blackrock, Co. Dublin: Columba Press.

Dummett, M. (2001) *On Immigration and Refugees*. London: Routledge.

England, H. (1986) *Social Work as Art: Making Sense for Good Practice*. London: Allen and Unwin.

Fell, P. (2002) Personal communication from member of local authority asylum team.

Fook, J. (2002) *Social Work: Critical Theory and Practice*. London: Sage.

Foucault, M. (1975) *Surveiller et Punir*. Paris: Gallimard.

Foucault, M. (1976) *Histoire de la Sexualité (I) – La Volonté de Savoir.* Paris: Gallimard.

Gergan, K. (1999) *Invitation to Social Construction.* London: Sage.

Graham, M. (2002) *Social Work and African-Centred Worldviews.* Birmingham: Venture Press.

Home Office (2002) *The Democratic Republic of Congo, October 2002.* Home Office Country Information and Policy Unit.

Home Office (2003) *Asylum Statistics: 4th Quarter 2002 United Kingdom.* London: The Home Office.

Howe, D. (1995) *Attachment Theory for Social Work Practice.* Basingstoke: Macmillan.

Howe, D. (1998) 'Psychosocial work.' In R. Adams, L. Dominelli and M. Payne (eds) *Social Work – Themes, Issues and Critical Debates.* Basingstoke: Macmillan.

JCWI (Joint Council for the Welfare of Immigrants) (2001) *Manifesto for the Reform of British Immigration Policy.* London: JCWI.

Jordan, B. (2001) 'Tough love: Social work, social exclusion and the third way.' *British Journal of Social Work 31*, 527–546.

Jordan, B. and Jordan, C. (2000) *Social Work and the Third Way: Tough Love as Social Policy.* London: Sage.

Martiniello, M. 'Citizenship of the European Union: A critical view.' In R. Bauböck (1994) (ed) *From Aliens to Citizens.* Aldershot: Avebury.

Pierson, J. (2002) *Tackling Social Exclusion.* London: Routledge.

Sale, A.U. (2003) 'Cut adrift.' *Community Care,* 20–26 February, 26–27.

Sales, R. (2002) 'The deserving and the undeserving? Refugees, asylum-seekers and welfare in Britain.' *Critical Social Policy 22,* 3, 456–478.

Taylor, C. and White, S. (2000) *Practising Reflexivity in Health and Social Care: Making Knowledge.* Buckingham: Open University Press.

Travis, A. (2003a) 'Appeal Court upholds asylum ruling.' *The Guardian,* 19 March.

Travis, A. (2003b) 'Increase in asylum-seekers "threatens unrest".' *The Guardian,* 8 May.

Woods, M.E. and Hollis, F. (2000) *Casework: A Psychosocial Therapy (5th edition).* Boston: McGraw Hill.

Chapter 8

Social Work Responses to Accompanied Asylum-seeking Children

Pete Grady

Introduction

Social work with asylum-seeking children and their families is a growing area of practice at the moment. Agencies are coming into contact with such families through a variety of situations, yet there is very little understanding of the needs or circumstances of such children. What we may be more conscious of is the fact that asylum-seekers occupy a particular place within the policy context that can be characterised by the notion of undeserving of welfare support (Sales 2002), and social work has struggled to respond appropriately (Humphries 2001). The establishment of specific teams to deal with asylum-seekers, often within the remit of the National Asylum Support Service (NASS), may actually be hiding the reality of the problems faced by those children and their families who find themselves within the systems (Parker 2000). This chapter sets out to explore some of the tensions that exist within policy for asylum-seeking children and their families and to highlight how the growing knowledge and practice around supporting children in need may contribute to an understanding of the potential harm that immigration and asylum policies may be constructing for those subject to them.

Immigration and asylum-seeking is a vast area of practice, in terms of the range of situations and families that may come within its remit: for example, accompanied asylum-seeking children, unaccompanied children seeking asylum, those with exceptional leave to remain and those other families with children who are subject to immigration controls. The numbers of children involved are also hard to define, as different agencies keep different kinds of statistics (Refugee Council and BAAF 2001). However, in terms of asylum-seeking children recent estimates suggest that 23,000 accompanied children were receiving services from social work agencies, alongside 6,000 unaccompanied minors (Community Care 2001a). These figures are clearly those known to social work departments; the Home Office records the numbers of families who enter the UK seeking asylum legally, rather than specific members of those families, so the number of accompanied children is not known at the national level.

Even the use of the term 'family' is problematic when considering children who are asylum-seekers. The Home Office, and consequently NASS, make decisions about children's status on the basis of adults who accompany them when they claim asylum (Jones 2001). There is little done to check the relationship of these children to the adults who accompany them, either because immigration officials are unable to do so due to a lack of documentary proof, or perhaps because it is more expedient to allow a child to remain with an adult than to treat him or her as unaccompanied. Whilst I would not seek to suggest that families are the only place that children can receive adequate care and support (Colton, Sanders and Williams 2001) – indeed we must acknowledge that concerned adults can provide a more supportive environment than birth families to many children – this situation can still lead to issues of concern. First, there is the issue of who has parental responsibility (PR) for such children, if they do not live with their parents. British law is clear that PR rests and remains with the parents of a child whatever that child's relationship is with the state (see Children Act 1989, ss.2–4), unless he or she is adopted; indeed, it remains as a check and balance to the power of the state. The issue is that some (the exact numbers are not known) of these children remain with adults who have no legal responsibility for them and who may not, as a consequence, have the power to challenge the decisions that are made on a welfare basis about them.

Within the constraints of these considerations this chapter will now focus on some of the areas of concern for all asylum-seeking 'families'. It will also seek to draw out issues which are relevant to all asylum-seeking children, and to build upon the wider range of materials that is available with regard to unaccompanied children (see for example Refugee Council and BAAF 2001;

Stanley 2001; Save the Children 2003a and b) and, ultimately, seek to develop ideas which construct a response to the potential harm of the policy position that is developing in the UK. Central to this debate is the value and knowledge base of social work that is built upon experiences of migration and the effects of oppression on those who are seen as 'outsiders' within the context of practice.

The current policy context

Without reiterating the details of policy that have been covered elsewhere, it is important to remember that children within the UK occupy a particular policy space that has been constructed around notions of childhood and the nature of expectations of children's experiences (Colton *et al.* 2001; James, Jenks and Prout 1998). There has been a consensus within the UK about childcare policy for a number of years, and the Children Act 1989 remains the central piece of legislation that prescribes the state's responsibility not only for children but also for families and communities (Colton *et al.* 2001). The concept of protection through support, and the acknowledgement of vulnerability have remained key aspects of social policy for children and their families (DoH 2000), and local authorities have been required to respond to these through the introduction of a number of Department of Health led initiatives, including *Quality Protects* (DoH 1998), and the *Framework for the Assessment of Children in Need and their Families* (DoH *et al.* 2000).

This policy direction is clearly located within a concern by Government that all children should achieve the best possible outcomes, and that families and agencies should play a role in providing services that enable children to achieve that level. Situations where children fail to achieve then become a concern of the state and welfare intervention may become a necessity in order to provide those children with adequate chances (DoH 1998). Social work is seen primarily as a service that is targeted towards those children in need of support rather than, as it was perceived previously, a service that is focused purely on issues of protection, in order that service users may gain the full benefit from the range and depth of services available (DoH 1998). Indeed, there is a growing body of evidence which suggests that effective support may reduce the need for protection and so reduce the degree of state intervention required to protect families (DoH 2001).

Yet this policy position does not apply to all children. Asylum and immigration policy in the UK has consistently developed a discourse of exclusion for those who are not seen as citizens (Hayes 2001; Humphries 2001; Sales

2002). For children in the UK there is a growing debate about the nature of citizenship (Miller 2000), and the consequences of failing to meet the requirements of citizenship standards (see Blunkett 2002). The citizenship debate has focused on the nature of the relationship between the individual and the state, and has been used to justify the exclusion of particular groups from mainstream discourses on rights and responsibilities. The New Labour position can be summarised as a desire to make access to services commensurate with active participation in society (Community Care 2001b; Jordan 2000, 2001; Tate 2000), and the implementation of this has been constructed within the current education framework.

Children's exclusion from welfare

As practitioners it is important to understand how asylum-seekers and their children are excluded from welfare services, and to consider the consequences of such exclusion. The asylum system in the UK is very clear about the limitation of services to particular groups of children and young people. The most obvious case is the Government's specific reservation on Article 22 of the United Nations Convention on the Rights of the Child, which states: '…a child…whether unaccompanied or accompanied by his or her parents or by any other person, [should] receive appropriate protection and humanitarian assistance in the enjoyment of applicable rights' (United Nations 1989, Article 22 [1]).

This reservation, which allows the UK to act outside of the letter and spirit of the Convention, was further confirmed in the Nationality, Immigration and Asylum Act 2002. Section 47 of this Act amends Section 122 of the Immigration and Asylum Act 1999, so that a family which is receiving support from the Secretary of State (sic) via NASS shall not be entitled to support from a local authority by way of destitution. In essence, the children of destitute asylum-seekers – i.e. those able to apply to NASS because they are homeless, have no means of support and have entered the UK for their own protection – are not entitled to support of the state through the Children Act as a child in need, under Section 17. The principle rests on the fact that NASS provides the same support elsewhere. There is growing concern about the ability of NASS to provide such support to children and their families and indeed as an organization they have defined their role as one of housing and financial support rather than welfare (Harvey 2001). NASS has also sought to subcontract its responsibilities primarily to welfare agencies (Sales 2002), which leaves local authorities in the contradictory position of being asked to assist children to whom they cannot by law provide services. How this dilemma is resolved is dependent upon local agreement and interpretation.

Such a position is justified with reference to the need to contain and deter (bogus) asylum-seekers from draining state resources through welfare systems. On the one hand it seems inconceivable that the UK would seek to exclude children from access to organized welfare, on the other the rhetoric of asylum that constructs the bogus and criminal nature of such individuals justifies the position occupied by Government (Humphries 2001). This has caused concern among those working with asylum-seekers at all levels of welfare provision. International concern has been such that the matter has been raised in the House of Lords, following the publication of a report by the United Nations Committee on the Rights of the Child in 2002, on the position occupied by the UK in relation to the implementation of the Convention rights for children. Baroness Walmsley posed the following question to the Health Minister:

> The [second] matter that I would like to highlight is the committee's [UNCRC] concern about the Government's refusal to withdraw their reservation on Article 22 of the convention with regard to immigration. We do not treat asylum-seeking children well in this country. Many of them are detained with their families outside the general community; they have access to only 76 per cent of the benefits available to other families and often have no access to the normal health, welfare and educational facilities that resident children have. (House of Lords, *Hansard* 10 March 2003, Column 1186)

The UN is continually concerned about the UK's position in relation to asylum-seeking children. The exclusion of Article 22 and the use of that exclusion to justify the use of alternative welfare systems means that Government can divert such children from welfare into the NASS structures which, as we shall see, may or may not be able to cope with them. What is also of interest is the response of Government to the expressed concerns.

> The noble Baroness, Lady Walmsley, spoke about the interests of asylum-seeking children. I accept that we are always looking for ways in which we can support them more effectively. *But the level of support for children who are part of an asylum-seeking family is identical to the support that is provided for children in families on income support...* However, the noble Baroness's points will be passed on to my noble friend in the Home Office.

(My emphasis) (Baroness Ashton of Upholland, in reply on behalf of the Government. *Hansard* 10 March 2003, Column 1201)

The state is confident in its position that the level of support is the same as for children in families who receive income support, and indeed, continually reiterates this point (Home Office 2002). In reality it may be very different, as financial support may be provided to the same level, although even this is in dispute, since other support that is available to such families is denied to asylum-seekers. In effect, social work provision for such children is not available unless the NASS framework can provide it. This raises a number of questions about the type of services that may actually come into contact with children and young people in asylum-seeking families and the way that they may develop their relationships with such families in terms of developing patterns of support. The drive for a multi-agency approach to welfare services (DoH 2000) also appears absent from the asylum-seeking debate. NASS operates in almost total isolation from other services, and asylum teams that do exist may often find it difficult to engage other services in debate about the provision of welfare.

If we think of patterns of social work provision to vulnerable families, those who are affected by poverty and other significant inequalities, structural inequalities are often key markers in identifying the *typical* consumer of children's services (Colton *et al.* 2002). The fact of the matter is that such children and their families go on to access many more services through that contact – day care, financial assistance, parenting support, etc. For asylum-seeking children and their families there is no access to such a breadth of services.

The implications of this position are manifold. Principal is the concern that asylum-seeking families may not come into contact with welfare professionals at all, or if they do, it will be at a point when things have reached a deepening crisis that is irresolvable. The issue is that failing to access welfare early enough (a constant message from Government about social work services generally and childcare in particular) (DoH *et al.* 2000) means that problems become so great that families become unable to offer adequate protection to their children. One can immediately draw parallels with the Climbié case (Laming 2003), where concern about late professional involvement and failure to recognize the signs of abuse or neglect may be repeated with asylum-seeking families, whose only recourse to the protection of the state is through other areas of the Children Act, specifically those connected with child protection concerns.

As previously suggested, NASS, through its position as a Government agency, does not have a duty to provide welfare support to the same level as social services. For example, it is not required to provide travel expenses or money for toys or recreational activities (Reg 9[4] Immigration and Asylum Act 1999). For those with children these may be key areas of provision that social work offers. When considering the role of social work it is often focused around the developmental aspects of childcare, particularly play and socialization, which are seen as the most important aspects of a child's experience, and which are the focus of Section 17 support. The Government is very clear about the failure to provide such services:

> Children who are defined as in need…are those whose vulnerability is such that they are unlikely to reach or maintain a satisfactory level of health and development, or their health and development will be significantly impaired without the provision of services. (DoH *et al.* 2000, p.5)

Yet these children may be excluded by NASS from receiving any services because of their status rather than any other factor. Asylum-seeking children, perhaps more than any others, may be in need of services that address issues of development, partly because their experiences may reflect a need for increased attention to developmental issues and partly because their development may be increasingly affected by the lack of resources available to their families (Parker 2000). So we are left with the question: how do we seek to understand some of these issues and translate them into effective practice with asylum-seeking children and their families?

Understanding the potential for harm – the Assessment Framework in practice

The exclusion of asylum-seeking children appears to be at odds with the Government's position, or at least the Department of Health's position, in terms of promoting services for children, with its intention of raising awareness of the need to offer broad-based childcare services (DoH 1998). The extension of these policies to looked after services, crystallizes a position that is welfare orientated. Indeed, the *Framework for the Assessment of Children in Need and Their Families* can be seen as the expression of these principles in a practice focus (DoH 2000). It characterizes the shift of policy away from a protection focus into an arena that relies on welfare provision to prevent children requiring protection and enables the practitioners involved to detect at an early stage the signs of risk that may otherwise require more in-depth support and protective services.

Such ideas are immediately at odds with the position that asylum-seeking children occupy. The marginalization of these children excludes them from the principles on which the modern welfare system is based. It could also be suggested that this exclusion may in itself create some of the factors which increase the risks to children living in the community.

Quality Protects, for example, is constructed on a language of inclusion and expectation for children, with constant references to peers and achievement that is in line with expected outcomes for all children, yet it remains the language of the inclusion of those within particular systems (DoH 1998).

The Department of Health's construction of the Assessment Framework as a way forward for social work services in meeting the needs of vulnerable children needs to be considered in the context of asylum-seeking families. The Framework provides useful insight into the relationship between particular factors and the potential for children to be in need or at risk and as such can inform practice. Of particular note is its attention to the presence of certain issues in determining the likelihood of concern and this predictive quality may be useful in the consideration of asylum-seeking children (DoH *et al.* 2000, DoH 2000). When considering the Assessment Framework implementation particular attention should be given to the role of resilience and developmental issues in relation to children.

Resilience and protective factors

A key aspect of the theoretical basis of the Framework is that of protective factors which include 'family, community and environmental factors'. Social workers familiar with this aspect of assessments will be aware of the impact of social isolation, mental and physical health needs of parents or carers, and children's health needs (DoH 2000) in determining those most in need of services. Indeed, to quote from the guidance provided for social workers highlights the way that such factors may contribute to the experience of being a child in need:

> Where social isolation is combined with fears for personal safety because of a hostile neighbourhood, cumulative negative factors can have an impact on parents' mental health...there is considerable evidence which catalogues the impact of the environment on parental capacity. The

impact on families' health and well-being is well known. (DoH 2000, p.14)

There is a growing catalogue of evidence to suggest that asylum-seeking families experience social isolation and fear in their daily lives. Violence from host communities is a common feature of dispersal policy (Travis 2003); enforced detention (BBC 2003) may lead to a sense of complete isolation and dispersal often leaves families and individuals alone in strange host communities (Kohli 2000; Stanley 2001). The role of NASS in dispersal and the lack of welfare-orientated services do contribute to this isolation, and sense of abandonment by the state, which is felt by many asylum-seekers (Sales 2002).

It appears to be at least ironic and at worst criminal that we create the very factors for asylum-seeking families that we seek to reduce in those who deserve the attention of welfare services. Asylum-seeking in the UK means being subjected to the potentially dangerous environments which promote concern, through dispersal, use of poor standard of housing and failing to acknowledge the evidence which is most important to practitioners in other areas of life.

The other area to consider in terms of the contribution of the Assessment Framework to practice is the nature of resilience amongst children. Resilience is seen as the way that children respond to particular factors, and accounts for the qualitative differences that occur between children who experience deprivation and poverty which may lead some to be in need and some to lead lives which require less intervention from welfare agencies (DoH *et al.* 2000). It is clear that we can make assumptions about the resilience of asylum-seeking children, that they have a higher level of resilience that has enabled them to survive their experiences so far (Okitikpi and Aymer 2000). This should also call into question our perceptions of asylum-seeking families, rather than our knowledge of their experiences. There is little evidence of what asylum-seekers have to go through to enter the UK and certainly no universal standard or minimum requirement (although this may be an area of development for third way regulators in the future). There is a growing body of evidence to suggest that trauma may characterize the types of experience that asylum-seekers have (Brinkman 1998) but what remains generally unclear is the way that they respond to that trauma, and indeed the best way for services to respond to them.

What is clear is that we cannot take the position that all asylum-seeking children are by their nature resilient. The test of resilience rests on outcomes, i.e. surviving, and social work services have taken this test enough times already, if we consider the Climbié case (Laming 2003) and other similar inquiries that have taken place into the deaths of children in receipt of social work services.

We could argue equally that experience of asylum systems in the UK is traumatic; dispersal and relocation outside of established communities is most likely to produce feelings of helplessness and a sense of continued oppression. Lack of funding, housing and access to services may compound rather than alleviate the traumatic nature of the experiences. It is clear that we cannot rely on the fact that asylum-seeking children are by their nature resilient any more than we can rely on other facts supposedly known about them to be other than generalizations about a very diverse group of people.

Child development

Another area of consideration in terms of current practice is the notion of child development as a marker of children in need. The call to utilize evidence, specifically medically based evidence, to establish the 'in need' status of children has led to a change in focus for consideration of how assessments can be completed. Within the context of asylum-seeking children, again there is a tension between knowledge as a eurocentric concept and the use of that in practice. Asylum-seeking children may not meet our expectations in terms of their development for a number of reasons, including the impact of their experiences, the nature of the welfare system in their country of origin, their experiences of poverty and the ability of their families to adapt to the conditions of the UK. There is a dangerous exclusivity in the Assessment Framework's call to knowledge-based practice, which suggests that it is the only way that children can be assessed (DoH 2001).

Culturally appropriate services may take second place to regulatory responses in terms of service provision. How we use child development scales, tables and evidence is important. By definition a child who is undernourished due to his or her circumstances will be a child in need, because development has been impaired, unless of course he or she is an asylum-seeker. The concerns about the use of particular methods to determine the status of children is an important one; we need only look to attachment theory for an example of the translation of British research into an international method of judging the relationships that children can establish with their caregivers (Bowlby 1969). Attachment, and its developed notions of the quality of relationships that may be deduced from observation and questioning, calls into question the validity of transferable knowledge and the methods that practitioners may use to understand children's behaviour. This can be further compounded by the presence of unknown factors, and again when we think about asylum-seeking families we must try to account for their experiences. For children who have experienced (possibly) multiple traumatic losses and find themselves in a strange culture it would be unrealistic to expect their behaviour to follow 'normal' patterns. To make decisions about psychological development based upon the principles of a theory, which is based in a particular culture, time and space is problematic to say the least.

That said, the principles of child development might give us an insight into the general progress of asylum-seeking children within very broad boundaries. Failing to thrive or continued infections may be strong indicators of the impact of poverty on child development. It is the awareness of such issues that is the key to enabling children to access services, and account has to be taken of the experiences of asylum-seeking children in constructing such outcomes.

The potential of the Assessment Framework

The Assessment Framework may be seen, then, to provide indicators of the likelihood of children to be exposed to risk, either through material circumstances or the effects of family life on parenting capability and the development of children. It is clear that the application of the Assessment Framework to asylum-seeking families immediately identifies areas that may cause concern to practitioners. The circumstances of asylum-seeking replicate those that cause most concern for citizen children; professional knowledge and practice would suggest that these families are more in need of services than some of their citizen counterparts. The Assessment Framework represents a potential tool not only to identify areas of concern but also to utilize practice skills to address some of these concerns effectively.

The dilemma for practitioners is how to use the Framework to access services, and how to enable asylum-seeking families to use welfare services effectively. Some of these issues may only be resolved by changes in policy. However, there is much to be gained from a consideration of previous social work developments and the position that engaging with contentious issues around the oppressive nature of the state has developed in the past, in particular, around areas of race and culture and its impact on the provision of services to children generally (Barn, Sinclair and Ferdinand 1997).

Learning from the past – race, culture and social work development

Social work in general, and children's services in particular, have continued to struggle with the impact of race and culture in British society (Barn *et al.* 1997). The impact of difference on the experiences of children and their families, and the impact of difference on their treatment by welfare and 'caring' professions has caused concern for the past 50 years, as the issues of race and whiteness have permeated social policy (Barn *et al.* 1997; Garrett 2002). Social work has responded to this by embracing issues of discrimination and attempting to construct a meaningful challenge to the disadvantages experienced by some members of society (Dalrymple and Burke 1995; Dominelli 1997, 2002). This has had mixed success, however, since cultural issues continue to blight social work practice. Transracial placements, the perceived problems of mixed race children, the appropriateness of carers to meet children's needs and acceptable methods of assessment have all led to a continuing discourse within children's services social work about the adequacy of services to meet children's needs (Barn *et al.* 1997; DoH 1998; DoH 2000; Parker 2000).

That social work has failed to resolve these issues highlights the inability of one part of the welfare state to challenge and overcome such structural inequalities on its own. The persistence of institutional racism within a number of public bodies, and the need for a public enquiry to confirm what social work and others had believed for some time, indicates the difficulties in bringing forward such contentious issues (Macpherson 1999). Indeed, it could be suggested, when social work did begin a genuine attempt to challenge structural inequalities in Britain, it was silenced with the charge of 'political correctness' and the threat of dissolution should it continue to make waves (Pierson 1999).

On a number of levels then, the issues of race and culture continue to challenge social work practice at both the policy and practical level (Barn *et al.* 1997; DoH 2000). It could also be argued that those on-going issues are as a direct result of previous migration, particularly of former Commonwealth citizens in the mid-20th century (Dominelli 1997; Parker 2000). In terms of working with asylum-seeking families, perhaps the most useful learning from the past is to see the previous experiences of the profession as akin to the current situation, with similar discourses framing the experiences of asylum-seekers in the 21st century as were used to understand migrants in the 1950/60s.

Examples of how race and culture have impacted upon service delivery may be seen in the way that models of care have been regulated and monitored within the UK. Foster care and adoption services are beginning to address the issues of race and culture as important factors in determining the potential success of placements. Policy is also beginning to reflect the realization that cultural and religious specificity are important aspects of planning and implementing services (DoH *et al.* 2000). The Assessment Framework has made inroads into the need for culturally appropriate assessments that take account of children's experiences both at the global and personal level (DoH 2000), such as in the area of private fostering (Bostock 2003; Holman 1973). What is clear is that such children might well be experiencing placements that were not matched to their cultural, religious or personal needs, and that there is a growing potential for 'agencies' to arrange the placement of children for financial reward (Holman 2002).

There continues to be professional concern about the relationship between private fostering and those who are subject to immigration controls. Whilst West African children and their parents may be more willing to acknowledge their status as privately fostered individuals, Bostock (2003) highlights the position of unaccompanied asylum-seeking children, those whose parents have been deported and those who have entered the country as domestic workers, as being problematic in regard to effective registration. Practitioner responses to concerns about the welfare of such children have led to moves to challenge the status quo. Continuing concerns about the exposure of such children to potentially abusive situations have meant that government has had to consider tighter regulation.

It can be seen from a historical perspective that culture, race, ethnicity and social work practice have been inextricably linked to immigration issues throughout the past 50 years (and more). Race and concerns about the impact of *foreign* groups on English society have constructed social work practice in a number of ways. The place of discrimination in the consciousness of practitioners and the mixed response to its impact on service users highlight the tension that exists for practice in managing structural concerns in a reality that is bounded by those same structures. What is clear is that such a tension continues to construct practice which is both resistant to and tolerant of the disadvantage experienced by service users, and which may often be seen to be following the path of least resistance when it comes to pursuing services. It would also be true to say that the continued commitment of social work services, through education and training as well as practice, has kept such issues on a national agenda, and has been contributing factors to the change that has occurred in other areas of policy in relation to such issues. The struggle within social work over the past 30 years has allowed other developments to take place in relation to the provision of public sector services.

Conclusion: the way forward for social work with accompanied asylum-seeking children

The first challenge, then, for social work with children and families who are seeking asylum is to recognize the constraints of current policy and guidance which construct asylum-seekers as not worthy of welfare owing to their status. The second is to acknowledge the potentially oppressive effects of asylum systems in isolating families and nurturing the very factors which government policy seeks to reduce for the population as a whole.

Social work agencies are charged with the duty to protect and promote the welfare of vulnerable members of our communities, and to recognise and act upon the circumstances that may lead to the reduction in welfare for children in particular, and to take account of structural inequalities that produce disadvantage within society. The struggle to recognize the historical impact of race and culture on children's lives, and of the need for effective services to remedy this, can be seen as a struggle that was led by social work agencies and is held within the continuing commitment to anti-discriminatory practice within social work training and education.

Acknowledging the discriminatory nature of current immigration legislation (Mynott 2001) and its use to exclude particular groups from access to welfare services is a first step in constructing practice which accounts for the needs of asylum-seeking children and their families within the mainstream discourses of welfare, and begins the process of reducing the marginalization of this vulnerable group. However, practice needs to go beyond the simple recognition of oppressive circumstances, for practice implies action.

Social work practitioners have at their disposal a range of resources that would enable asylum-seeking families to engage with welfare systems in effective ways. A way into these systems is through the *Framework for the Assessment of Children in Need and their Families*, which provides a legitimate analysis of the experiences of families to identify vulnerability and risk. Whether in a specific asylum service team or in children's services, practitioners can use this as a vehicle to draw attention to the plight of asylum-seeking children and their families and to construct assessments that show how the need for services can resolve these issues. Using assessments to highlight need will allow practitioners to begin to argue for appropriate services. It may also draw attention to the inadequacies of NASS in meeting the most basic welfare needs of asylum-seekers, and to the contradictions that are inherent in the current legislative position.

Practitioners need also to update their knowledge: the constantly changing regulation and legislation in relation to asylum-seekers means that practice knowledge can soon be outdated. Use of practice materials such as legal handbooks (JCWI 2002) and Refugee Council briefings (Refugee Council 2002) allows knowledge to develop with practice. Asylum-seekers should be an area of concern for agencies as well as for individuals. We can draw upon the many examples of good practice that are beginning to characterize European professional practice in relation to these issues, especially the impact of external factors in asylum-seekers' experiences (Brinkman 1998; Okitikpi and Aymer 2000; Valtonen 2002). The growing recognition of asylum-seeking as a European concern (Bloch and Schuster 2002; Düvell and Jordan 2002) may open up the possibility of practice that is led by sharing experiences across national boundaries and breaking down some of the fears that have led to the resurgence of the need for a 'British' identity in the first place (Hall 2000). We need a more open focus on responding to asylum-seekers as individuals with specific problems that can be met by effective social work services (Valtonen 2002).

The continual fight for recognition of need and resistance to oppressive systems that has characterized the development of children's services over the past 30 years lends itself to the issue of asylum-seeking. Assessments that are well constructed will enable practitioners to argue for appropriate resources and may begin to highlight the real deficits in current service provision (see also Brown in this volume). The responsibilities of NASS and local authorities to meet the welfare needs of asylum-seeking families over and above the financial commitment of government means that these assessments could form the basis for action within a variety of agencies. The potential for inter-agency teamwork and the imperative for multidisciplinary working open up the possibility of raising consciousness across a number of agencies in terms of the provision of services (see Mather and Kerac 2002, for example). The imperative to use information and knowledge effectively and to build working relationships that allow the implementation of such knowledge in practice – see, for example, Richman (1998) – in relation to the psychological effects of race and culture can only be explored in a multi-agency setting.

Social work's tradition of challenging attitudes to difference and taking up the cases of those who are disadvantaged means that it is ideally situated to develop effective practice with asylum-seeking children and their families. The impact of the media and government position cannot be denied when thinking about practice; however, professional practice must seek to (re)establish a critical position in relation to asylum-seeking families, and to move away from the culture of suspicion that already surrounds their presence in the UK. As Parker (2000) notes in relation to such practice: 'The onus on social workers is to ensure that specific knowledge develops within the context of existing knowledge and values for social work practice' (p.70).

The use of existing knowledge should allow practitioners to move to a more critical position about the nature of asylum-seekers' experiences, and away from the current ambivalence that exists. This ambivalence is highlighted by recent reporting of a conference; in terms of the poverty experienced by asylum-seekers, speakers were clear that:

> many pregnant asylum-seekers were facing extreme hardship because of rules that meant they were not eligible for a maternity grant...the dispersal system is now taking up to eight months, and many women were left to cope with a single NASS grant of £50 for baby equipment and clothes. (Community Care 2002)

However the conference also reported that: 'some parents who would normally have breastfed were turning to bottle feeding simply to supplement their income' (Community Care 2002). The maximum value of milk tokens is £5 per week, yet the conference devoted time to this point rather than to a consideration of the reasons why such actions may be necessary, or indeed if such actions would be as concerning within the indigenous communities. It is worrying that practitioners would see this aspect of the work as more problematic than challenging the way that systems are administered and used to construct asylum-seekers as an economic threat to society.

The discourse of difference, which currently informs and leads practice, should be incorporated into a discourse of inclusion that the United Nations Charter enshrines in terms of our understanding of childhood. All children in the UK deserve the right to access welfare services by nature of their status as children, not because of their economic or social circumstances. Social work is well positioned to begin to raise the consciousness of individuals and agencies to this fact now.

References

Barn, R., Sinclair, R. and Ferdinand, D. (1997) *Acting on Principle: An Examination of Race and Ethnicity in Social Services Provision for Children and Families.* London: BAAF.

BBC (2003) 'Asylum children policy "Immoral".' At www.bbc.co.uk/news

Bloch, A. and Schuster, L. (2002) 'Asylum and welfare: Contemporary debates.' *Critical Social Policy 22* 3, 393–414.

Blunkett, D. (2002) 'What does citizenship mean today?' At www.guardian.co.uk

Bostock, L. (2003) *Effectiveness of Childminding Registration and Its Implications for Private Fostering.* SCIE Position Paper No.1. London: SCIE.

Bowlby, J. (1969) *Attachment and Loss, Vol. 1 Attachment.* London: Hogarth.

Brinkman, J. (1998) 'Social work for refugees: Overcoming trauma and cultural difference.' *Social Work in Europe 5* 1, 21–24.

Children Act (1989) London: HMSO.

Cohen, S., Humphries B. and Mynott E. (eds) (2001) *From Immigration Controls to Welfare Controls.* London: Routledge.

Colton, M., Sanders, R. and Williams, M. (2001) *An Introduction to Working with Children: A Guide for Social Workers.* Basingstoke: Palgrave.

Community Care (2001a) *Stretched and Underfunded Services Place Refugee Children in Jeopardy.* At www.community-care.co.uk/articles

Community Care (2001b) 'Citizenship programmes boosted but Blunkett queries children's services.' Located at www.community-care.co.uk/articles

Community Care (2002) 'Home alone children at risk.' Located at www.community-care.co.uk/articles

Dalrymple, J. and Burke, B. (1995) *Anti-oppressive Practice: Social Care and the Law.* Buckingham: Open University Press.

Department of Health (1998) *Quality Protects: Transforming Children's Services.* Local Authority Circular (LAC[98]28).

Department of Health (2000) *Assessing Children in Need and Their Families: Practice Guidance.* London: HMSO.

Department of Health (2001) *Studies Informing the Framework for the Assessment of Children in Need and Their Families.* London: HMSO.

Department of Health, Department for Education and Employment, Home Office (2000) *Framework for the Assessment of Children in Need and Their Families.* London: HMSO.

Dominelli, L. (1997) *Anti-Racist Social Work.* Basingstoke: Macmillan.

Dominelli, L. (2002) *Anti-oppressive Social Work Theory and Practice.* Basingstoke: Palgrave Macmillan.

Düvell, F. and Jordan, B. (2002) 'Immigration, asylum and welfare: The European context.' *Critical Social Policy 22* 3, 498–517.

Garrett, P. (2002) '"No Irish need apply": Social work in Britain and the history and politics of exclusionary paradigms and practices.' *British Journal of Social Work 32*, 477–494.

Hall, S. (2000) 'Multicultural citizens, monocultural citizenship?' In N. Pearce and J. Hallgarten, (eds) (2000) *Tomorrow's Citizens: Critical Debates in Citizenship and Education.* London: IPPR.

Hansard (2003) Located at www.parliament.the-stationery-office.co.uk

Harvey, A. (2001), 'The 1999 Immigration and Asylum Act and How to Challenge it: A Legal View.' In S. Cohen, B. Humphries and E. Mynott (eds) *From Immigration to Welfare Controls.* London: Jessica Kingsley Publishers.

Hayes, D. (2001), 'From Aliens to Asylum-seekers: A History of Immigration Controls and Welfare in Britain.' In S. Cohen, B. Humphries and E. Mynott (eds) *From Immigration to Welfare Controls.* London: Jessica Kingsley Publishers.

Holman, B. (1973) *Trading in Children.* London: Routledge and Kegan Paul.

Holman, B. (2002) *The Unknown Fostering: A Study of Private Fostering.* Lyme Regis: Russell House Publishing.

Home Office (2002) *Secure Borders, Safe Haven: Integration with Diversity in Modern Britain.* London: HMSO.

Humphries, B. (2001) 'From welfare to authoritarianism: The role of social work in immigration controls.' In S. Cohen, B. Humphries and E. Mynott (eds) *From Immigration to Welfare Controls.* London: Jessica Kingsley Publishers.

Immigration and Asylum Act (1999) London: HMSO.

James, A., Jenks, C. and Prout, A. (1998) *Theorising Childhood.* Cambridge: Polity Press.

Joint Council for the Welfare of Immigrants (2002) *Immigration, Nationality and Refugee Law Handbook.* London: JCWI.

Jones, A. (2001) *Family Life and the Pursuit of Immigration Controls.* In S. Cohen, B. Humphries and E. Mynott (eds) *From Immigration to Welfare Controls.* London: Jessica Kingsley Publishers.

Jordan, B. (2000) *Social Work and the Third Way: Tough Love as Social Policy.* London: Sage

Jordan, B. (2001), 'Tough love: Social work, social exclusion and the third way.' *British Journal of Social Work 31*, 527–546.

Kohli, R. (2000) 'Breaking the silence.' *Professional Social Work June 2000*, 6–7.

Laming, H. (Lord) (2003) *The Victoria Climbié Inquiry.* London: HMSO.

Macpherson, W. (1999) *The Stephen Lawrence Inquiry.* London: HMSO.

Mather, M. and Kerac, M. (2002) 'Caring for the health of children brought into the UK from abroad.' *Adoption and Fostering 26*, 4, 44–54.

Miller, D. (2000) 'Citizenship: What Does it Mean and Why is it Important?' In N. Pearce and J. Hallgarten (eds) *Tomorrow's Citizens: Critical Debates in Citizenship and Education.* London: IPPR.

Mynott, E (2001) 'From a shambles to the new apartheid: lLocal authorities, dispersal and the struggle to defend asylum-seekers.' In S. Cohen, B. Humphries and E. Mynott (eds) *From Immigration to Welfare Controls.* London: Jessica Kingsley Publishers.

Nationality, Immigration and Asylum Act (2002) London: HMSO.

Okitikpi, T. and Aymer, C. (2000) 'The price of safety: Refugee children and the challenge for social work.' *Social Work in Europe 7*, 1, 51–58.

Parker, J. (2000) 'Social work with refugees and asylum-seekers: A rationale for developing practice.' *Practice 12*, 3, 61–76.

Pierson, J. (1999) 'Social work and civil society: The mixed legacy of radical anti-oppressive practice.' In T. Philpott (ed) *Political Correctness and Social Work.* London: IEA.

Refugee Council (2002) *The Nationality, Immigration and Asylum Act 2002: Changes to the Asylum System in the UK.* London: Refugee Council.

Refugee Council and BAAF (2001) *Where are the Children?* London: Refugee Council and BAAF.

Richman, N. (1998) *In the Midst of the Whirlwind: A Manual for Helping Refugee Children.* London: Trentham Books.

Sales, R. (2002) 'The deserving and the undeserving? Refugees, asylum-seekers and welfare in Britain.' *Critical Social Policy 22*, 3, 456–478.

Save the Children (2003a) *Young Refugees: A Guide to the Rights and Entitlements of Separated Refugee Children.* London: Save the Children.

Save the Children (2003b) *Young Refugees: Providing Emotional Support to Young Separated Refugees in the UK.* London: Save the Children.

Stanley, K. (2001) *Cold Comfort: Young Separated Refugees in England.* London: Save the Children.

Tate, N. (2000) 'Citizenship education in a liberal democracy.' In N. Pearce and J. Hallgarten(eds) *Tomorrow's Citizens: Critical Debates in Citizenship and Education.* London: IPPR.

Travis, A. (2003) 'Shame of violence to asylum family.' *The Guardian,* Thursday 17 April.

United Nations (1989) *International Convention on the Rights of the Child.*

Valtonen, K. (2002) 'Social work with immigrants and refugees: Developing a participation-based framework for anti-oppressive practice.' *British Journal of Social Work 32*, 113–120.

Chapter 9

'Not our Problem': The Provision of Services to Disabled Refugees and Asylum-seekers

Jennifer Harris and Keri Roberts

Introduction

In post-modern Britain, it is easy to imagine that the majority of people defined as 'in need' will have recourse to basic levels of service provision from the community care system. This is because the system appears comprehensive and sufficiently reactive to cater for the requirements of the various groups of people who might be considered 'at risk' in the event of non-provision.

In this chapter, we explore service provision for a group of people for whom it is problematic in the extreme, owing to a lack of clear guidance from policy makers and legislators. Disabled refugees and asylum-seekers frequently experience hardship and poverty in Britain owing to a lack of basic service provision. This, we will demonstrate, has its roots in the conflict over responsibilities between two macro level services, the National Asylum-seekers Support Service (NASS) and local authorities (social services). This unresolved conflict engenders confusion and inaction at the ground level of face-to-face service provision, with workers from both services attempting to refer applicants to the other service whilst denying responsibility.

The roots of these issues are ignorance of the current law and responsibilities for service provision, inflexibility in service provision and a punitive system that seeks to deter applicants.

This chapter is based upon original research conducted by the authors as part of a three-year project funded by the Community Fund and the Joseph Rowntree Foundation (Roberts and Harris 2002). Here we focus upon disabled refugees' and asylum-seekers' requirements for services by examining the perspectives of service providers from local authority social services and refugee reception assistant organizations. The latter organizations were established following the Immigration and Asylum Act 1999. Both these organizations have a legal responsibility and a mandate to be involved in the provision of social and welfare services to disabled refugees and asylum-seekers.

Local authority social services have a legal duty to assess *all* disabled people who are considered to be in need under the NHS and Community Care Act 1990 (Rummery, Ellis and Davis 1999). However, several cases in the late 1990s established that, once assessment is completed, service provision thereafter may be blocked in situations where a local authority claims insufficient resources to provide the required services (Valios 1997).

Disabled refugees have identical rights to British citizens with regard to all social and welfare benefits and services and may apply for benefits and services in exactly the same manner as all other citizens. As refugees they have been granted the protection of the British Government after fleeing persecution in their country of origin.

The law is rather more complicated in relation to disabled asylum-seekers. Asylum-seekers have asked the British Government for protection, but have yet to hear whether the Home Office will grant them refugee status. Their status should not be viewed as inferior to that of refugees but rather that they are at an earlier stage of the asylum process. Disabled asylum-seekers are entitled to apply for local authority support under the community care system, in exactly the same manner as the indigenous population. Local authorities may have a duty to assist asylum-seekers when it can be demonstrated they have needs arising *other than* solely though destitution under the National Assistance Act 1948.

Under the Immigration and Asylum Act 1999 asylum-seekers came to be expected to support themselves, but if they are classed as 'destitute' they can apply for subsistence and accommodation support to the National Asylum Support Service (NASS). NASS provides accommodation on a 'no-choice basis' and is charged with dispersing asylum-seekers across Britain. Subsistence levels are currently 70 per cent of income support levels. There is very limited extra provision within the NASS system for additional financial support for *disabled* asylum-seekers. The latter have been debarred from applying for disability benefits since February 1996 and although the Immigration and Asylum Act 1999 allows NASS to make special payments to meet particular needs, there are currently no set procedures for making such a claim.

A test case that established the basis of law was Westminster City Council v NASS (April 2001), the judgment being that the local authority's responsibilities took precedence in cases of provision of support to disabled asylum-seekers. Three further cases followed: London boroughs of Enfield and Lambeth: R (Mani) v Lambeth; R (Tasci) v Enfield and R (J) v Enfield. All four cases confirmed that local authorities have a responsibility for meeting the community care needs of disabled asylum-seekers.

Policy background

It is currently difficult to obtain accurate statistics concerning refugees and asylum-seekers in Britain and basic information, such as community size, age and gender structures, is impossible to obtain at a local level[1] (London Research Centre 1999). Hence, research projects such as the one described here encounter problems in attempting to explore the experiences of sub-populations, such as disabled people within these populations. Lack of data means that service providers are largely ill informed about specific needs of these groups, which 'makes it difficult for them to respond' (Robinson 1998, p.153). This situation engenders a climate within which diversity within the refugee population, be it in terms of age, gender, religion, country of origin, ethnicity, or disability may be unaccounted.

There is currently no means of determining how many of the refugees and asylum-seekers living in Britain are disabled (Harris and Roberts 2003; Roberts and Harris 2002). Both the refugee and disability literature are largely silent in relation to disabled refugees, although the former are attempting to rectify this situation with recent items on these issues (Datta 2000; Davis 2000).

Government publications such as the White Paper *Fairer, Faster, Firmer: A Modern Approach to Immigration and Asylum*, the subsequent Immigration and Asylum Act 1999, the consultation paper on the integration of recognized refugees in the UK (Home Office 1999) and the White Paper *Secure Borders, Safe Haven: Integration with Diversity in Modern Britain* (Home Office 2002) all largely leave undiscussed issues relating to *disabled* refugees and asylum-seekers.

Local authority social service departments have a responsibility to 'carry out an assessment of care needs…and ensure that care being given was what that person needed' (Department of Health 1998, p.13). However, a series of legal challenges has shown that local authorities can claim that they are unable to provide the required services because of resource limitations (Valios 1997). Therefore, although an individual's service requirements are recognized, legally, they can continue to remain unmet. Despite this, Blackman (1998) argues that 'at present, social care assessments appear to offer the best approach to identifying need' (p.193). A confounding issue here is that many local authorities charge for services (Department of Health 1998), which may deter those who require services from obtaining them.

Recent research demonstrates, however, that many disabled people experience difficulty in gaining access to assessment (Rummery *et al.* 1999). Lack of information about the services on offer (Chesson and Sutherland 1992) and failure by social services to provide information in accessible formats (Harris and Bamford 2001) have both been shown to deter applicants.

There has been much media coverage concerning the expectations placed upon local authority social services departments to provide destitute asylum-seekers with housing and subsistence under the National Assistance Act (1949) (Vaux 1998). This requirement was dissolved from April 2000 by the implementation of the Immigration and Asylum Act 1999 which formally ended entitlements to social security benefits for all new asylum-seekers and transferred responsibility for destitute asylum-seekers from local authorities to the National Asylum Support Service (NASS). The Act also instigated a policy of dispersal, with asylum-seekers being sent to areas of the UK that had not previously housed significant numbers of refugees and asylum-seekers. Nevertheless, recent court cases (for example, in Westminster) have confirmed that local authorities retain their obligation to undertake community care assessments of disabled asylum-seekers' need for services.

Method

In this study, 18 interviews were conducted during the summer and autumn of 2001, with 7 workers from social services and 11 representatives from reception assistant organizations across Britain. The purpose of the interviews was to focus upon current practices in provision of support to disabled refugees and asylum-seekers and to gauge respondent knowledge of entitlements to social and welfare services for these particular groups.

Social service interviews

The social services respondents were aware of their responsibility to assess all disabled people (irrespective of immigration status). However, considerable confusion was expressed concerning the implications of the Westminster case (see above) even though this confirmed that local authorities have a duty of care towards disabled asylum-seekers. The situation was complicated by the fact that the Immigration and Asylum Act 1999 removed their duty towards *destitute* asylum-seekers. Confusion was expressed therefore concerning situations in which a person might be destitute and therefore requesting help from the local authority (which they are not obliged to provide), but if they are a disabled asylum-seeker, then the Westminster case gave them the duty to act. However, dissent was expressed on the question of whether the ruling actually meant that disabled asylum-seekers *had* to be offered services and more explicitly, whose responsibility it would be to pay for those services:

> [In] the Westminster [case] there are two points really. The difficulty that I think many Authorities have (and we have) is that it's incredible that NASS can take responsibility for the fate of an individual and then decline any financial responsibility for them. We've sought certain legal advice here and we've agreed that we will support people in those circumstances. But equally, you know, we're quite happy to meet our Community Care needs but NASS would be paying for accommodation and support for those individuals anyway. It seems only fair that they ought to be paying that element. We're not asking them to pay the balance of it, because we don't do that for children in school, we don't do that for special needs, you know, for English language classes and so on, we meet them reluctantly. (Social services respondent)

Several social services respondents expressed similar sentiments to these; namely, that they are willing to assess and, in cases of eligibility criteria being met, provide services to disabled asylum-seekers. However, the majority of respondents were still taking the line that the situation following the Westminster judgment was not finalized and therefore they should not appear too hasty in coming forward with services, especially in cases where provision is likely to prove expensive.

The organization of social services into specialist teams, dealing with 'disability' in one team and 'asylum-seekers' in another, created further confusion over responsibility and in many cases disabled asylum-seekers were effectively passed between the two teams. This situation inevitably increased waiting times for often desperately needed support:

> What my team actually does, we provide the basic needs to most of the asylum-seekers we deal with…my team deals with about…two hundred and seventy-five asylum-seekers across the county. Asylum-seekers whose needs fall outside what my team provide are referred to our mainstream services and then that's it – things that fall outside of what we can do, i.e. those needs, then they provide Community Care services and then there would have to be, you know, using our generic services for that. (Social services respondent: asylum-seekers' team)

This respondent acknowledged that, in these cases, disabled asylum-seekers would be referred to the disability team and must then be placed on a waiting list for assessment, and that this process could take a considerable time.

We found that the response of local authority social services departments to requests for community care assessments from disabled refugees and asylum-seekers varied in terms of perceived urgency of their cases. Whilst some local authorities appeared to be operating a humanitarian policy and categorizing requests for community care assessments as urgent, others applied a strictly chronological system, with new applicants being given no special priority. Yet others were operating a policy based on the view that community care assessments should not be carried out until the person had been dispersed. The danger we identified here is that disabled asylum-seekers with significant personal care needs may then be without support for prolonged periods of time.

In general, access to community care assessment was low, but even once an assessment has been completed, service provision does not always result. The legal obligation is to conduct the assessment, rather than to provide services to meet identified needs. Again practice varied widely, with some social services waiving fees for services provided to destitute disabled asylum-seekers, others applying charges even in cases where it was clear the client could not afford them.

The 'leniency' of local authorities in response to requests for community care assessments appeared to be directly related to the number of requests in discrete geographical areas. Where large numbers of disabled asylum-seekers were present in communities, it was common to find resistance to carrying out assessments based on costs:

> There has been no communication between the Home Office and the local authorities... There is a lot of passing the parcel of cases like this [as] there is no clarity about whether that money can be reclaimed. (Social services respondent)

Reception assistant organizations

Reception assistant organizations (RAOs) have a key role in referring refugees and asylum-seekers to other service providers such as social services, housing providers and primary health care practitioners. RAOs were established after the Immigration and Asylum Act 1999 to implement dispersal of asylum-seekers and support established refugees. They are funded by central government but do not form part of it. They are not part of NASS but they distribute vouchers, provide advice and support and assist in form-filling to make applications for support. They are generally operated by charities with experience of supporting asylum-seekers, such as Refugee Action. Under this confusing system, RAOs are implementers of NASS policy, but they have no control over the latter and NASS is their funder but not directly their 'boss'. However, they must follow NASS rules. NASS supplies lists of asylum-seekers arriving in the RAO's area. In practice, these lists are often inadequate, with few or no details of 'special needs'. In order to be able to refer people effectively and advocate on their behalf, reception assistant organization staff need to be in possession of detailed and accurate information concerning disabled refugees' and asylum-seekers' rights and entitlements to services.

However, our respondents from the RAOs were often ill-informed about disabled refugees' and asylum-seekers' entitlements to services. In general, there was little awareness of the disability specific services and support which social services and NASS might be able to offer. Inevitably, this had repercussions in terms of their ability to advise disabled clients and this then placed them at a disadvantage when attempting to negotiate with both their local social services departments and NASS. From our sample of 11 RAO respondents, we found only one who was well-informed and had up-to-date information to hand on the entitlements issue. This respondent below understates the issue thus:

> Sometimes social services department people are not sure whether they could take asylum-seekers, so often we have to tell them their responsibil-

ity and quote legislations and all that and then they become aware that, yes, it is their responsibility... In all the local authorities, not everybody's aware about all this, everybody goes about doing their own thing. (Reception assistant organization respondent)

A general atmosphere of defensiveness prevails concerning responsibility for provision of services for disabled asylum-seekers. Not only is the law still unclear, providing loopholes for inactivity or disclaiming responsibility, but the fact that disabled asylum-seekers have two statuses (disabled person and asylum-seeker) creates yet more opportunities for 'buck passing', as this respondent stated:

What about asylum-seekers? Nothing to do with them! [Social Services] So it is our responsibility, those who are directly seeing them [asylum-seekers] on a daily basis to explain to people what their roles are, what their responsibilities are if we refer clients to them.

[The] council is saying 'We can't do anything'. I think they are getting huge bills for community care assessments and they say they can't manage.

Further difficulties are created for the reception assistant organizations by the fact that NASS does not communicate in advance any special requirements concerning dispersed persons. This is demonstrated in the following excerpt from one of the interviews:

Q. Were you aware that the disabled person – before they arrived, that they were going to be disabled?

A. No.

Q. You didn't get any notification of that?

A. No, and in actual fact, our stipulation, when we signed the contract, was that we really hadn't got suitable property for anybody severely disabled; fortunately this lady is not severely disabled.

We found no instances where NASS had informed an RAO in advance that a member of an arriving group of asylum-seekers was disabled. When this situation occurs, the RAOs are placed in a difficult position since, like the respondent above, they may not have accessible accommodation available.

Conclusion

Poor communication between all agencies involved in the care of disabled asylum-seekers has resulted in a fragmented experience of service provision, with many of this group experiencing a form of 'pass the parcel' as they move from one agency to another. In our study, NASS was particularly criticized by respondents from both social services and reception assistant organizations since, being the arm of the Home Office in charge of dispersal to their local geographical areas, they were in possession of crucial information. In situations where they fail to pass on information concerning impairment/s and requirements for accessible housing, service providers are left in a difficult position in which they may be forced from necessity to admit the client to unsuitable accommodation.

Inter-agency communication appears to be at a minimum, with each sector operating defensively. Most agencies appear confused about their obligations under the law towards disabled asylum-seekers and this situation seems likely to continue whilst further legal challenges are mounted and contested. In the meantime, there is an urgent need for staff training, both in alerting staff to the possibility of disability within the applicant population and in understanding the means of securing appropriate service provision for these applicants. In general, the rigidity of the NASS system in terms of failing to take account of impairment and related needs of disabled asylum-seekers (especially in relation to forced dispersal) requires a radical overhaul on humanitarian grounds.

The fragmented system detailed above is the product of the lack of clarity in the law, dragged feet by policy makers and, on the ground, failure to take the initiative by service providers. Put succinctly, NASS operates a rigid, inhumane system of dispersal that fails to inform or acknowledge the impact of disability in the system when sending people to the reception assistant organizations. The latter flounder to make the best of a poor deal, often having to place people in unsuitable accommodation. Social services have, in the main, attempted to deny their responsibilities under the NHS and Community Care Act 1990 to assess disabled asylum-seekers, claiming that NASS takes care of all issues for this group. Our study reveals that these issues are fuelled by panic over the financial implications of admitting responsibility and the impact upon local authority budgets. Even where disabled asylum-seekers manage to get through the gate to social services, they face being passed between asylum-seeker and disability teams, with consequent long delays in attending to urgent requirements.

The issues raised by our research are not merely about better coordination of services and ambiguities in the law, but also particularly about the existence of NASS itself. The problems generated are in many respects inevitably caused by the implementation of a separate, parallel and inferior system of welfare support for asylum-seekers.

Notes

1   Carey-Wood, Duke and Karn (1995) found that 10% of their sample of 263 people (of various nationalities) with refugee status or exceptional leave to remain reported 'some sort of disability sufficient to affect their daily life' (p. 77). Girbash (1991) reported that 4.5% of Vietnamese refugees living in Manchester were disabled, and Duke and Marshall (1995) reported that 3% of refugees from Vietnam who arrived in Britain after 1982 were either chronically sick or disabled.

References

Blackman, T. (1998) 'Facing up to underfunding: Equity and retrenchment in community care.' *Social Policy and Administration 32*, 2, 182–195.

Carey-Wood, J., Duke, K. And Karn, V. (1995) 'The resettlement of refugees in Britain.' *Home Office Research Study 141*. London: HMSO.

Chesson, R. and Sutherland, A. (1992) 'General practice and the provision of information and services for physically disabled people aged 16 to 65 years.' *British Journal of General Practice 42*, 364, 473–476.

Datta, S. (2000) 'Interim arrangements for asylum-seekers.' *Disability Rights Bulletin*, Spring 2000, 14–15.

Davis, V. (2000) 'Asylum-seekers after April.' *Disability Rights Bulletin*, Spring 2000, 15.

Department of Health (1998) *Modernising Social Services: Promoting Independence, Improving Protection, Raising Standards*. London: HMSO.

Duke, K. and Marshall, T. (1995) 'Vietnamese refugees since 1982'. *Home Office Research Study 142*. London: HMSO.

Girbash, C. (1991) 'Manchester Vietnamese Refugees since 1982.' *Home Office Research Study 142*. London: HMSO.

Harris, J. and Bamford, C. (2001) 'The uphill struggle: Services for deaf and hard of hearing people: Issues of equality, participation and access.' *Disability and Society 16*, 7, 969–979.

Harris, J. and Roberts, K. (2003) '"All doors are closed to us": A social model analysis of the experiences of disabled refugees and asylum-seekers in Britain.' *Disability and Society 18*, 4.

Home Office (1999) *A Consultation Paper on the Integration of Recognised Refugees in the UK*. London: Home Office.

Home Office (2002) *Secure Borders, Safe Haven: Integration with Diversity in Modern Britain*. Norwich: HMSO.

London Research Centre (1999) 'Refugee demographic data sources.' *Population Advice Note 98*, 5, 3–7.

Roberts K. and Harris J. (2002) *Disabled People in Refugee and Asylum-seeking Communities.* Bristol: Joseph Rowntree Foundation/Policy Press.

Robinson, V. (1998) 'The importance of information in the resettlement of refugees in the UK.' *Journal of Refugee Studies 11*, 2, 146–160.

Rummery, K., Ellis, K. and Davis, A. (1999) 'Negotiating access to community care assessments: Perspectives of front-line workers, people with a disability and carers.' *Health and Social Care in the Community 7*, 4, 296–300.

Valios, N. (1997) 'Law lords give green light to slash services.' *Community Care*, 1164:1.

Vaux, G. (1998) 'Paying the price for a society that doesn't care.' *Community Care*, 1219: 29.

Chapter 10

Asylum-seekers as Offenders and Victims within the Criminal Justice System

Angela Montgomery

Introduction

There are many dilemmas and ethical issues which face probation practitioners when working with individuals, whether as offenders or as victims,
within the criminal justice system. The ethical issues in respect of working
with those who are asylum-seekers in the UK have seldom been more marked.
Many of the difficulties faced by this group of offenders in respect of being
processed by the criminal justice system mirror those faced by the minority
ethnic communities in the UK. However, these difficulties are exacerbated by
bearing the legal status of an asylum-seeker, refugee or non-British national.
The difficulties which beset this group of offenders commence at the point of
arrest and follow the individual through the remand/bail process and trial to
the point of sentencing.

The Probation Service, in engaging with asylum-seekers who have been
convicted, has a responsibility for working with those offenders in respect of
both community and custodial sentences. It should be noted that the Probation Service's focus on working with offenders has changed from a befriend-
ing role to more focused work with the offender, preventing re-offending and
protecting the public. The Probation Service was an organization which acted
as an advocate for offenders, helping them with housing, benefits and so on.

However, little work was done with offenders in terms of challenging their offending behaviour or the use of evidence-based methods of working with offenders – specifically the use of accredited programmes where peer-challenging is an integral part of the process. The change has recently been further accentuated by the appointment of Martin Narey as the Commissioner of the newly formed Correctional Services Department.

The National Probation Service

The National Probation Service came into existence on 1 April 2000 as a result of the Criminal Justice and Court Services Act 2000. The aims of the new national service are to protect the public, to reduce re-offending and to ensure the proper punishment of offenders. Additionally, the Service has a responsibility to ensure that offenders are made aware of the effects of crime on their victims. As part of this responsibility, the Service has a role in ascertaining and promoting the concerns of victims of violent and sexual offenders. The Service is organised into 42 different areas which are co-terminus with local police authorities. Each Service has a Board appointed by the Secretary of State, which has a responsibility for ensuring that the national aims, objectives and targets are met. The Board also acts as the employer for all staff within the Service. The responsibility for local operational delivery ultimately rests with the Chief Probation Officer who is directly employed by the National Probation Directorate.

The provision of the Probation Service's statutory responsibilities in respect of asylum-seekers is additionally affected by its diversity strategy, which is outlined in some detail by *The Heart of the Dance* (NPD 2003). The diversity strategy also incorporates the statutory duties outlined within the Race Relations (Amendment) Act 2000 as well as *The Stephen Lawrence Inquiry* (Macpherson 1999). *The Heart of the Dance* makes a commitment that offenders, victims of crime and communities will receive an equal service. This is translated by the Service as recognizing and valuing the differences of each individual and by so doing ensuring both justice and reduction of risk to the general public.

Asylum-seekers within the criminal justice system

The position of asylum-seekers within the criminal justice system (CJS) is a necessarily complex one in that they can be identified as offenders, victims and as a community which can be subject to particular types of criminal behaviour. The status of being an asylum-seeker within society, and more specifically within the CJS, is one that in many ways can result in a different and detrimental service being afforded. This applies whether the asylum-seeker is an offender, victim or becomes part of an asylum-seeking community.

The position of asylum-seekers who are offenders must be seen against a background in which asylum-seekers are afforded a provision of state support which is less than that of the host population. Since 1996, in some cases asylum-seekers have been afforded no support at all; this is where it is deemed that an application for asylum has failed to be made in good time. This has been further compounded by the fact that in July 2002 legislation was passed which prevents asylum-seekers from working, whereas the previous position had been that prohibition of employment lasted only for the first six months (Merali 2003). Asylum-seekers can thus be contrasted with the offending population at large by the fact that they as a group are required to manage their day-to-day lives on less than that of an individual on benefits. It has long been recognized that poverty and destitution are features of criminal behaviour as are poor housing conditions (Merton 1968). Asylum-seekers, by virtue of current legislation and policy, have less financial resources and often inhabit poor quality private rented accommodation and thus are not afforded the same starting point as the general offending population.

Asylum-seekers as offenders

Asylum-seekers as a section of the offending population have needs which are similar to those who offend from minority ethnic communities. These needs can be summarized as follows:

1.   appropriate interpreter facilities

2.   cultural sensitivity and understanding

3.   understanding of the impact that racism can have in respect of minority ethnic offenders

4.   awareness and understanding of the differing health needs of minority ethnic offenders.

Criminal justice agencies and thus the Probation Service have a legal requirement to comply with the Race Relations Amendment Act 2000. This requires public authorities to:

- eliminate unlawful racial discrimination

- promote equality of opportunity, and

- promote good relations between people of different racial groups. (CRE 2002)

This legal obligation is outlined in the National Probation Service's diversity strategy; thus probation officers working with asylum-seeking offenders should be mindful of these duties in the provision of information to the Court and in the supervision of offenders subject to community and custodial sentences. In practical terms, these considerations should apply from the pre-sentence stage right through to the supervision of an offender's licence, when he has been released from prison.

Pre-sentence reports

First, at the pre-sentence stage, it is necessary to ascertain whether an interpreter is required. Whilst this may appear straightforward it can be fraught with difficulties, especially where the offender's solicitor and the Court which has convicted him/her has deemed this to be not necessary. However, if it is believed that a detailed discussion of the offence and the factors relating to it merit an interpreter, then this must happen regardless of the embarrassment this may cause the offender's own solicitor and the convicting Court. A further dilemma for the probation staff is that, having secured an appropriate interpreter, it is conceivable that the offender may well give a version of events which would alert the staff member to the fact that the offender has not received a fair trial. Depending on the seriousness of the offence, this may well impact on the asylum-seeker's claim to remain in the UK.

The next difficulty is to ascertain the language of interpretation and the relevance of any dialect. The use of 'Language Line' which is available in most Courts is a first step to identification, if identifying the relevant language is problematic. 'Language Line' is an interpretation service provided via telephone, involving the use of an interpreter using a three-way telephone conferencing facility. Many asylum-seekers can speak a number of languages but the best language in which to interview an offender is their first language. The more serious and complicated the offence, e.g. a sexual offence, the greater the need to interview in the offender's first language.

Having ascertained the offender's first language, it is necessary to locate an accredited interpreter. In the case of an area that has a diverse ethnic population, this should cause no difficulty. However, if the asylum-seeking offender is isolated, in that the area in which they are resident does not have a 'matching' minority ethnic population, it can be difficult to obtain a suitably qualified interpreter. The policy of dispersal by which asylum-seekers are placed in areas where there are small or no minority ethnic communities can make engaging an appropriate interpreter impossible. In these cases, the Probation Service may be required to pay for an interpreter to travel from out of area. This involves a degree of knowledge and persistence as well as cost; to find, for example, an interpreter out of area to speak a specified dialect of a difficult-to-source language can be both time consuming and costly.

The Home Office has targets to reduce the number of successful asylum claims. This makes the role of the Probation Service a difficult one, because it can be argued that the commission of a criminal offence has penalties for asylum-seekers which are disproportionate when compared with the treatment of UK nationals. On the one hand, 42 local probation areas are directed from the National Probation Directorate whose policies are heavily influenced by the Home Office. On the other hand, local probation areas are required to implement a local race equality scheme, which is concerned with the elimination of racial discrimination, promotion of equality of opportunity, and the promotion of good relations between different racial groups. Additionally, they are required amongst other things to ensure that individual offenders are equitably and justly treated.

The tension between Home Office policy in respect of reducing the number of successful asylum applications, and the policies of the National Probation Service in promoting equality and justice within minority ethnic communities, places probation officers at the forefront of the current debate on asylum-seekers and whether their continued stay is to be deemed 'not conducive to the public good'. The concept of an asylum-seeker being not conducive to the public good is used as grounds for deportation. The interpretation of this statutory concept is one which has resulted in a significant amount of case law. It is fair to say that the Secretary of State, in making a decision that an individual's presence in the UK is not conducive to the public good, has to consider the concept of proportionality contained within the European Convention on Human Rights. The move to inter-agency working and joined-up thinking begs the question as to what extent the Probation Service, the Home Office, and Customs and Excise should work closely together and how transparent and accountable such working arrangements should be.

The new proposals, whereby the Probation Service along with the Prison Service are under the same umbrella organization as the judiciary Courts and the Crown Prosecution Service as a newly created Ministry of Justice, would enable all criminal justice agencies to support asylum-seekers without the dilemma as to whether the pursuit of justice for an individual contravenes

Home Office policy. The current location of the Probation Service along with other criminal justice agencies within the Home Office represents a conflict at strategic level between policy considerations regarding a reduction in the numbers of asylum-seekers and the National Probation Service's commitment to diversity, and in particular the legal requirements that all offenders should receive fair and equal treatment. Probation Service staff in undertaking work with asylum-seekers may well find that the course of action they wish to take in addressing an asylum-seeker's offending behaviour contradicts Home Office policy, as in, for example, the encouraging of employment skills with a view to full-time employment.

There may be a requirement to obtain advice and guidance in respect of cultural norms and values and this can be provided by the interpreter or by a consultant/adviser with the relevant knowledge. It should not be assumed that the interpreter has specific knowledge about an asylum-seeker's culture because he/she speaks the same language. Again, the policy of dispersal has made the task of obtaining appropriate advice for this group of offenders problematic even where there is a resident minority ethnic community, as language and customs may have significant differences which can result in serious misunderstandings. This can impact on the quality of the risk assessment in respect of the preparation of a pre-sentence report or the shorter specific sentence report. The role of reports for the Courts is to provide the best risk assessment and recommendation for sentencing purposes. In this context, being able to obtain the best possible information is essential in order to produce a correct risk assessment and appropriate recommendation. The *Thematic Inspection Report: Towards Race Equality* (HMIP 2000) highlighted the differentials which exist in respect of pre-sentence reports written for minority ethnic offenders and white offenders. In particular, the former were less likely to include a recommendation and if there was a recommendation it was more likely to focus on community punishment or custody. In response, the National Probation Service's target for the production of pre-sentence reports for ethnic minorities states that there must be a clear recommendation for disposal in 90 per cent of cases. Reports on asylum-seekers will inevitably be included in this target as they are likely to have pre-sentence reports completed which do not make a firm recommendation. In the absence of any statistics, it could safely be predicted that because of the additional needs which asylum-seekers have, they are likely to have pre-sentence reports completed which do not make firm recommendations. Many services have set up processes to ensure that a significant proportion of pre-sentence reports on ethnic minorities will be overseen by a second member of staff to ensure quality, consistency and sensitivity to cultural issues. In terms of sensitivity to diversity issues, some probation services have entered into partnerships with minority ethnic communities in order to access such services (NPD 2002). The UMMID Project, a voluntary sector organisation, was established in Bradford and Keighley to support the work of the West Yorkshire Probation Service. The co-working of core tasks has enabled the Probation Service to address offending behaviour and thereby improve the quality and effectiveness of supervision.

Community disposals

The Probation Service, in assessing risk, has to give consideration to a range of issues and make a recommendation in respect of community disposals. The introduction of accredited programmes as an effective method of working with offenders whilst being supervised by the Probation Service has impacted upon all offenders. There is anecdotal evidence that offenders from minority groups do not have access to these programmes. The reason for this is a lack of fluency in English or fear by probation staff of placing a lone ethnic minority offender in all-white groups. As a result, minority ethnic offenders and more specifically, asylum-seekers, are likely to be offered one-to-one work which is statistically less effective. The National Probation Service in response to these concerns has agreed that targets in respect of ethnic minority offenders will be set by November 2008 (NPD 2003). It is expected that these targets will be based on the percentage of a specific minority group within the offending population on the caseload.

In order to be eligible to attend accredited programmes such as the 'Think First Programme' or 'The Sex Offender Treatment Programme', it is a prerequisite that the offender must have a specified level of literacy. Both of these programmes deal with changing the behaviour of offenders by improvement of thinking skills brought about by constructive peer interaction. Many ethnic minority offenders do not possess the degree of literacy required and are not able to benefit from the programmes, and in the case of asylum-seeking offenders who are newly arrived in the UK, the proportion is likely to be greater than for the minority ethnic community generally. Accredited programmes are shown to have an impact on the rate of re-offending and much of this is down to the fact that it is a group work programme, where offenders are challenged by their peers. There is currently no national guidance as to the impact of using interpreters within a group work programme, although it is a widely held belief that it is not possible to undertake this programme with an interpreter present as this would affect the group dynamic, which is necessary to maximize its effectiveness. Currently, accredited programmes are not offered in any other language but English. Thus, asylum-seekers in many cases are effectively excluded from this form of treatment and, it could be argued, suffer a detriment in respect of a reduction in their rate of re-offending.

Offenders can also be made subject to a community punishment order where an offender carries out unpaid work for the benefit of the community. Traditionally, this work has involved groups of offenders undertaking practical work such as gardening, clearing ponds and collecting litter. There have been difficulties placing minority ethnic offenders on these programmes because of the racist behaviour of other offenders. For this reason, many are often allocated singleton placements where the risk to their personal safety can be minimized. Community Punishment is being revised and will be known as Enhanced Community Punishment from 1st October 2003. It is clear that the objectives of Enhanced Community Punishment are to improve an offender's employability by means of enabling them to obtain some level of basic educational qualifications through the process of reparation work. The current thinking is that having been employed and obtaining qualifications to verify the quality of the work undertaken, offenders are in a better position to obtain paid employment on completion of the order. It is clear that there are difficulties with asylum-seekers being subject to Community Punishment Orders because, whilst they would be able to fulfil the order in itself, by undertaking unpaid employment as reparation to the community against which they offended, the current requirements that asylum-seekers are barred from working would make one of the policy objectives of Enhanced Community Punishment redundant.

Hostels and prisons

One of the services which the Probation Service provides is residence at bail and probation hostels for those who have been charged with offences or are being released from prison and who do not have a suitable home address. Some asylum-seekers may be placed in this category because they are not receiving any state benefits and are of no fixed abode. Additionally, other asylum-seekers may well need to access bail hostels because the seriousness of their offence is such that the strict supervision present in hostels is necessary in order that the public be protected in the period leading up to trial.

There are difficulties for individual probation services in funding such hostel placements because the benefits agency is not able to cover the cost of hostel accommodation for asylum-seekers. Thus probation services may well be reluctant to offer places in their hostels knowing that there will be a deficit in the hostel budget. This is a particular difficulty in areas where there are large numbers of asylum-seekers who offend. There may well be some financial pressure in respect of those who commit serious offences, or even where the offences are minor but there is no fixed address, for probation services not to proactively allocate hostel places to this group of offenders with the result that they are highly likely to be remanded in custody. This in itself represents a detriment to asylum-seekers that is born out of policy considerations rather than appropriate risk assessment, and ensuring that equality of opportunity exists.

Asylum-seekers who do acquire hostel placements may well find it difficult to reside within the placement as they may feel that their needs are not being fully met. This may well be true in terms of the food that is offered and the lack of awareness of their cultural/religious needs. It is well documented that prisons have had difficulties in meeting the needs of minority ethnic offenders, not only in terms of religion and culture, but also in protecting these offenders from the racism of other offenders within the prison system. The CRE has criticized Feltham Prison in the case of a murder of a young man who was killed by a racist cell-mate. Additionally, there are difficulties where asylum-seekers have poor English and are unable to understand the rules of the prison or hostel. This may well lead, particularly within the prison regime, to additional days being added to a prisoner's sentence where rules are consistently broken. Some probation services, in order to combat discrimination, have developed initiatives which enable 'cultural assessments' to take place within hostels. Additionally, tailored support is also being provided to minority ethnic residents as well as to hostel staff.

Generally, it is difficult to cater for asylum-seekers within the CJS where there are language difficulties and the asylum-seekers themselves have a poor understanding of British culture, legislation and policy. It is further compounded by the fact that often asylum-seekers have significant health considerations, particularly in terms of the trauma they have suffered either fleeing from their country of origin or in the process of making the journey to the UK. Asylum-seekers traditionally have had difficulty accessing basic health services, but this is compounded where there is a mental health need as a result of serious trauma in fleeing from violence and/or persecution. Mental health services have a poor record in dealing with minority ethnic offenders as a result of stereotyping and clinical judgements being made within a Eurocentric approach to psychiatry. Where there are significant language difficulties, this may well mean that an offender who should be receiving psychiatric treatment finds him/herself engaged with by the CJS and sometimes incarcerated, where appropriate out-patient or in-patient treatment should have been provided. The persecution experienced by many asylum-seekers impacts on their ability to negotiate their way through the asylum maze and no doubt results in many of them missing crucial deadlines.

Additionally, the experience of dispersal has resulted in many asylum-seekers being moved from metropolitan conurbations to largely poor white areas in the UK. The lack of an appropriate infrastructure to meet the cultural needs of asylum-seekers in accessing a range of services is a particular difficulty in such areas. At the time that the dispersal policy was being introduced, the Medical Foundation for the Care of Victims of Torture, which offers a service to those who have experienced violence, raised concerns that many asylum-seekers would no longer have access to such services, resulting in the absence of medical evidence for their asylum claim.

Deportation as an element of sentencing

Where asylum-seekers, or indeed any offender who is not a British national, are convicted of an offence but particularly a serious offence, the Courts have the option as part of the sentence to make a Notice of Intention to Deport on completion of the custodial sentence. In the case of asylum-seekers, the commission of a serious criminal offence jeopardizes their chances of making a successful application, for by committing such an offence, it can be argued that their continued presence in the UK is not conducive to the public good, which is ground for deportation. This is a particularly difficult dilemma in that an individual asylum-seeker may well have fled his or her country of origin having been subject to persecution and may be in fear of his or her life. The commission of a serious offence would appear to negate the need for asylum. Deportation to the country of origin carries two risks: one of persecution and ultimate death, and the other to the public in the country to which the asylum seeker is being deported, if he is, for example, a serious sex offender.

Currently, there is no clear system of balancing these competing needs, which it can be argued constitute a triangle of an asylum-seeker needing to pay his debt to society whilst at the same time receiving protection because of a well-founded fear of persecution, and the threat he may constitute. It could be argued that where the UK is intending to deport a violent or sexual offender, a duty of care is owed to the receiving country in terms of information and risk assessments which have already been made in respect of that individual. The Probation Service's role in protecting the public from violent/sexual offenders is one which is clear in respect of the UK but is less clear regarding protection of the public in other countries. Currently, the issue of responsibility for the protection of vulnerable communities outside the UK is a subject for discussion. It is submitted that whilst there may be no legal responsibility in respect of serious offenders, there is clearly a moral responsibility to ensure that re-offending by the asylum-seeker is reduced whether by the sharing of sensitive risk-assessment information, or by an acknowledgement that deportation is not practicable to some countries which do not have an adequate infrastructure to supervise specified asylum-seeking offenders.

Where individuals are asylum-seekers, refugees or non-British nationals, there are particular difficulties where a Court makes a decision permanently to remove such an individual from the UK. A Court can recommend deportation as part of the sentencing process (Immigration Act 1971). The grounds upon which a Court can make a recommendation are where the offender is over 17 and convicted of an imprisonable offence. A recommendation for deportation can be made by any of the criminal Courts (Magistrates, Crown, Court of Appeal). It is important for probation practitioners to realize that such a recommendation is part of the sentence. Probation staff are in many ways faced with a dilemma in dealing with offenders upon whom such a sentence can be passed, as to whether this should be considered in the preparation of a pre-sentence report. The dilemma is that the Court may not realize or may not have considered such a sentencing option. The question is whether a probation officer as an Officer of the Court, should draw to the Court's attention all available sentencing options, a practice often followed by probation officers.

Legislation as it currently stands states that when making a recommendation to deport the Court must concern itself with criminal behaviour and not immigration policy (as in the case of R v Caird, (1970) 54, Cr. App. Rep. CA). Additionally, the Criminal Courts in reaching their decision are concerned with the concept of potential detriment to the UK and the assessment of such detriment is to be decided on a case-by-case basis as a question of fact. This suggests that a risk assessment regarding the offender's dangerousness and risk of re-offending is key to the decision-making process and the Probation

Service should be required to provide an up-to-date risk assessment. Additionally, it should be noted that Articles 6 and 8 of the Human Rights Act 1988 must be adhered to in arriving at a decision that deportation is a component part of a sentence, and that the individual's home country circumstances and his/her right to a family life should also be a consideration.

Non-British nationals who have been resident in the UK for a long time often have families and children here who are full British citizens. The decision to fight the Notice of Intention to Deport will have to be made on the basis that the removal of the non-British nationals is not conducive to the public good. The Probation Service, in its role of risk assessment and reducing the risk of re-offending, may well have a role in the presentation of reports in respect of a particular offender. These individuals may have strong support from local ethnic minority communities, and the Probation Service is in a difficult position in terms of promoting good relationships with these communities whilst at the same time ensuring proper punishment and rehabilitation of individual offenders. There is also a question as to whether serving a lengthy custodial sentence and then being deported to a country where there are no community ties or links and where behaviour cannot be effectively monitored, constitutes proper punishment or effective rehabilitation. The Probation Service's role in supporting such offenders should focus on the rehabilitative element of sentencing as well as protecting the general public. The involvement of local communities in supporting such offenders in their battle against deportation would appear to fulfil the Probation Service's role under the Race Relations Amendment Act.

Asylum-seekers as victims

Both the CJS and the Probation Service have a responsibility for victims of crime. There have been concerns that ethnic minority groups do not receive an appropriate service to meet their needs as victims of offences. The Stephen Lawrence Enquiry was particularly critical of the way in which ethnic minority victims/witnesses were treated by the CJS, particularly where they were victims of racially motivated offenders (Macpherson 1999). The difficulties which ethnic minority communities have in respect of accessing victim support, whether that be from the victim support service or from the Probation Service's Victim Liaison Officer, will be affected by those similar concerns which have already been detailed in respect of asylum-seeking offenders. However, in terms of racially motivated offences, there have been difficulties not only in enabling asylum-seekers to report offences being committed against them but also in progressing these through the Courts.

The high level of media coverage given to asylum-seekers and the response by both central and local governments to the placing of asylum-seekers under dispersal has often resulted in their being placed in largely white areas where there has been no history of ethnic minority settlement or communities. As a result of their newly arrived status, and a perception by the indigenous population that they are receiving significantly more through the benefits system than they themselves are, asylum-seekers are often subject to violence. The lack of tolerance by what are often poor and vulnerable communities in largely deprived city areas has led to asylum-seekers being openly attacked by those communities. An example of such an offence was where Kent County Council sought to relocate a number of asylum-seekers within the local authority area of Salford, in what had been previously a residential setting. This resulted in the premises coming under attack and threats being made against the asylum-seekers themselves. There is some anecdotal evidence suggesting that ethnic minority communities themselves are not sympathetic to or supportive of asylum-seekers being located within their communities and that such attacks may well be made by second or third generation migrants. This appears to have been the case in an attack on asylum-seekers outside a local hostel which was known for housing asylum-seekers in Liverpool. Asylum-seekers themselves may well have been subject to intimidation and violence from agents of the state, including the police. They may be reluctant to report incidents of violence against them and as a result may engage in defending themselves, only to be arrested for committing offences of violence themselves. Language and cultural difficulties certainly play a part in this process as do locally held perceptions that asylum-seekers somehow bring offending upon themselves.

The increase in the numbers of racially motivated offences, whether these are against ethnic minority communities or asylum-seekers, can in part be traced to increased security concerns as a result of the attack on New York on 11 September 2001. It should be noted that the Anti-Terrorism and Security Act 2001 enables an individual who is suspected of being a terrorist to be detained or even removed. Concern about Al Qaeda has led to Muslim communities within the UK being targeted in much the same way as were members of the Irish community living in the UK in the late 1970s and early 1980s. The resultant miscarriages of justice had wide repercussions for the CJS and those communities themselves, who lost faith in the system because they perceived that the state had made them scapegoats for the criminal activities of a few. The death of a police officer in Manchester highlights the security risks posed by terrorist organizations, and their cynical use of the asylum-seeking community as a convenient cover for their activities. This makes asylum-seekers particularly vulnerable, both in terms of state interest and of involvement in their activities. The media coverage of such security concerns and the explicit links made by the popular and tabloid press also makes them more vulnerable than the wider community. Additionally, it gives legitimacy to the racism directed at asylum-seekers, which is sadly encouraged by senior politicians for perceived political gain. In order to combat the vulnerability of asylum-seekers, particularly where they have been subject to dispersal throughout the UK, some criminal justice agencies have engaged in multi-agency work to support them. This has involved partnerships, ostensibly between police, local authorities and in some cases the Probation Service. Asylum-seekers are encouraged to report offences committed against them and are then supported during the process of taking these offenders through the Court system. Recently, the Crime and Disorder Act 1998 has created specific racially motivated offences with the hope that this will inspire greater confidence amongst the ethnic minority communities, whether asylum-seeking or not, and that more racially motivated offenders will be brought to justice. Whilst it is too early to say with any degree of certainty whether this has made a impact, anecdotally it would appear that the number of convictions for what could loosely be termed as racially motivated offences has increased.

The Heart of the Dance specifically makes one of its priority objectives that of communicating and connecting with local communities and promoting good relations between people of different racial groups. It can be argued that asylum-seekers make up a definable community, particularly where significant numbers of a specified ethnicity, culture and language are dispersed and housed in the same locality to make up such a community. The National Probation Service has given a commitment via its priority objectives to increase its profile and credibility within such community groups. Their commitment in so doing has yet to be measured but some of it would appear to be based on employing members of such communities. There are clearly difficulties in respect of this approach because of the requirement for asylum-seekers not to take paid employment. It is clear that the courts, in responding to asylum-seekers, whether as offenders, victims or communities which are vulnerable to crime, struggle with the dichotomy of preventing crime and disorder and implementing central government policy regarding their dispersal and monitoring. Where asylum-seekers have significant needs which can involve mental health services, the system finds it difficult to provide appropriate and meaningful services.

Conclusion

The Probation Service has an important role in working with asylum-seeker offenders, in ensuring that there is appropriate and adequate supervision. In delivering an equitable service, Probation Service staff are required to have a good understanding of the impact of being non-English speaking. It is essential that they are aware of the range of language needs and cultural/religious support which such offenders may require. Probation practitioners also need to be aware of the effect that racism can have on asylum-seekers at all stages of the criminal justice process. This has been well documented in respect of minority ethnic communities as evidenced by numerous inspection reports within the CJS. In working with asylum-seekers probation practitioners need be aware of the impact of Government policy, in particular the fact that basic funding for this group is below that of all other benefit claimants and in many cases asylum-seekers are legally prevented from working.

At this time the Probation Service has found itself situated at the forefront of the discussion about the rights, privileges (as perceived) and benefits available to asylum-seekers. The Probation Service's work with offenders and victims places it in the unenviable position of working with communities as they struggle to maintain themselves within the law, and as they come under increased scrutiny from the state. There is also rising hostility from the wider community including minority ethnic communities, who themselves are facing hostility which some perceive to be as a result of the increased presence of asylum-seekers. The issues raised by the deportation of serious offenders, whether asylum-seekers or other non-British nationals, raises questions in terms of the management of risk either in the UK or abroad. Whilst it might be attractive to deport high-risk offenders on the basis that this would eliminate risk of offending in this country, this invariably means an increased risk to the receiving country, particularly where the system of supervision and risk assessment is poor. It could be argued that the British Government has a responsibility in this respect to other countries.

References

Commission for Racial Equality (2002) *The Duty to Promote Race Equality: The Statutory Code of Practice and Non-Statutory Guides for Public Authorities.* London: CRE.

Commission for Racial Equality (2003) *A Formal Investigation by the CRE into Her Majesty's Prison Service of England and Wales: Part 1: The Murder of Zahid Mubarek.* London: CRE.

Her Majesty's Inspector of Prisons (2000) *Thematic Inspection Report: Towards Race Equality.* London: Home Office.

Macpherson, Sir W. (1999) *The Stephen Lawrence Inquiry: Report of an Inquiry by Sir William Macpherson of Cluny.* London: HMSO.

Merali, S. (2003) 'If your name's not down, you're not coming in.' In *Leeds and Yorkshire Lawyer 21*, 9–11.

Merton, R. K. (1968) *Social Theory and Social Structure.* New York: The Free Press.

National Probation Directorate (2002) *Working with Minority Ethnic Communities.* London: Home Office.

National Probation Directorate (2003) *The Heart of the Dance: A Diversity Strategy for the National Probation Service for England and Wales 2002–2006.* London: Home Office.

Chapter 11

A Comparison of Two European Resettlement Programmes for Young Separated Refugees

Michael Wells and Susanna Hoikkala

Introduction

Young separated refugees can suffer acutely from the persecution of family members, the generalized violence that is associated with refugee flight and the very distressing act of leaving home, leaving behind family, parents, friends and all that is familiar to them during their flight (UNHCR 1999). Despite differing approaches within Europe, there are some similarities emerging. European opinion has tended to turn against immigrant and refugee flows especially with reference to non-European immigrants. This social construction often results in separated children in Europe receiving inadequate care and being discriminated against in strict, unfriendly asylum procedures. Given the loss and the vulnerability that may occur in resettlement, it raises important questions about the quality of support afforded to young separated children. There is evidence to suggest a need for complementary strategies. Examining two contrasting systems, in Finland and in the UK, the effect of these restrictive immigration and welfare practices upon separated refugee children's well-being will be presented. Illustrating the process of asylum among separated children, the chapter concludes by drawing recommendations from the two contrasting contexts.

Public opinion and European harmonisation

As late as the mid 1980s, when the famine of Ethiopia and the pictures of the starving millions produced guilty and charitable feelings, people often saw refugees as victims of oppression, circumstance and regimes. But in the last decades Western Europe has witnessed new refugee flows from non-European regions. With increased numbers of persons seeking asylum from countries such as Somalia, the former Yugoslavia, Iraq, Iran and Congo, negative public opinion has grown accordingly. Now these asylum-seekers are rejected, used as scapegoats and spoken of with contempt and suspicion (Taviani 1988, p.78). As with the most robust of stereotypes, the scenario of Europe swamped by 'economic migrants' seeking financial betterment rather than those fleeing persecution now persists, despite academic resistance to dilute it. Alarmism seems to be an inevitable by-product of media coverage of asylum-seekers and, for the mass media, the increasing numbers applying for asylum is an irresistible topic. Banner headlines emphasizing the large numbers of applicants for asylum, stating that the problem is unprecedented, are inevitably likely to provoke an adverse public reaction, whilst images on the conditions of famine victims have been shown to gain public sympathy (Joly and Nettleton 1990). Adjectives regrettably used to define asylum-seekers range from at best 'bogus' to at worst 'tunnel rats'. Opinion in Europe has experienced an about-turn and, increasingly, discourses concentrate on restricting the flow of 'illegal economic' immigrants rather than tackling factors such as the role of global market forces and Third World debt, which are root causes of poverty and oppression.

Simultaneously, inward migratory patterns from humanitarian emergencies have substantially influenced Euro-asylum policies. It has become increasingly difficult to claim asylum from non-European regions (Miles and Thränhardt 1995). From the process of harmonization via the Single European Act and the Amsterdam Treaty 1997, when member states agreed to harmonize their national asylum systems into a common EU policy, the restriction of non-desirable migrants is illustrated in a number of different policies:

1.   the pursuit of effective pre-entry controls including increased visa controls, common visa procedures and airline carrier liabilities, returning the 'uninvited' (Harding 2000, p.23) to the point of departure

2.   the introduction of *accelerated status determination*; faster and more efficient measures have focused upon relieving the pressure of the

backlogs of asylum applications within national asylum systems. Contained within the Schengen Agreement and the Dublin Convention are requirements for member states to operate effective pre-entry and entry controls, to make sure one EU country takes responsibility for an individual asylum application to deter multiple applications, and to make decisions at the port of entry to prevent backlogs in the system (Findlater 1999, p.43). As things stood in 2000 and 2001, on average European member states recognized merely 10.6 per cent (2000) and 11.2 per cent (2001) of asylum-seekers (Eurasylum 2003). Applying fast and effective asylum controls has been an efficient way of recognising very small numbers of 'genuine' asylum-seekers and quite bluntly deterring the inflow of so-called 'illegal migration'

3. In response to concerns about 'asylum shopping', the Schengen information system (personal data that can be exchanged amongst member states) will prevent asylum-seekers searching for a country with a more generous liberal policy in order to apply for asylum there. Nor, if they are refused asylum in a particular country, will they be allowed to travel on to a second country; the first country will, in most cases, be required to take them back and either grant them asylum or expel them (European Research Forum on Migration and Ethnic Relations 2001 et al. p.43; Gordon 1989, p.14)

4. With the increased economic demands of granting asylum and the deteriorating public attitudes towards asylum-seekers, member states seek to maintain their international responsibility and their duty to provide sanctuary under the 1951 Geneva Convention. They actually avoid breaching the principle of non-refoulement (asylum-seekers should not be returned from the places they have fled) and have developed an alternative legal device. For example, in countries such as Denmark, Finland, The Netherlands, Portugal, Sweden and the UK, large percentages of asylum applications are granted temporary asylum but denied full refugee status. The temporary protection system allows individuals to stay in the member country from a period ranging from six months to five years.

So though we may suspect politicians who suggest waves of asylum-seekers represent a present danger to socio-economic conditions, their efforts to deter the flow of non-Europeans and provide only temporary protection suggest the international safeguards to the right to claim asylum are being distorted by an abuse of executive power. It has never been apparent whether the monetary and social costs of protection are arguments enough when the largest cost resulting from waves of 'undesirable migrants' is the cost of Europe's fears for its own stability (Harding 2000, p.9). Under pressure from the populations in the receiving countries and spurred by right wing politicians, the authenticity of asylum-seeking has ultimately become viewed as externally manipulated. Asylum-seekers are accused of 'shopping around' before making an asylum claim or re-identified (as recently applied to Islamic immigrants) as being part of an axis of evil. In other words, socially or economically, individual countries in one way or another are affirming the notion that asylum-seekers are bogus and a particular threat.

One of the most worrying aspects of restrictive refugee policies is the impact upon young separated refugees. Despite the grounds for their special protection established within international law, countries have responded in an ad hoc way. Young separated refugees must enjoy basic human rights as enshrined in the 1989 UN Convention on the Rights on the Child (UNCRC). Briefly, this binds signatories to ensure protection and rights in virtually every aspect of a child's life including health, education, social and political rights. Because there is protection against discrimination, whatever provisions and protection a state gives to the children who are its citizens must also be given to all children without discrimination (Article 2) – including young refugees and those who are 'illegal' within its territory (UNHCR 1999). The UNCRC's provisions cover all refugee and displaced children within a signatory country. Refugee children are given particular attention in Article 22, which binds states to ensure any child under 18 seeking refugee status or who is considered a refugee receives appropriate protection and humanitarian assistance.

International *Guidelines on Policies and Procedures in Dealing with Unaccompanied Children Seeking Asylum* (UNHCR 1997) also encourage states to recast the issue of asylum processes and emphasize the 'best interest' principle as the primary consideration in all matters concerning separated children. With continuous standards in mind, the *Guidelines* make specific reference to the UNCRC Article 3, paragraph 1, which demands that 'in all actions concerning children, whether undertaken by public or private social welfare institutions, courts of law, administrative authorities or legislative bodies, the best interests of the child shall be a primary consideration'.

Taken together, the UNCRC and *Guidelines* (UNHCR 1997) require an absolute respect for the rights of children to seek asylum. However, a move towards protecting the rights of young refugees was spurred by reports that drew attention to inadequate levels of protection for these vulnerable migrants within the context of broader 'internationalist' issues (Jones 1998). An exhaustive report written by Ruxton (2000) revealed the clash in perspectives of many EU members and the rights afforded to young separated refugees. It is young separated refugees who, as a most vulnerable group of migrants, have lost most through the process of harmonization. There have been calls for improvements and wider advocacy; for example the Separated Children in Europe Program and Unaccompanied Minor Migrants as a Vulnerable Group (European Research Forum on Migration and Ethnic Relations *et al.* 2001) provide periodic information and country recommendations. However, their subsequent reviews have looked at the position of separated children and confirmed that these children may share with their adult compatriots some implications of the restrictive refugee policies. Before considering the impact of restrictive asylum controls on young separated refugees in Finland and the UK, we will consider the general context of social work in the respective countries and its implications for resettlement support.

Finland and the UK

The models of welfare systems differ by countries and are dependent on political, economical and social situations (e.g. Mayo 1998). National and international social policies and professional social work practices are linked intensively to the development of each welfare state. Consequently, the contexts and models of resettlement services in Finland and the UK reflect such differences. In this chapter we have defined Finnish resettlement services as 'institutional-based' and British as 'community-based' services. In our terms the description is suggestive and may sound generalized, but it is based on the differences in resettlement services for unaccompanied minors in these two countries. The development of resettlement services is linked to the development of child welfare and child protection policies and practices. So to understand differences of social services provision and resettlement support, we have to discuss the historical context.

In Finland, the declaration of independence in 1917 and the civil war were very significant events for developing national integration and administration (e.g. Satka 1996). Finland, like other Nordic countries, has a high provision of public and statutory services: for example, income support and subsistence, education, health and social care. Equality, social protection and integration are the key objectives. By the provision of social services and social security benefits, the state aims to reject social risks and marginalization such as unemployment and poverty. Municipalities are responsible for organizing and providing services, which are defined in current legislation. Using social services and benefits is not stigmatizing in Finland (e.g. Herberts 2001, p.75; Rauhala 1996; Satka 1996).

Pringle (1998, p.99) notes that the British welfare model was similar to that of Nordic countries 20 years ago, but is different nowadays. Local authorities, social services departments and a variety of related agencies provide social services in the UK and local authorities are responsible for financing and regulating services (Johnson 2001, p.267). However, the role of the state as a service provider has been reduced in the UK during recent decades. Increasingly the third sector, including private organizations, civil society organizations and NGOs, provides services. It has been argued that the transformation from public to private services has increased, for example income equality and social exclusion in the UK (Walker and Walker 1998, p.46, p.53).

In Finland, institutionalization has been a typical feature of social services provision. In the second half of the 19th century, workhouses and poorhouses were established for poor people (e.g. Satka 1996). This institutionalized system led to the control and isolation of these people, who were recognized as 'non-decent citizens'. The children's day care system became institutionalized at the end of the 19th century. In addition, 'homes for misbehaving young people' and mental health institutions were established. The state has retained a strong role in looking after children's well-being and their best interest. A relatively high number of children are taken into care and placed outside families (in children's homes, foster families and professional family homes). However, during the last decades large institutions have been divided into smaller units and community care services have been developed to allow rehabilitation, self-sufficiency and integration into society (Herberts 2001, p.75; Pringle 1998; Rauhala 1996; Satka 1996).

In the UK, the switch from residential to community foster care has been faster than in Finland. One reason for this development is that the quality of residential care has been questioned. There have been incidents in which staff members of residential homes have abused children. Pringle (1998) notes that suspicion of physical and sexual abuse of children by staff in residential units remains. In addition, the development of community work and anti-oppressive practices has been significant. According to Mayo (1998) community work has generally been associated with holistic, collective, preventive and anti-discriminatory approaches to meeting social needs. It has been based on values of participation and empowerment. It is used to encourage self-help as informal caring (Mayo 1998, p.172, p.165). Payne (2001) argues that community care is boundary work in social work and links it to decentralization, de-bureaucratization, self-help, local community action, advice work and welfare rights. We use the concept 'community-orientated practice' in its wide meaning, when it is extended to mean both practical and conceptual approaches (e.g. Mayo 1998, p.162).

The resettlement of separated children in Finland and the UK

In Finland, the Integration of Immigrants and Reception of Asylum-seekers Act 1999 and the Child Welfare Act 1983 are the most significant Acts to regulate the resettlement process of unaccompanied minors. Correspondingly, in the UK, the Immigration and Asylum Act 1999 and the Children Act 1989 are the most important. The main focus of child welfare legislation in both countries is the 'best interest and well-being of a child'. According to the existing legislation, all unaccompanied minors should be treated as children first and as asylum-seekers second.

There is one significant difference in Finnish and British legislation. In Finland, unaccompanied minors are not treated under the Child Welfare Act 1983 unless there is a need for child protection intervention (community care interventions or being taken into custody and placement), but remain under national asylum legislation. Child protection interventions might be needed when a child's behaviour is harmful for him/herself or for other people. These cases among unaccompanied minors are rare. In the UK, unaccompanied minors are assessed under the Children Act 1989 and the resettlement arrangements depend on the level of 'need' of a child.

In both countries, there are national and local authorities that influence the resettlement process. In Finland, at the national level, the Ministry of Interior (Directorate of Immigration [DI], border authorities and police) and the Ministry of Labour (Immigration Affairs) are responsible for the arrangements for asylum-seekers. The local authorities in municipalities are responsible for practical arrangements. The Immigrant Service Unit, as part of the local social services department, together with the Employment and Development Centre, organize the resettlement of asylum-seekers in the municipality (for example, the establishment of family group homes). In relation to unaccompanied minors, there are currently two group homes and three family group homes, which are responsible for the resettlement of these minors (MOL 2003).

In the UK, the Home Secretary administers immigration control through the Home Office's Immigration and Nationality Department (IDN). The National Asylum Support Service (NASS) is part of IDN. As in Finland, the local authorities are responsible for practical arrangements for asylum-seekers. Unaccompanied minors are assessed by local social services. There are different practices in the UK for making resettlement arrangements for unaccompanied minors. They may be referred either to the children and families team or to the asylum team. Both are part of local social services departments. Generally, it depends on the assessed 'need' as to which team a minor is placed with. This causes inequality for unaccompanied minors.

The reception and support of an unaccompanied child in Finland is as follows:

> **ENTRY** at port → the police and the border authority (DI) who will contact the nearest reception centre OR directly to the group home (sometimes only after arrival into country)
>
> **INTERVIEW** and **ASSESSMENT** by police (matters relating to travelling route and identity) and DI (trained interviewers), the right to use interpreter and legal adviser → representative → accommodation in group home, combined home or relative family while awaiting status → application for family reunification (DI) → age assessment (an 18-year-old does not have the right to a family reunification, a legal representative, attend school and cannot be placed in a group home) → care and integration plan.

There are defined support arrangements for asylum-seekers in the Integration and Reception Act 1999 in Finland. 'The reception of asylum-seekers shall include temporary accommodation, social assistance, interpretation services, work and training activities, and satisfaction of all other basic needs.' 'A group home may be organized at a reception centre to receive an asylum-seeker who is a minor and arrives without a guardian.' 'In the reception of a minor, other services required because the child's age and developmental level shall be provided' (Integration Act, Chapter 4, Section 19). The state operates reception centres and covers all expenses for municipalities. Multi-agency forums, consisting of the employment and economic development centres, local authorities, joint municipal boards, other public sector bodies or private bodies or associations, agree on arranging reception systems. There are no local variations of procedures and support arrangements. All unaccompanied minors are treated according to the same procedure (Integration Act, Chapter 4, Sections 20 and 21; Helander and Mikkonen 2002, p.36).

A representative may be assigned to an unaccompanied child and s/he exercises a guardian's right to be heard in matters pertaining to the child's person and assets, decides on the child's living arrangements, shall protect the child's interest, taking his/her ethnic, linguistic, religious and educational background into account. (Legally, a representative does not have all those equal rights that a guardian normally has in Finland. The role of the representative has been confusing, but it has been clarified recently.) When making decisions, the representative shall take the child's opinions and wishes into consideration. S/he is not to undertake the daily care or upbringing of the child (Integration Act, Chapter 5, Section 26). A representative is a trained, suitable and a consenting person. The assignment of a representative or a release must be made by the district court (Helander and Mikkonen 2002).

> **Status**: (Minors' applications should be handled as expeditiously as possible.) Usually minors receive a residence permit. Family reunification OR no family reunification → accommodation after status confirmed: family group home OR combined home OR relative family (unless reunited with family before)
>
> **Appeal**: of the asylum application OR application for family reunification
>
> **18th birthday**: Independent living OR supported independent living. If a child has been taken into custody before his/her 18th birthday, s/he is allowed to remain with care services until 21 years old. (Practically, this means more organized support. According to Helander and Mikkonen [2002] there are some local variations in Finland.)

The accommodation is arranged at the group home, combined home, family group home or with a relative's family. Group homes are located near to reception centres. The combined home is a joint group and family group home. In practice, once placed in a combined home, a child doesn't have to move away before his/her 18th birthday or family reunification. Family group homes are small homely units. There are eight places in each unit and five workers. These homes are not child welfare units, which impacts on the qualification requirements of staff members. In addition, unaccompanied minors do not have access to after-care services (Helander and Mikkonen 2002.)

The reception and support arrangements for an unaccompanied child in the UK are as follows:

ENTRY at port → the border authority → referred to local social services or NASS

ENTRY: after entry into country → social services

DISPERSAL POLICY → ad hoc arrangements around the UK.

ASSESSMENT by local social services → defined as child 'in need' under Section 17 of the Children Act (1989) → accommodation, financial support, in some cases continuous assessment OR defined as child 'in need' under Section 20 of the Children Act (1989) → care plan and support, financial support, placement in foster care, residential home or other approved accommodation.

As discussed above, the current resettlement arrangements depend on a needs assessment in the UK. In practice, children assessed under Section 17 get less support than those who are designated under Section 20. In our experience, 16- and 17-year-old unaccompanied minors are in an 'at risk group' which does not get support and services under Section 20 – in practice, these are probably the most vulnerable group of young people who do not always receive appropriate support.

Unaccompanied minors under Section 17 are placed within 'supported housing'. Private landlords accommodate these young people and are responsible for 'signposting' them. In addition, landlords receive financial support from local social services and pay the weekly allowance to a young person. According to our experiences, the condition of accommodation is sometimes very inappropriate and the young person often receives only minimal support from the landlord.

Status: Refugee status (full entitlement to citizen benefits) OR ELR (Exceptional Leave to Remain, transfer to mainstream support services) OR ILR (Indefinite Leave to Remain, after four years with ELR, full entitlement to citizen benefits).

Appeal: lose → return to country of origin/asylum application successful → full entitlements.

18th birthday: Children Act Section 17 → if immigration status unresolved (transfer to adult system OR financial support and possible dispersal by NASS)/Children Act Section 20 → if immigration status unresolved (financial support by NASS OR leaving care services which means on-going services).

In both countries there are service gaps for both under-18s and over-18s. First, there is a lack of organised support for 18+ minors. The exception is a minor who has a right to after-care services until reaching his 21st year. The most disadvantaged group is those minors who arrive in the country when they are 17 years old, as they will soon be too old for the services provided.

Second, in both countries there is a service gap in the provision of primary health care services. A causal connection exists between the experiences and presenting problems of young separated refugees and their ability to cope with the particular asylum system. Within cognitive psychology (e.g. Garmezy 1987; Rutter 1985; Sourander 1998, p.724) it has been argued that the ability to cope successfully is lessened considerably with multiple stressors. It has been argued (Hodes 1998, p.793) that there is a need for immediate linkages between primary health care services and young refugees. These direct practices would reduce young refugees' vulnerability as 'the experience of traumas can both affect the cognitive competence of the child and the ability of the child to pass on clear and accurate information during interviews in the asylum process' (Danish Refugee Council 2000, p.15). When interviewing young refugees, authorities require precise and correct information to make decisions concerning their entry or refusal, regarding their distribution and what further support they are entitled to (European Research Forum on Migration and Ethnic Relations *et al.* 2001, p.14). The asylum process must take these experiences into account when considering whether the individual child is sufficiently mature to take part in the initial and further asylum interviews. To meet this special need, and in accordance with Article 24 of the UNCRC, children should be assisted by the highest attainable standards of health. In addition, England can learn from the practice of Finland and the *Guidelines* (UNHCR 1997, para. 5.12, 5.13) that recommend that qualified persons trained in refugee and children's issues undertake all interviews.

The psycho-social impact of asylum controls upon unaccompanied minors in Finland and the UK

Not surprisingly and even more than for voluntary migrants, the experience of being a young separated refugee increases the risk of psychological trauma. For instance, there is a body of research which illustrates that social and emotional adjustment problems of young immigrants are exacerbated by migration (see Aronowitz 1984 for a review of the literature), where the primary antecedent of the young person's crisis is more articulated amongst children experiencing traumatic separation. Such labelling of trauma can be explained as a 'uni-dimensional approach' as it is particularly concerned to account for the trauma during the movement of the refugee and to distinguish this experience from the safe normality of the host country (Donà 2002, p.46). For example, post-flight psycho-social symptoms include post-traumatic stress, depression, anxiety, increased behavioural problems and aggression (Sourander 1998; Danish Refugee Council 2000).

But as we continue with this theme, we would like to pay attention once again to the theme of restrictionism. It is important to counter the idea that young separated refugees are locked into inevitable cycles of depression and psycho-somatic symptoms of trauma, and dependent upon caring professionals. The psycho-social adjustment of young separated refugees is one aspect of something a little broader. As Donà reminds us:

> it lies within the person and not with system, in past experiences of war and not in current resettlement programs that undermine asylum-seekers' sense of dignity and the fulfilment of their potential as productive human beings (2002, p.47).

Essentially then, it can also be about evaluating the young person in the context of social relations, so that finally there is a tendency to view the stress induced during resettlement as being bi-polar, pre- and post-flight. Rather than this view, we favour the development of an understanding of the wider impact of oppression and discrimination – a process which inevitably links with the resettlement through various social representations. Not all young separated refugees require mental health interventions.

A theoretical framework that has been largely neglected when applied to humanitarian groups is the acculturation research into the impact of individuals from different cultural backgrounds resettling within different cultures. One of the best known models of acculturation is that advocated by Berry (1988). The model has its limitations in that it was devised earlier for immigrant adult populations, but Berry linked this approach to the study of refugees. According to Berry, psychological problems such as anxiety, depression, marginality, alienation and identity confusion may materialize during acculturation. These stress indicators are linked with the orientation the young person has towards maintenance of his or her cultural identity and which characteristics are considered to be of value, or will maintain relationships with the larger society. Berry proposed that these formative questions – the acculturative stress – be mediated by adopting one of four acculturative attitudes. Briefly, the four stages are:

1. Assimilation is the outcome when migrants choose to identify with the host culture, and sever ties with their traditional culture.

2. Integration is a strong identification with host and traditional culture.

3. Marginalization is a lack of involvement in host and traditional culture.

4. Separation is an exclusive interaction within one's traditional culture, with no interaction with members of the host society.

Berry's model may serve as a useful tool for social workers to understand that the well-being of young separated refugees is becoming more concerned with the wider impact of current policies. The resettlement experience of young people is varied in both the push factors from the country of origin and the reception in the host country. But the uni-dimensional assumption of 'trauma' which we absorb into our professional knowledge as a psychosocial characteristic of separated refugees does not materialize in a context-free environment. With these thoughts in mind, let us turn our attention once again to the Finnish and UK contexts and focus upon the structural processes that have a potentially oppressive affect on young separated refugees.

Assimilation

Assimilation would be the orientation in which a powerful asylum control articulates young refugees to a dominant culture and then via structural and defined processes absorbs them into the larger society. Young refugees are a relatively powerless group and an imbalance of political, economic relations with the dominant host group is likely to produce a great deal of stress (Berry 1988, p.108). Asylum stressors and controls manipulate individual change and adaptation to the mainstream culture for social and economic reasons.

In Finland, for example, there may be a tendency to assimilate young people into Finnish society because it has traditionally been a homogenous and monistic country (e.g. Kunz 1981, p.48). Finland has no history of being a colonial country or a destination for labour migration. Finland as a country of asylum is less able to permit full participation of the young people, and the lack of personal power is inevitably likely to produce stress for a young person. The institutional-based resettlement process has indeed been criticized for these reasons. The handling times of the applications are long and young people may live for several years in an institution, often far from multicultural areas (Sourander 1998, p.725). Assimilation might be the result of long application handling times even though the applications of unaccompanied minors should be handled faster than other applications. This may be a very significant problem when the family reunification process is completed and the child's family arrives in Finland. There is also a risk of institutionalization, which may cause dependencies or make the minor passive. Nevertheless, according to the research of Helander and Mikkonen (2002), institutionalization and alienation among unaccompanied minors in these institutions were not significant.

Given the UK's post-war migratory history of de-colonialization, one could assume that cultural diversity would limit the possible psycho-social problems existent in an assimilationist monistic ideology. But in the UK, the paradox remains in the community-based accommodation arrangements. As we have noted, the support for integration is either independent of or with the support of the community. Individual adaptation, including to the physical conditions of housing, political isolation, economic losses, and cultural and social isolation is likely to have a negative effect on mental health (Berry 1988, p.108). To relieve this stress, young people alienated in a community without formal or informal supports may assimilate or merge effectively into the host culture (e.g. Kunz 1981).

Integration

An integration orientated policy, the optimum resettlement outcome, would reflect the ease or difficulty with which young people maintain networks with their ethnic group and join with the dominant group in the host society. The psycho-social benefits of such remedial action have been illustrated in research. Van Tran (1987) and Rosenthal and Feldman (1992), for example, used acculturation to show that the availability and strengths of 'ethnic community supports' were essential to psychological well-being. The well-being of adolescents was linked to the integration of their peers, the maintenance of cultural traditions, their socio-economic status and the participation of the ethnic group in the broader host society.

The Finnish resettlement system is well organized (Okitikpi and Aymer 2000) and to an extent includes these needs of retaining cultural identity and building relations with the broader Finnish society. The accommodation arrangements support the learning of the Finnish language and developing cultural knowledge, because almost all workers in these residential homes are Finns. In addition, it is possible to learn Finnish norms and values in a safe environment. Hypothetically, the accommodation arrangements guarantee everything necessary for everyday living, for example, nutrition, a sanitary, safe environment and a weekly allowance. Unaccompanied minors have access to education, including Finnish language and preparatory courses, at Finnish schools (in the beginning minors attend classes for immigrants, but are transferred to mainstream classes).

In Finland, each unaccompanied minor participates in an integration plan and openly plans together with authorities (social worker) and his/her own representative. Through accessing leisure, hobbies and activities in the community, minors are supported to integrate to local culture. It is possible to arrange a Finnish support worker and/or support family for an unaccompanied minor. In the institutional-orientated arrangement it is possible to receive peer support, structured routines and stability. The relationships with relatives and parents are supported. Young people are able to call their parents weekly if their location is known. Their own cultural aspects, like food, religion and dress, are supported.

In the UK integration may also be considered as an aspect of the asylum system. Unaccompanied minors are accommodated within communities, in supported lodgings, according to Section 17. Typically, several young people share a flat; they have their own room, but a shared kitchen, living room and bathroom. They will receive a weekly allowance from their landlords. The placements into communities reduce dependency upon formal agencies, minimizing exclusion by geographical location and supporting through ethnocultural community (e.g. Valtonen 2002, p.115); personal friendships provide the link between the individual, culture and broader community relations. Unlike the Finnish system, however, unaccompanied minors have no direct access to education, for example, to English language courses.

Marginalization

At the heart of such an orientation are the deterministic roles of the young person and the attitudinal position of the host. Separated asylum-seeking children are undoubtedly the most vulnerable group of asylum-seekers. At a period of vulnerability in the refugee flight they are strangers in a foreign culture and language context without parents or carers. The attitudinal position of the host (Kunz 1981, p.42) inevitably affects settlement and well-being. The experience of trauma, confusion about identity and low self-esteem combined with racist postures of the host are likely to develop feelings of marginalization, whereas a positive and supportive attitudinal position of the host society would inevitably allow the development of feelings of belonging, self-worth and integration.

It is difficult but not impossible to live illegally in Finland because of the high control and state-orientated services. Most of the immigrants live in the southern part of Finland, which has been the general tendency in recent years. Nevertheless, some unaccompanied minors may feel themselves marginalized because of the location of the first accommodation, far away from multicultural areas. Two group homes, which are responsible for accommodating unaccompanied minors at an early stage, are located far away from the refugees' cultural and ethnic communities. Consequently, this poses concerns over the appropriateness and length of residence in first-tier accommodation in reception centres. In research by Sourander (1998) the conditions in reception centres in Finland have led to high levels of post-traumatic stress, anxiety and depression among separated children. Marginalization and exclusion are also significant when the minor comes of age. As discussed already, there is a lack of after-care services and support. But in addition, Valtonen (2002) argues that the meaning of employment in the resettlement process becomes important when a minor reaches 18. There is a high degree of unemployment amongst immigrants in Finland. In terms of labour market opportunities, 'the industrial, catering, cleaning, and care branches appeared to be the key employers' (Forsander 2000, p.11) and unemployment is a risk for marginalization.

It is easier to become marginalized, alienated and excluded in the UK than in Finland. One reason is the high number of unaccompanied minors. Even though the formal procedure is structured, it may be inappropriate. Vulnerable young people may be dispersed around the country and have to survive mainly by themselves. It is particularly important for young refugees that measures should be taken to effect the child's basic need to develop a sense of belonging. Resettlement is a period of stress; it is essential for young people who are faced with the uncertainty of asylum, that personal arrangements be made to assist the process and future support arrangements (Kidane 2001). Access to public services, for example to GPs, may become difficult. Unaccompanied minors may also be dispersed to the cluster areas, in which there is social exclusion and marginalization already (e.g. Zetter and Pearl 2000, p.680).

Separation

Depending on how the asylum process manipulates the young person's situation, it may be desired by the political will of the regime to create what Berry refers to as a 'separatist movement' – maintaining divisions between asylum-seekers and the larger society to 'keep people in their place' (1988, p.102).

In both countries there is evidence to suggest that separated children face many restrictive measures during their asylum applications. For example, similarities exist when the refugee application is refused and the child is granted a temporary residence as it poses great risks that the child 'will fall between two stools' (Danish Refugee Council 2000, p.18). Temporary protection means enormous psychological stress for young people. It leaves the child for a long time in a vacuum of insecurity, separated from both acculturating worlds, and the implications of uncertainty while residing in Finland or the UK make it more difficult to integrate.

But at the same time, the maintenance of traditions distinct from integrated social life in host societies can mediate some of the impact of restrictive refugee policies. For example, the importance of the child's own cultural group as a protective buffer makes the difference between certainty and chaos for the child. In Yinger's work (1981) discrimination directed towards the ethnocultural group of the child has been linked to the 'exclusion' and a 'rejection' of the host majority and a reaffirmation of traditional culture. In the UK this orientation is recognized via the dispersal in ethnocultural communities. In Finland this orientation is actively pursued as every unaccompanied child has a right to apply for family reunification. Unfortunately, the process is often very slow, partly because of the difficulties with documentation and the identification of a minor. It has been argued that some children may have been sent to Finland as 'satellite children'. In these cases it has been assumed that children arrive in Finland with the hope of a positive decision regarding their family reunification application. Based on this argument, a new status has been created for these children. According to status 'A4', a child is allowed to live in Finland and has access to services, but s/he is not allowed family reunification.

Conclusions

According to Berry's model, integration as an acculturation strategy is the optimum. In terms of support services provision, it means a relevant balance between 'cultural' and 'dominant' services. As described, there are advantages and disadvantages in the Finnish and UK systems. Neither is the optimum situation and the combination of them would be the ideal. Probably the professional family homes would be the ideal model. Parents with similar ethnic backgrounds living within communities would accommodate a separated child. Parents would receive education, guidance and continuous support from social workers. A child would have access to services such as education, counselling and leisure activities. Ideally, the community would consist equally of minority and majority people. This kind of placement would guarantee a safe and stable environment for a minor while waiting for family reunification.

Another option is to increase the number of 'family workers' for separated children. In this model a child could be accommodated as in the UK model in the communities, but would receive more support from social workers on a regular basis. A child would have independence, but would not be alienated and isolated. It is possible to avoid the worst scenario, marginalization, by appropriate support arrangements.

So what else can be done? Are there better ways of responding to the needs of separated children? In Finland and the UK there are a variety of responses, ranging from community dispersal to institutionalization within first- and second-tier accommodation. The following is a minimum list of recommendations:

Non-discrimination

The policy direction begins from the option of understanding asylum as a symptom of social injustice and reciprocates by improvement: improvement offered as a safeguard to protection and care and as a democratic embrace underpinning democratic values. Where improvements are not on offer, or migration is further interpreted as bogus, there may be further efforts to undermine it, involving increased systematic restrictive measures to prevent individuals seeking asylum.

Information

At the heart of the matter remains the issue of alarmism, and public opinion if it is not to be ill informed. Questions remain for those who keep the European institutional system up and running, while matters concerning alarmism and asylum-seekers have attracted little attention or attempted to persuade electorates by means of pro-refugee debates. Only an assumption of a pan-European drive to establish a positive public consensus – overcoming the pervasive lack of clarity over the nature of the threat which society faces – against the harsh realities, the persecution, flight and reception conditions of asylum-seekers would be adequate.

Child-friendly procedures

So far the question of whether the rights of young separated refugees are compatible with asylum integration regimes remains unanswered. Most of the asylum processes such as detention, interviewing, dispersal, or deportation depend on information. Can such information be obtained from young people without being oppressive or being a danger to individual rights in itself? For the children's support and integration into the community, interviews should be conducted by persons trained in refugee and children's issues. When young separated children are presented in the first instance, 'culturally appropriate mental health care should be developed and qualified psycho-social counselling be provided' (UNHCR 1997, *Guidelines*, para 7.11).

Education

It is essential for those responsible for the training of caring and social work professionals to respond, and to demand a level of training that teaches the nature and dynamics of refugeeism. Such training should incorporate persecution, flight, the psycho-social conditions, reception support, and also reflect the needs of young separated refugees. For the child's 'best interests' to be adequately protected, and to make the asylum process transparent by providing information on rights and process, there is a clear need for all children under 18 years of age to be supported by a guardian or adviser at all stages of the asylum process (Spindler 2001). Guidelines and training regarding the functions of a guardian should be developed and adopted by social work education.

Realization of Rights

On the whole, the asylum programmes provide unsuitable interim provision and young separated refugees are most vulnerable to its limited resources. A change would begin by concerned parties demanding the signatory implementation of the UNCRC. According to the UNCRC, member states are obliged to provide: special protection and appropriate alternative care arrangements for children separated from their family environment, taking into account the child's best interests and their ethnic, religious, cultural and linguistic background (Article 20); the highest attainable standards of health (Article 24); periodic reviews of placement and treatment of the child (Article 25); a standard of living adequate for the child's physical, mental, spiritual, moral and social development (Article 26).

Comparative research and international exchange programme for workers

Exchange of knowledge by practitioners and professionals in different countries is needed. There are different systems of support arrangements and it would be valuable to exchange experiences and 'know-how' in practice. This would be a system similar to student exchange programmes, but it could be systematized. By familiarizing oneself with other systems in practice, it is possible to learn something new. In addition, the inevitable distance from one's own system enables critical reflection upon it.

Power, values and ethics

The traditional 'hierarchical relationship' between client and social worker has to be questioned. Separated children, who are probably the most vulnerable children in society, should especially be heard. Less bureaucratic and formal social work systems and practices are needed and power relationships should be recognized. The unequal situation between child and worker should be compensated for by an equal and dialectical relationship. This relationship is possible by internalizing basic social work values and sustaining a commitment to them. Separated children are children first and they deserve ethical and high value social work interventions.

Redefining formal social work practices

In both countries, volunteer work and informal support should be recognized as important social work models. The limits and boundaries of welfare systems often support accountability and the formality of social work practices. Nevertheless, the importance of informal support practices should not be ignored.

References

Aronowitz, M. (1984) 'The social and emotional adjustment of immigrant children: A literature review.' *International Migration Review 18*, 2, 237–25.

Berry, J.W. (1988) 'Acculturation and psychological adaptation among refugees.' In D. Miserez *et al.* (1988) *Refugees: The Trauma of Exile, The Humanitarian role of Red Cross and Red Crescent.* Dordrecht: Martinus Nijhoff.

Danish Refugee Council (2000) *Unaccompanied Children in the Danish Asylum Process – Experiences from Counselling of and Assistance to Children.* http//www.drc.dk/publications/unacc/ulflrapport.pdf

Donà, G. (2002) 'Refugees' well-being in countries of resettlement.' In *Social Work in Europe 9*, 1, 41–48.

Eurasylum (2003) *Asylum Applications and Recognition of Asylum-Seekers in the European Union.* http://www.eurasylum.org/portal/docs/statistics.doc

European Research Forum on Migration and Ethnic Relations , Berliner Institut für Vergleichende Soziet forschung, The Family Federation of Finland and Università Degli Studi di Firenze (2001) *Unaccompanied Minor Migrants as a Vulnerable Group – Information and Recommendations.* Berlin: Edition Parabolis.

Findlater, J. (1999) 'Asylum-seekers in Europe: What difference has the EU made?' *Social Work in Europe 6*, 2, 42–47.

Forsander, A. (2000) *Immigrant Employment and Work Government: Who, How, and to Where?* Helsinki: Ministry of Labour.

Garmezy, N. (1987) 'Stress, competence and development: Continuities in the study of schizophrenic adults, children vulnerable to psychopathology, and the search for stress-resistant children.' *American Journal of Orthopsychiatry 57*, 159–174.

Gordon, P. (1989) *Fortress Europe – The Meaning of 1992.* London: Runnymede Trust.

Harding, J. (2000) *The Uninvited, Refugees at the Rich Man's Gate.* London: Profile Books.

Helander, R. and Mikkonen, A. (2002) 'Ikävä äitiä... Ilman huoltajaa tulleet pakolaislapset Suomessa.' *Katsauksia E13/2002.* Helsinki: Väestöliitto.

Herberts, K. (2001) 'Finland.' In H. K. Anheier (ed) *Social Services in Europe. Annotated Bibliography.* Frankfurt a.M.: Observatory for the Development of Social Services in Europe.

Hodes, M. (1998) 'Refugee children may need a lot of psychiatric help.' *British Medical Journal 316*, 793–794.

Johnson, N. (2001) 'UK.' In H. K. Anheier (ed) *Social Services in Europe. Annotated Bibliography.* Frankfurt a.M.: Observatory for the Development of Social Services in Europe.

Joly, D. and Nettleton, C. (1990) *Refugees in Europe.* London: Minority Rights Publications.

Jones, A.D. (1998) *The Child Welfare Implications of UK Immigration and Asylum Policy.* Manchester: The Manchester Metropolitan University.

Kidane, S. (2001) *Food, Shelter and Half a Chance: Assessing the Needs of Unaccompanied Asylum-seeking and Refugee Children.* London: British Agencies for Adoption and Fostering.

Kunz, E.F. (1981) 'Exile and resettlement: Refugee theory.' *International Migration Review 15,* 1, 42–51.

Mayo, M. (1998) 'Community work.' In R. Adams, L. Dominelli and M. Payne (eds) *Social Work – Themes, Issues and Critical Debates.* Basingstoke: Macmillan.

Miles, M. and Thränhardt, D. (eds) (1995) *Migration and European Integration.* London: Pinter Publishers.

MOL (2003) *Immigration Affairs in 2002.* http://www.mol.fi/migration/a2002tieteng.pdf

Okitikpi, T. and Aymer, C. (2000) 'Refugee children and the challenge for social work.' *Social Work in Europe 7,* 51–58.

Payne, M. (2001) 'Community work: Origins and Research.' Unpublished lecture notes. Helsinki: Helsinki University Department of Social Policy and Social Work.

Pringle, K. (1998) *Children and Social Welfare in Europe.* Buckingham: Open University Press.

Rauhala, P. (1996) 'Miten sosiaalipalvelut ovat tulleet osaksi suomalaista sosiaaliturvaa?' *Tampere: Acta Universitatis Tamperensis, Ser A, Vol 477.* Tampere: University of Tampere.

Rosenthal, D.A. and Feldman, S.S. (1992) 'The nature and stability of ethnic identity in Chinese youth.' *Journal of Cross Cultural Psychology 23,* 214–227.

Rutter, M. (1985) 'Resilience in the face of adversity: Protective factors and resistance to psychiatric disorders.' *British Journal of Psychiatry 147,* 598–611.

Ruxton, S. (2000) *Separated Children Seeking Asylum in Europe: A Programme for Action.* Save the Children: UNHCR.

Satka, Mirja (1996, 2nd ed) *Making Social Citizenship – Conceptual Practices from Finnish Poor Law to Professional Social Work.* Jyväskylä: SoPhi.

Sourander, A. (1998) 'Behaviour problems and traumatic events of unaccompanied minors.' *Child Abuse and Neglect, 22,* 7, 719–727.

Spindler, W. (2001) *The Situation of Separated Children in Central Europe and the Baltic States.* Separated Children in Europe Programme.

Taviani, H. (1988) 'The perspectives of a host country.' In D. Miserez (ed) (1988) *Refugees: The Trauma of Exile, The Humanitarian role of Red Cross and Red Crescent.* Dordrecht: Martinus Nijhoff.

UNHCR (1997) *Guidelines on Policies and Procedures in Dealing with Unaccompanied Children.* Geneva: UNHCR.

UNHCR (1999) *Protecting Refugees, A Field Guide for N.G.O.s.* Geneva: UNHCR.

Valtonen, K. (2002) 'Social work with immigrants and refugees: Developing participation based framework for anti-oppressive practice, Part 2.' *British Journal of Social Work 32,* 113–120.

Van Tran, T. (1987) 'Ethnic community supports and psychological well-being of Vietnamese refugees.' *International Migration Review 21,* 833–843.

Walker, C. and Walker, A. (1998) 'Social policy and social work.' In R. Adams, L. Dominelli and M. Payne (eds) *Social Work – Themes, Issues and Critical Debates.* Basingstoke: Macmillan.

Yinger, J.M. (1981) 'Toward a theory of assimilation and dissimulation.' *Ethnic and Racial Studies 4*, 3, 249–264.

Zetter, P. and Pearl, M. (2000) 'The minority in the minority: Refugee community-based organisations in the UK and the impact of restrictionism on asylum-seekers.' *Journal of Ethnic and Migration Studies 26*, 4, 675–697.

Chapter 12

Asylum-seeker and Migrant Children in Ireland: Racism, Institutional Neglect and Social Work

Bryan Fanning

Introduction

This chapter examines responses by statutory and voluntary sector service providers in Ireland to the children of asylum-seekers and other migrants and to unaccompanied minors, with a specific emphasis on the challenges facing social workers. It draws on recent research undertaken in Ireland and on interviews with statutory and voluntary sector service providers. There is also a specific emphasis on the consequences of institutional barriers resulting from racism and on how lesser rights and entitlements can contribute to the risk of institutional neglect. Between 1995 and 2000 approximately one quarter of a million people migrated to Ireland. This amounted to an aggregate figure of seven per cent of the total population as recorded in the 1996 census. About half were returning Irish (MacEinri 2001, p.53). Asylum-seekers are a small minority within this population. Refugees and asylum-seekers from over 100 countries form just one part of a larger wave of immigration consisting of returned emigrants, people from other European Union (EU) countries and immigrant workers from non-EU countries. Some 32 per cent of immigrants who arrived in the year ending in April 2001 came from non-EU countries. More than 18,000 work permits were granted to non-EU nationals in 2000. This rose to 47,000 during 2001 (Woods and Humphries 2002, p.5). Some

78 per cent of those who arrived in 2001 came from eastern Europe, the Baltic states and the Russian Federation. Migrant workers have come to greatly outnumber asylum-seekers. To these must be added a population of illegal migrants. These include the children of undocumented migrants and the undocumented children of adults with work permits.

Racism and rights

Racism can be expressed through the acts of individuals or in the values, presumptions, structures and processes of social, economic, cultural and political institutions. For example, Article 2 of the UNESCO Declaration on Race and Racial Prejudice emphasizes the role of structural and institutional barriers in producing racist barriers in society:

> Racism includes racist ideologies, prejudiced attitudes, discriminatory behaviour, structural arrangements and institutional practices resulting in racial inequality as well as the fallacious notion that discriminatory relations between groups are morally and scientifically justifiable; it is reflected in discriminatory provisions in legislation or regulations and discriminatory practices as well as in anti-social beliefs and acts...[1]

There has been considerable debate, in the wake of the Macpherson report, about how institutional racism impacts upon black and ethnic minorities. This defined institutional racism in the following terms:

> The collective failure of an organisation to provide an appropriate and professional service to people because of their colour, culture or ethnic origin. It can be seen in processes, attitudes and behaviour which amount to discrimination through unwitting prejudice, ignorance, thoughtlessness and racist stereotyping which disadvantage ethnic minority people. (Macpherson 1999, p.22).

The consequences of institutional racism include unequal access to services and unequal outcomes on the basis of ethnicity. Services configured towards the cultures, expectations and needs of majority groups which wittingly or unwittingly neglect those of minority ethnic groups are likely to produce unequal outcomes for minority ethnic groups.

The issue of structural racism warrants similar consideration. The migrants who comprise the new minority ethnic groups within Irish society, as in other European countries, often have lesser rights and entitlements than citizen ethnic minorities. These encounter structural barriers to participation in society that compound institutional barriers resulting from racism. Non-citizens face exclusion on a number of levels within Irish social policy. First, they tend to have lesser social rights and entitlements. They may be categorized by the state as outside the remit of a range of policies and programmes aimed at tackling disadvantage. Second, they may be excluded from official equality discourse, that is, excluded from how inequalities in society are conceptualized and discussed in official research, reports and within the remit of policies. In this context, social policy considerations may become subordinate to policies of excluding such groups or of limiting their rights and entitlements. A dominant logic, which distinguishes between the citizen and the non-citizen, allows non-citizen groups to be categorized as outside of the communities within which they live. It supposes that the fate of these communities can be disconnected from the fate of non-citizen neighbours. The resulting exclusions can be understood as the institutionalization of a narrow definition of community increasingly at odds with the real social membership of Irish society (Fanning 2002, p.184).

The Irish state stratifies groups of non-citizens on the basis of decisions about their entitlements. A distinction between citizen rights and social citizenship and what Joppke (2001, p.345) refers to as 'alien rights' underlies a state process which allows non-citizen/alien groups to be treated differently from each other by the state. Migrant workers, immigrants with Irish-born children, people with refugee status and asylum-seekers are each deemed by the state to have different levels of rights and entitlements. In all cases, these are less than the entitlements of EU citizens living in Ireland. The current entitlements and non-entitlements of such non-citizen groups have been shaped by a mixture of court rulings, government policy (administrative decisions), legislation and international agreement. For example, in 1987 the High Court ruled (*Fajujonu v Minister for Justice*) that all Irish-born children were entitled to Irish citizenship and as such had a constitutional right to family life[2]. As a result, the asylum-seeker and migrant families with Irish-born children were deemed to be entitled to 'leave to remain' in Ireland. This ruling was successfully overturned by the Minister for Justice, Equality and Law Reform in April 2002 (*Lobe v Minister of Justice*). A system of direct provision was introduced in 1999 following the introduction of a similar system in the UK. This reduced the benefit entitlements of asylum-seekers. The Aliens Act (1935) and the Refugee Act (1996) disallow various groups from engaging in paid employment. The result has been a hierarchy of differential rights – less than those of citizens in each case – which shape the responses of social policy and social work service providers to migrants and non-citizen ethnic minorities.

Such inequalities and welfare stratifications sit uneasily with Ireland's obligations under the UN Convention on the Rights of the Child that was ratified by the government in 1991 and applies to all children within the jurisdiction of the state (Stapleton and Fanning 2002, p.26). Article 2 states that all children should be entitled to basic rights without discrimination. Article 3(1) states that the best interests of children should be a primary consideration in all actions concerning children (whether undertaken by public or private social welfare institutions, courts of law, administrative authorities or legislative bodies). Other articles specify a right to the highest attainable standard of health and to have access to health and medical services (Article 24); a right to benefit from social security (Article 26); a right to an adequate standard of living with a duty on the state to assist parents, where necessary, in fulfilling this right (Article 27); and a right to participate in leisure, recreational and cultural activities (Article 31).

The roles of social work

In the case of asylum-seeker and migrant children, a range of potential roles for social work in Ireland can be identified. The roles of social workers as agents of social control and as service providers occur with respect to asylum-seekers and migrants within a context where the services which they provide are inevitably stratified by the fact that non-citizen groups have lesser social and economic rights and welfare entitlements. It is arguably the case that the advocacy role with respect to such groups is more problematic than with respect to clients who are Irish citizens. For example, social workers may have fewer options when seeking to support clients who are not deemed entitled to social housing. Clients who experience lesser rights and entitlements are likely to present more challenges to social workers than citizen clients. Groups such as asylum-seekers and migrants will have distinct advocacy needs relating to the specific barriers they experience. Examples include language barriers in accessing services, information and advocacy issues relating to asylum and immigration processes and, of course, racism.

Since the mid-1990s social workers have been increasingly drawn into more explicit 'policing' of the internal and external boundaries of the state (Humphries 2002, p.131). Christie argues that the social work profession in Ireland, as elsewhere, has acquired a potential role in regulating national and super-national boundaries by working with asylum-seekers as residents and as 'potential citizens' (2002a, p.188). He draws upon Bauman's description of the welfare state as a gardening state (Bauman 1991, cited in Christie 2002a, p.188). Within this analogy social workers are depicted as maintaining borders and regulating the growth of the different parts of the 'garden' or, more specifically, by using social work practices to integrate families and individuals within society using techniques of moralization, normalization and tutelage. Insofar as social work may reflect the dominant culture the social control role can be affected by cultural differences and by racism. For example, assessments relating to child protection are likely to be affected by attitudes to and understandings of clients from black and ethnic minorities amongst social workers.

The advocacy and social control roles of social work will inevitably be affected by the power inequalities wrought by lesser rights and entitlements. They will be affected by the specific social control circumstances of immigration processes. The advocacy role may be undermined by the strictures of asylum application processes whereby social workers become involved in the assessment of such applications (Humphries 2002, p.131). In the Irish case, social workers working with unaccompanied minors have a role in supporting them in making asylum applications yet there are indications that they may be ill-equipped for such a role. A report by the Irish Refugee Council and Save the Children emphasized the need for every unaccompanied minor to have a court appointed *guardian ad litem* (MacNeice and Almirall, 1999, p.17). However, most unaccompanied minors do not have access to such support. Social workers working with unaccompanied minors often lack the necessary training and expertise to support them in this context (Christie 2002b, p.15).

Racism and institutional neglect

There is some evidence that suggests that the anti-racist critique of British social work, put forward by writers such as Dominelli, is relevant in the Irish case. This critique emphasizes the importance of addressing racism within social work as well as the role of social work in addressing the racist experiences of clients from black and ethnic minorities (Dominelli 1992, p.170). For example, Moroney describes the experiences of a black social worker in Dublin being rejected by her clients because of her colour. Furthermore, the social worker's children experienced racist harassment from other children and her home had been attacked on a number of occasions (Moroney 1999). The lack of a historical focus on racism in Irish social work suggests that issues identified by Dominelli such as institutional racism, social dumping and avoidance may be problematic.

The complexities of addressing racism in social work in an era where welfare stratifications discriminate against non-citizen members of black and ethnic minority communities have recently been highlighted by the Report of the Inquiry into the Death of Victoria Climbié (Laming 2003). The inquiry examined how the relevant services failed to prevent her death. Victoria had come into contact with four social services departments, two specialist child protection teams and three housing departments. She had been admitted to two different hospitals. The inquiry highlighted a number of factors that may have contributed to her death but placed particular emphasis on the poor coordination of child protection services. It concluded that racism 'did play its part' in Victoria's death (Laming 2003, p.12). The inquiry report quoted the Director of Haringey's Race Equality Unit:

> There is some evidence to suggest that one of the consequences of an exclusive focus on 'culture' in work with black children and families is (that) it leaves black and ethnic minority children in potentially dangerous situations, because the assessment has failed to address a child's fundamental care and protection needs. (Cited in Laming 2003, p.345)

The report of the inquiry stated that 'it may be assumptions made about Victoria and her situation diverted caring people noting and acting on signs of neglect and abuse' (ibid.). It described how, on more than one occasion, medical practitioners who noted marks on Victoria's body considered the possibility that children who have grown up in Africa may be expected to have more marks on their bodies than children who have been raised in Europe. It noted that such assumptions may have prevented a full assessment of those marks on Victoria having being made. The report referred to other assumptions made in this case, including those relating to discipline in Afro-Caribbean families (Victoria was African). Other factors, noted by the inquiry, included fear amongst white workers of being accused of racism and feelings amongst white workers that they were not as qualified as black workers to make decisions about black children. The report quoted a statement by one QC who participated in the inquiry to illustrate this point:

> Assumptions based on race can be just as corrosive as blatant racism...racism can affect the way people conduct themselves in other ways. Fear of being accused of racism can stop people acting when otherwise they would. (Cited in Laming 2003, p.345)

The context of Victoria's death was one of inadequate access to services, advocacy and support due both to lesser rights and entitlements and because of lack of responsiveness from service providers. She received inadequate support from a welfare system poorly configured to meet the needs of vulnerable migrants. Arguably, the Climbié inquiry points to the risks engendered by lesser status as well as due to racism. Marginal non-citizen populations can be seen as particularly at risk from institutional neglect in areas such as child protection.

Some insight into the causes of institutional neglect is suggested by Lipsky's 'street level bureaucracy' thesis. Lipsky argues that workers in public services have wide discretion over the dispensation of benefits and public sanctions (Lipsky 1993, p.381). It is argued that street level bureaucrats – these can be professionals or non-professionals – have enormous power over the consumers of services but also considerable autonomy from their employing agency through the exercise of discretion and demand control. A number of forms of demand control are open to officials such as perpetuating delay, withholding information and stigmatizing the process of service delivery (Hudson 1993, p.388). Street level bureaucrats do not simply deal with occupational hazards by limiting client demand. They modify their own activities, perceptions of their jobs and their perceptions of their clients to better match their ability to perform. This may result in psychological withdrawal resulting in a workforce relatively unbothered by the discrepancy between what they are supposed to do and what they actually do (Hudson 1993, p.339). Lipsky argues that street level bureaucrats who are unable to provide all clients with their best efforts develop conceptual mechanisms to divide up the client population and rationalize the division, even though the consequence of this may be at variance with the formal goals of the organization, by 'creaming off' those clients who seem most likely to succeed in terms of bureaucratic success criteria or distinguishing between those clients deemed to be deserving and undeserving (Hudson 1993, p.339). The 'street level bureaucracy' thesis suggests that 'hard to help' clients, such as migrants with lesser rights, may be particularly vulnerable.

The risks of institutional neglect can be illustrated in the Irish context by a study of asylum-seeker mothers in Ireland by Kennedy and Murphy-Lawless (2002). The study noted that some women respondents choose to remain in violent relationships with their children because of fear of risking status. It described how some women felt 'not listened to' when they came into contact with doctors and midwives (Kennedy and Murphy-Lawless 2002, p.120).

The potential for institutional neglect resulting from a cocktail of bad practices, racism and lesser rights is suggested by one example included in the study. This describes the dismissive treatment by a midwife of a woman experiencing domestic abuse. The woman had become distressed about being unable to breastfeed her baby soon after its birth:

> The baby was crying and she felt helpless... A midwife came back and rebuked her saying that she was 'too demanding'. And her husband, when he came to see her a few minutes later, agreed with the midwife. When she came home with the baby, there was no one to help her and she felt weak and depressed. Her partner began to abuse her physically at this point. (2002, p.106)

The dangers of institutional neglect in such cases are potentially exacerbated by inadequate coordination of services for children in the Republic of Ireland. The 1998 report by the UN Committee on the Rights of the Child on Ireland's implementation of the UN Convention on the Rights of the Child identified poor coordination between and within the nine government departments involved in the area of early childhood. It also identified a history of poor communication and coordination between statutory and voluntary providers of early years care and education (Horgan and Douglas 2001, p.139). With respect to social work, there is a need for a focus on potential risks facing asylum-seeker children, unaccompanied minors and other categories of 'hard to help' migrant children emanating from institutional neglect.

Asylum-seeker children in direct provision

The Irish Government introduced a system of 'direct provision' for asylum-seekers that drastically lessened their welfare entitlements following similar developments in the UK. There were some crucial differences between each case. In Ireland, asylum-seekers received small cash allowances, rather than vouchers, in addition to meals and accommodation. The weekly rates have not been increased since the direct provision was piloted in 1999. In 2003 these remained at   19.05 Euros per adult and 9.53 Euros per child. In the Irish case, responsibility for the care of asylum-seekers was effectively privatized. Many asylum-seekers were accommodated in overcrowded, minimally staffed private sector hostels, hotels and bed and breakfasts with little or no statutory infrastructure. The conditions of people in direct provision often resembled those experienced by homeless persons in emergency accommodation, except that benefit rates were lower. A report by the Irish Refugee Council, 18 months after the introduction of direct provision, described it as 'wholly inadequate', 'inhumane and discriminatory' (2001, pp.11–13).

In a number of cases poor accommodation combined with extreme income poverty has led to serious deprivation amongst asylum-seeker families. Even taking into account child benefits, the combined entitlements of asylum-seeker families provided incomes that typically placed them below the 20 per cent poverty line (Fanning, Veale and O'Connor 2001, p.5). A number of studies have documented the consequences of such poverty. Two studies undertaken in 2001 found that, in some cases, hostel food was inadequate to meet the dietary needs of pregnant women and babies (Fanning, Veale and O'Connor 2001; Kennedy and Murphy-Lawless 2002). Most respondents in direct provision (92% in one study) considered that it was necessary to buy extra food to supplement the food provided by the hostels. However, most respondents on 'direct provision' (69%) stated that they were unable to afford to purchase extra food (Fanning, Veale and O'Connor 2001, pp.35–6). Parents had to purchase extra food for themselves and their children in the face of competing demands for items such as non-prescription medicines (not covered by the medical card), clothes for children, nappies and toiletries. Some of their children had special dietary needs that could only be met at considerable hardship to other

members of the household. The consequences of extreme material deprivation for some respondents included some cases of malnutrition amongst expectant mothers, ill-health related to diet amongst babies, weight loss amongst children and hunger amongst adults as a result of 'within household rationing' of available resources in an effort to provide for the needs of children and babies (Fanning, Veale and O'Connor 2001, p.35). In some cases the absence of an adequate diet for pregnant women and mothers with young babies caused difficulties in breastfeeding. Women in hostels tended to give up breastfeeding within a few weeks of the birth of their babies. They were compelled to switch to expensive baby formula which they could ill afford on direct provision (Fanning, Veale and O'Connor 2001; Kennedy and Murphy-Lawless 2002).

A number of studies have found that material deprivation was exacerbated by extreme accommodation deprivation as the result of chronic overcrowding in hostels. Three studies of asylum-seekers in direct provision found that respondent families living in hostels and hotels generally shared a single room irrespective of the age of children (Comhlamh 2001; Fanning, Veale and

O'Connor 2001; Kennedy and Murphy-Lawless 2002). The inappropriateness of such accommodation is illustrated by the following example:

> Three generations of a Polish family shared one bedroom, which measured about 12 by 12 feet. The grandparents slept on the floor on two single mattresses. The 17-year-old mother slept on a mattress on the floor while her baby slept nearby in her pram. There was no room for a cot. The young mother explained that she had to stop breastfeeding, as it was too difficult during the nights in such close proximity to her father. (Kennedy and Murphy Lawless 2002, p.62)

Inadequate accommodation has been found to have a detrimental impact upon the developmental well-being of asylum-seeker children in a number of ways. For example, overcrowding has impeded the toilet training of small children. Some children living in direct provision have experienced stress-related illnesses. Some parents have described communal areas as being unsafe for children. For example, inappropriate leisure activities, such as the watching of over-18 videos, took place in communal areas used by children. Tensions within hostels have detrimentally impacted on family life. Children have reported becoming very upset as a result of conflict or being shouted at by non-parental adults. Some parents have described their children as becoming psychologically withdrawn as a result of these tensions (Fanning, Veale and O'Connor 2001, pp.35–43). Such conditions present considerable challenges to social workers and health workers with respect to child welfare.

Unaccompanied minors

These challenges are particularly acute in the case of separated children under 18 years of age seeking asylum in Ireland. Eight hundred and sixty-one such unaccompanied minors arrived in Ireland in 2002. Of these, 506 were subsequently reunited with parents or relatives. These are predominantly accommodated in the Dublin area and are the responsibility of a dedicated unit comprising social workers and link workers. Unaccompanied minors have been exempted from the dispersal programme. Accommodation centres for unaccompanied minors are subject to regulation. Every voluntary or private agency is required to register all non-statutory children's residential centres with the Registration and Inspection Service of the relevant Health Board (Department of Health and Children 2002, p. 2). The *National Standards for Children's Residential Centres* set out requirements for management, staffing, monitoring, children's rights, statutory care plans, child protection, education, health, safety and the role of social workers (Department of Health and Children 2002, p.2).

Supervising social workers have clear statutory obligations towards all young people, including unaccompanied minors in residential care. Staff members in centres are required to be trained in the principles and practices of child protection. They have a clear obligation to report any child protection concerns. The National Standards state explicitly that young people should have a room of their own and that centres must have age-appropriate play and recreational facilities. There is also a requirement that the Health Board be satisfied, by undertaking a proper risk assessment, that centres are safe and secure places for young people to live in. The National Standards also require that centres should be subject to outside monitoring on an annual basis by an authorized person appointed by the Health Board, in line with the Child Care (Placement of Children in Residential Care) Regulations 1995. The authorized person must ensure that all children have an allocated social worker and that a care plan has been prepared and looks for evidence that decisions have been acted upon (Department of Health and Children 2002, p.12).

It is questionable whether the care of at least some unaccompanied minors in Ireland meets the National Standards. For example, one centre that has been used exclusively for unaccompanied minors since September 2002 accommodates 66 young people from 12 years of age upwards. These generally share rooms with one or more other young people and have minimal facilities and support. No qualified care workers are employed on site. As a social worker employed by a voluntary sector drop-in centre for asylum-seekers said in February 2003, 'there is no care'. She described the level of support provided by Health Board social workers and project workers to the children as minimal.

There is just one dedicated long-term residential unit in Ireland for unaccompanied minors. Bellevue House in Tallaght is run by Clann Housing Association. It has 11 qualified staff members and provides care for 6 separated children between the ages of 7 and 15. According to the manager of the unit, such dedicated accommodation facilities for unaccompanied minors are vital because their needs are wholly distinct from those of other children in residential care (cited in Ross 2003). Unaccompanied minors may experience extreme psychological trauma as a result of both pre-migratory and post-migratory experiences. The former category includes bereavement, rape and torture. Post-migratory stressors can include racism, loneliness, insecurity and anxiety about the asylum process. According to Rylands, many unaccompanied minors are in danger of being overwhelmed by anxiety and loss (Rylands 2001). By definition, they have been thrust prematurely into independent life without family and community supports. As described by one 17-year-old unaccompanied minor: 'I miss someone to advise me and to take care of me. I am too young to have to do this alone' (Rylands 2001). A study of minors who had been living in Ireland between two and thirteen months with a mean age of 16.29 years found indications of 'moderate problem or severe problem behaviour' in more than 50 per cent (15 out 28) of respondents:

> Few had any contact with Irish people... The longer these adolescents were in Ireland, the greater the psychological distress. Current stressors contributed to psychological dysfunction and there was little integration into Irish culture. Social support networks consisted of other unaccompanied minors or asylum-seekers. Unaccompanied minors are a highly vulnerable group and current asylum policies may add to behaviour symptoms and psychological distress. (Rea 2001, p.4)

The study found that experiences of racist discrimination caused respondents to become more socially withdrawn. Most respondents (89%) were found to have experienced racist discrimination. Notwithstanding the exemption of unaccompanied minors from lower direct provision benefit rates, most respondents (71.4%) identified poverty as a problem. The study recommended that the number of dedicated social worker and project worker posts should be increased.

Migrant children

Asylum-seeker children in direct provision and unaccompanied minors account for just some of the potentially vulnerable migrant children living in Ireland. Large-scale labour immigration from non-EEA countries has generally been subject to restrictions upon the immigration of dependent children. Migrant workers on non-transferable work permits are currently not allowed to apply for visas for dependents during their first year in the country. However, there are indications that some migrant worker parents have sought to reunify their families in Ireland with the result that the number of undocumented children living in Ireland has risen. The formation of immigrant ethnic minority communities and households consisting of a potential mixture of documented and undocumented persons has a number of implications. Undocumented adults or children are particularly vulnerable members of Irish society. Households consisting of undocumented persons or of both documented and undocumented persons are likely to have low household incomes as a result of low pay and a lack of entitlement to child benefits and other forms of income support. Children in such households face potentially high risks of institutional neglect insofar as they may not come into contact with many children's services. They may encounter institutional barriers as a result of having lesser rights and entitlements and as a result of racism. Such marginal groups are often invisible within policy debates and programmes. In Ireland, the Revised National Anti-Poverty Strategy (NAPS) identified migrants and ethnic minorities as a distinct target group. It established a goal of ensuring that migrants and members of ethnic minority groups resident in Ireland are not more likely to experience poverty than majority group members (Department of Social Community and Family Affairs 2002, p.17). However, the current absence of data was identified within the Revised NAPS as an impediment to the establishment of specific targets with respect to poverty amongst migrants and ethnic minority groups and to the inclusion of minority ethnic groups within anti-poverty strategies in Ireland.

The difficulties suggested by the present exclusion of migrants from anti-poverty policies are likely to be reflected in other areas. These include a lack of strategic and administrative focus upon the needs of migrants within existing programmes (institutional barriers) as well as a lack of dedicated resources. In such a context, migrant children may come into contact with social services which are ill-prepared to acknowledge and address their needs. The risks of institutional neglect potentially faced by migrant children may exceed those of asylum children and unaccompanied minors who may be more visible to social workers.

The only area where social workers in Ireland have statutory responsibility to work with asylum-seekers and refugees is in the area of childcare (Christie 2002a, p.187). The Refugee Act (1996) specifically extends the provisions of the Child Care Act (1991) to refugees and asylum-seekers. Under the Child Care Act (1991) a health board is required to 'promote the welfare of children in its area who are not receiving adequate care and protection'. This obligation has been acknowledged in responses to unaccompanied minors. However, such children are more properly under the care of health boards rather than in their care (Christie 2002a, pp.191–2). Accommodation for unaccompanied minors often resembles the sorts of privatized minimalist and overcrowded provision experienced by asylum-seekers living in direct provision. The potential vulnerability of migrant and asylum-seeker children is partly due to lesser rights and entitlements. It is vital that social work responses to such groups address the needs of such children emanating from institutional barriers to welfare services. There is arguably a need for a broader definition of institutional racism than that set out in the Macpherson Report. Such a definition must take into account barriers relating to lesser rights and entitlements. In Ireland, as elsewhere, these disproportionately affect black and ethnic minorities. It also needs to take into account barriers that affect 'hard to help' persons with lesser rights, emanating from avoidance and social dumping, in areas not affected by lesser rights.

Conclusion

This chapter has emphasized the potential risks to vulnerable asylum-seeker and migrant children of institutional neglect. In essence, there is a danger that vulnerable children will fall through the cracks in the absence of a clear and sufficient collective focus on their needs by service providers. In the Irish case, asylum-seeker and migrant children have not been adequately defined as a target group by statutory services in the area of social work. Furthermore, there are indications that asylum-seeker and migrant children are disproportionately dependent upon the voluntary sector yet marginalized within this sector. In both sectors there is a need to address institutional racism.

In November 2000, the Irish Government launched a National Children's Strategy. This endorsed two of the guiding principles of the Convention on the Rights of the Child (1989): that all children should be entitled to basic rights without discrimination and that the best interests of the child should be a primary consideration in all actions concerning children (Government of Ireland 2000, p.10). There is a need for all policies and programmes that emanate from the National Children's Strategy to have a clear remit for asylum-seeking and migrant children. It is similarly crucial that all services for children, including those relating to social work and residential care, should not discriminate in responding to the needs of children on grounds of status or citizenship. Such a remit is particularly important given the profound gap which exists between commitments to children's rights adopted by the Irish state and existing policies and responses to asylum-seeker children, unaccompanied minors and migrant children in Ireland.

Notes

1   United Nations Educational Scientific and Cultural Organisation (UNESCO) General Conference 27 November 1978.

2   Article 41 of the Irish constitution sets out the rights of the family (notably 41.1.1. 'The state recognises the family as the natural primary and fundamental unit group of society, and as a moral institution possessing inalienable...rights, antecedent and superior to all positive law). Article 42 refers to the rights (and duties) of parents to provide for the religious and moral, intellectual, physical and social education of their children.

References

Bauman, Z. (1991) *Modernity and Ambivalence.* Cambridge: Polity Press.

Christie, A. (2002a) 'Responses of the social work profession to unaccompanied children seeking asylum in the Republic of Ireland.' *European Journal of Social Work 5*, 2, 187–198.

Christie, A. (2002b) 'Asylum-seekers and refugees in Ireland: Questions of racism and social work.' *Social Work in Europe 9*, 1, 10–17.

Comhlamh (2001) *Refugee Lives: The Failure of Direct Provision as a Social Response to the Needs of Asylum-seekers In Ireland.* Dublin: Comhlamh Refugee Solidarity Group.

Department of Health and Children (2002) *National Standards for Children's Residential Centres.* Dublin: Official Publications.

Department of Social Community and Family Affairs (2002) *Building an Inclusive Society: Review of the National Anti-Poverty Strategy under the Programme for Prosperity and Fairness.* Dublin: Official Publications.

Dominelli, L. (1992) 'An uncaring profession? An examination of racism in social work.' In P. Braham, A. Rattansi and R. Skellington (eds) *Racism and Anti-Racism.* London: Sage.

Fanning, B. (2002) *Racism and Social Change in the Republic of Ireland.* Manchester: Manchester University Press.

Fanning, B., Veale, A. and O'Connor, D. (2001) *Beyond the Pale: Asylum-seeking Children and Social Exclusion in Ireland.* Dublin: Irish Refugee Council.

Government of Ireland (2000) *The National Children's Strategy: Our Children – Their Lives.* Dublin: Official Publications.

Horgan, M. and Douglas, F. (2001) 'Some aspects of quality in early childhood education.' In A. Cleary, M. Nic Ghiolla Phadraig and S. Quin (eds) *Understanding Children: Volume 1: State, Education and Economy.* Dublin: Oak Tree Press.

Humphries. B, (2002) 'From welfare to authoritarianism: The role of social work in immigration controls.' In S. Cohen, B. Humphries and E. Mynott (eds) *From Immigration Controls to Welfare Controls.* London: Jessica Kingsley Publishers.

Hudson, B. (1993) 'Micheal Lipsky and street level bureaucracy.' In M. Hill (ed) *The Policy Process.* London: Harvester Wheatsheaf.

Irish Refugee Council (2001) *Regional Reception of Asylum-seekers in Ireland: Policy Recommendations.* Dublin: Irish Refugee Council.

Joppke, C. (2001) 'The legal–domestic sources of immigrant rights: The United States, Germany and the European Union.' *Comparative Political Studies 34*, 4, 345.

Kennedy, P. and Murphy-Lawless, J. (2002) *The Maternity Care Needs of Refugee and Asylum-seeking Women.* Dublin: Northern Area Health Board.

Laming (2003) *The Victoria Climbié Inquiry: Report of An Inquiry by Lord Laming.* London: HMSO.

Lipsky, M. (1993) 'Street level bureaucracy.' In M. Hill (ed) *The Policy Process.* London: Harvester Wheatsheaf.

MacEinri, P. (2001) 'Immigration policy in Ireland.' In F. Farrell and P. Watt (eds) *Responding to Racism in Ireland.* Dublin: Veritas.

MacNeice, S., and Almirall, L. (1999) *Separated Children Seeking Asylum in Ireland: A Report on Legal and Social Conditions.* Dublin: Irish Refugee Council.

Macpherson, W. (1999) *The Stephen Lawrence Inquiry: Report of an Inquiry by Sir William Macpherson of Cluny.* London: HMSO.

Moroney, A. (1999) 'Negotiating an island culture.' *Irish Social Worker 16,* 3, 4–5.

Rea, A. (2001) *Psychosocial Needs, Social Support and Estimates of Psychological Distress amongst Unaccompanied Refugee Minors in Ireland.* Conference on Unaccompanied Minors, Dublin Castle, June 2001.

Ross, E. (2003) 'How the needs of unaccompanied minors are being met in Ireland.' Unpublished.

Rylands, J. (2001) *Findings of a Research Project on Psychological Need, Social Support and Estimates of Psychological Distress amongst Unaccompanied Minors.* Conference on Unaccompanied Minors, Dublin Castle, June 2001.

Stapleton and Fanning (2002) 'Refugee and asylum-seeking children: A rights based perspective.' In Barnados (ed) *Diversity in Early Childhood.* Dublin: Barnados.

Woods, M. and Humphries, N. (2002) *Seeking Asylum in Ireland: Comparative Figures for Asylum-seekers and Refugees in Ireland and Europe in 2000 and 2001.* Dublin: Social Science Research Centre.

Chapter 13

Conclusion

Debra Hayes and Beth Humphries

Time and place

In its attempt to help social workers improve service delivery to those subject to immigration control, this book has always acknowledged the context within which this is taking place. The introduction sought to provide historical and ideological frameworks for understanding the racist nature of immigration control and, in particular, the current construction of the 'asylum-seeker'. We have argued that this construction allows for a separate and inferior welfare system for this group as well as more restrictive access to welfare resources for others subject to immigration control. The evidence in this book is that social work as a profession has become complicit in this and has been largely accepting of systems specifically designed to offer less to particular groups of people as a result of their immigration status. More worryingly, social work has itself been shown to be providing an inferior service to this group and has largely occupied itself with concerns over gatekeeping resources, rather than meeting need. As we go to press, tensions in dispersal areas show the ease with which asylum-seekers can be made scapegoats as the cause of long-term social problems and grinding poverty. When an Iraqi asylum-seeker, stranded in the UK as a result of the West's attempts to 'liberate' his people, lay critically ill in a Welsh hospital after being attacked by white youths on a Wrexham housing estate; it was the remaining asylum-seekers from the estate who were removed, ejected, further dispersed now 'for their own safety' (Al Yafai 2003). The seriousness of these negative constructions outlined in this book should not be underestimated in terms of racist attacks and murders. Neither are these attitudes confined to poor, white youths on grim housing estates; it seems for the Home Office and the police alike, it is asylum-seekers who threaten social unrest.

> Mass migration has brought with it a whole new range and a whole new type of crime, from the Nigerian fraudster, to the Eastern European who deals in drugs and prostitution to the Jamaican concentration on drug dealing. (Chris Fox, President of the Association of Chief Police Officers, cited in Ahmed 2003)

Reflections in the mirror

The book has been a call for social work as a profession to wake up and consider its attitudes and responses to this group. The inherent care and control tensions in the history of the profession, outlined in Chapter Two, result in a continual battle at the heart of the work. Those voices in social work who want a profession committed to supporting the poor and oppressed and who offer challenges to the current social order, have been drowned out in the era of budgetary constraints and resource control. Our attitudes to and practice with asylum-seekers and others subject to immigration control hold up a mirror, reflecting back to us the place we have reached as a profession. This book may not make comfortable reading for many in the job who do not like the direction the profession is taking, but it also offers us an opportunity to revisit some of those key questions about roles and responsibilities.

> The social work response to unaccompanied refugee children offers a good gauge to reflect on how much our professional value base and practice has been compromised by resource-led thinking and the prejudices with which we become stained through the creeping influence of the wider political agenda. (Masters 2003)

Whilst this conclusion will summarize some of the issues and problems identified in the book, it will also aim to offer good practice solutions where possible and will call for a withdrawal from some of the more repressive elements of the current arrangements.

Many of the chapters in the book (see Sales, Harris, Grady, Fanning, Humphries) evidence considerable uncertainty, confusion and abstention within social work teams concerning this work. A key area of contention has been about responsibility and in particular the relationship between mainstream social services teams and asylum teams. The, often inaccurate, assumption that 'the other team do that' does not help the service users when negotiating their way through complex systems. Linked to this is the conflicting status of those subject to immigration control, for example, disabled person/asylum-seeker, child/asylum-seeker, mental health service user/non-UK citizen, and this can contribute to that chasm of withholding services. It has become clear that workers themselves have been steeped in a culture, which accepts without question the need to gatekeep resources and make decisions about desirability and deservedness. Worryingly, the research presented by Sales and Hek in this book indicates that services and teams agreed with the generally negative stereotypes about asylum-seekers promoted in the media. They describe hostility towards asylum-seekers within social services offices, with teams in conflict with local refugee organizations, rather than working alongside them.

It has also become clear that social workers are now very much part of the army of workers in both the national and local state who, without their consent, indirectly and directly, form part of the internal policing of immigration. Being required to identify people's immigration status in order to ascertain eligibility raises questions about the ethics of excluding people from services as a result, but also colludes in the racist questioning of service users. In addition, social workers become part of a network of workers gathering information the Home Office would dearly love to access. The Efficiency Scrutiny in 1993, discussed in the opening chapter, understood completely that the policing of immigration internally requires information currently within the local state to be accessed by the national state. The agencies with that local information are in the main welfare agencies, including social services. Social workers need to consider if this is an acceptable role which for some local authority workers, for example, in housing, is a duty, not a voluntary arrangement. Those refugee organizations discussed in Chapter Four themselves perceived social workers as representatives of the state, interrogators from whom asylum-seekers seek to conceal information, rather than people to be trusted. That statement is perhaps the best wake-up call as to the place we have reached.

Voluntary?

Our focus should not be entirely on the statutory provision of services. The voluntary sector has a proud history of campaigning and developing services for those excluded, marginalized and poorly treated by mainstream statutory services. Immigration and asylum is no exception and much of the creative work in existence is rooted there. However, we need to be vigilant about cooption and independence. Resources which have to be relentlessly pursued by the voluntary sector for survival are increasingly given on condition that they are related to aspects of surveillance, control and cooperation with the Home Office. We should be very wary of this creeping agenda because many voluntary organizations now have a financial stake in the implementation of immigration controls. The Government itself has actively encouraged the participation of the voluntary sector in this work: 'The Government is particularly concerned to explore ways of harnessing the energy and expertise of voluntary and independent sector bodies in providing support for asylum-seekers' (Home Office cited in Cohen 2002, p.241).

Offering reception support and 'one stop services' are functions the Government has particularly assigned to the voluntary sector. Harmless enough, you might think, but these are fundamental to the work of NASS and part of the function of reception assistants is to identify alternatives to Directorate support and to take up offers of support outside the safety net scheme (NASS cited in Cohen 2002, p.147). Involvement in a system that allocates accommodation, in reality, means removing people from that accommodation when they reach the inevitable end of the asylum process. Taking Government money for support services may seem uncomplicated, but the recent reaction to National Lottery monies going to the National Committee for Anti-Deportation Campaigns (NCADC) illustrates the pressure to prove your work does not drift from support to campaigning, as this, of course, is not the purpose of Government money.

Good practice

And yet, social work's history of work with the marginalized, the oppressed and the poor makes it well armed to rise to this challenge. The social arrangements we have created for those subject to immigration control both increase need and increase risk, familiar concepts to workers in social care. As Grady and Fanning point out in this book, the factors social workers would consider significant in assessing risk are almost identical to the conditions we are placing asylum-seekers in; for example, extreme poverty, isolation, separation, negative labelling, external scapegoating and hostility. As a profession we have a knowledge base, so acknowledging the realities and confronting the problem must be the first step to improving practice.

Social work training is an area worthy of debate here, as to date only a very small number of courses have included the issues in their curriculum. Social work's professional body, the General Social Care Council (GSCC), has not insisted immigration issues are addressed in the curriculum, so there has been no imperative to do so. This reinforces the belief among social workers that immigration and asylum are 'none of their business' and sends newly qualified workers into the field with this mentality. Our experiences at integrating it into the curriculum at Manchester Metropolitan University have showed it is a most effective vehicle for exploring issues around racism, oppression, discrimination and the value base of social work, as well as some of the themes around roles and responsibilities. In addition to this, students are better prepared when they enter practice agencies as students and newly qualified workers. The numbers getting employment in immigration and asylum-led work now are an indicator that we were right to include immigration law, policy and practice in our core curriculum.

A unique scheme for social work students to work with asylum-seekers in Plymouth is an example of creative thinking. These students, supported by a community care worker, offer the support that statutory services and the voluntary sector alike are failing to deliver to vulnerable families (Community Care 2003a). Yet, in the arrangements for the new social work degree coming on line from 2003, the increasingly prescribed curriculum does not appear to include immigration or asylum. Educators need to address this gap as a matter of urgency, because the direction of the new degree follows the changes in social work practice towards managing, gatekeeping and controlling resources and behaviour, as cited in Chapter Two of this book.

There is also a need to focus on groups who have hitherto gone unrecognized. Ferguson and Barclay (2002) draw attention to the needs of women, especially lone parents with young children. They described problems of access to female practitioners and interpreters and the insensitivity of workers to this need. They call for separate spaces for women within service provision and this is a matter for practitioners now seriously to consider. The stereotype of the young, male asylum-seeker is actually some way from the truth and does not reflect the diversity within asylum-seeking communities.

Other chapters have focused on specific areas of practice which could be improved. Save the Children research cited in this book (Stanley 2001) called for Section 20 assessments under the Children Act, rather than Section 17, to ensure unaccompanied young people receive a full package of support and appropriate accommodation. A recent local authority circular (DOH 2003) seems to support this position; time will tell if assessments do fall into line for this group of children. Chapter Seven offers a humbling account of setting up an organization within the voluntary sector without Home Office funding, which offers advocacy, advice, counselling and support in the spirit of empowerment and has drawn asylum-seekers and refugees into delivering this work themselves within their own communities. Grady, in Chapter Eight, calls for the use of Children Act assessments to highlight need and battle for services for asylum-seeking children and their families. Comparative chapters presented by Fanning and by Wells and Hoikkala offer useful insights into improving systems here. Chapter Six offers a clear and helpful account of how social workers can intervene professionally in tribunal hearings by providing reports on those subject to immigration control. These reports can be extremely helpful in constructing arguments around the right to stay and their production is not a million miles from traditional social work skills, yet at present mainstream workers are neither trained nor encouraged to do this.

When all else fails

For many of the individuals and families subject to immigration control, the legal processes will run out and end simply in refusal. At this point workers need to consider whether campaigning for and on behalf of their service users can legitimately be added to their list of social work functions. In Manchester there is a long history of anti-deportation campaigns led by the black community, the most obvious of which is the Viraj Mendis campaign of the 1980s (see Cohen 1988). These campaigns have drawn in other layers of people, also appalled by the brutality of immigration systems. In some of these, professionals including teachers, doctors and social workers have been influential in building a case (see Gibbons 1999).

> Campaigning is never a waste of time and effort! We feel that every Anti-Deportation campaign, whether successful or not, highlights the inhumanity and social injustice of our immigration laws, and helps to educate and inform more people about the reality behind the rantings of the racist media and politicians. (Tayyip Oruc Campaign, NCADC, 2003)

Withdrawal?

What remains now is the question the book started with in the Forewo rd. Should social workers retreat from aspects of this work, given the openly repressive nature of the systems we are being drawn into, in particular, the National Asylum Support Service, NASS? The recent campaign against Section 55 of the NIA Act 2002, which requires asylum-seekers to lodge their claim for asylum 'as soon as reasonably practicable' after arrival in the UK, shows opposition can have an effect. A successful legal challenge meant the provision was declared illegal and contravened the Human Rights Act 1998. Similarly, a campaign led by the Child Poverty Action Group to give asylum-seekers milk tokens succeeded in changing Government policy. Prior to this, even HIV positive mothers, who were advised not to breastfeed, could not claim milk tokens (www.cpag.org.uk 16 May 2003).

Community Care have recently launched a campaign entitled *Right to Refuge: A Fair Deal for Asylum-seekers* which, in particular, calls for the end of the detention of children and treatment in line with the Children Act (Community Care 2003b). At the same time, they announced the results of a survey of social workers. The results show that 87 per cent of social workers working with asylum-seekers felt services were failing.

On some levels these examples also illustrate the weakness of the forces of opposition at the moment, because the focus has been on tinkering at the edges of legislation that is fundamentally and inherently unacceptable, draconian and discriminatory. Many of the contributors to this book share a commitment to opposing immigration control in its entirety. We do not believe immigration controls can be made fair because of their central purpose, as outlined in the opening chapter. Not only that, but they do not work (Hayter 2000) and are a very costly way of perpetuating a racist construction concerning who belongs and who does not.

Social work in the past has taken a stand against racism. During the 1980s, black people and other oppressed groups raised questions about issues such as their absence as users of some services and their over-representation at the more controlling end of provision. That movement effectively forced the profession to re-evaluate practices which had been taken for granted and seen as non-judgemental, but which were revealed to be exclusive, oppressive and discriminatory. When this clashed with the New Right and, subsequently, the New Labour project, the unruly profession was to be brought under control (Jones 1993). From 1995, the education and training of social workers diluted the expectation that students should challenge oppressive structures. Anti-racism and anti-discrimination have been reduced to tokenism and the immigration and asylum issue provides us with an opportunity now to retrieve those debates.

Even posing the question of refusal seems a step too far in the current climate for a demoralized and disoriented social work profession. Yet, when library workers in Plymouth were asked by the police to log internet activity by asylum-seekers, staff and bosses alike expressed quickly and resolutely their unwillingness to do so (Kundnani 2003). Non-compliance with aspects of the immigration system is only realistic with union support. Whilst unions like Unison have expressed concern about members being drawn into internal immigration control, they have discussed non-cooperation rather than non-compliance. At minimum, it is time for a call to refuse to report allegedly unlawful immigration status to the Home Office. The time is also right for a debate on withdrawal from NASS systems on the grounds that these are not support systems at all but designed specifically to reduce and deny support. The monolithic nature of immigration controls makes these points of conflict inevitable unless we collapse completely into the role of immigration officers by default.

This book has probably raised more questions than answers for those workers currently delivering social work and social care. We have offered some suggestions for improved practice, some models of good practice, argued for the legitimacy of campaigning and posed the difficult question of non-compliance. We hope the book will provide a stimulus to these debates and ultimately help improve the lived experiences of those individuals and families subject to immigration control who become recipients of social work services.

> Where does this leave us as social workers?... Should we simply turn our back on those human beings arriving on our shores who have already experienced horrendous abuse only to encounter more of the same? History books and films suggest that there was a word for this during 1939–1945: *collaboration...* Now is the time to speak out against such gross violation of human rights and remind ourselves of some of our most fundamental principles, that is to say, human dignity and worth, social justice and service to humanity. (Code of Ethics for Social Work cited by Mapstone 2003, p.1).

References

Ahmed, K. (2003) 'Immigrants behind crime wave.' *The Observer,* 18 May.

Al Yafai, F. (2003) 'The brick that turned fear and rumour into a riot.' *The Guardian,* 25 June.

Cohen, S. (1988) *From the Jews to the Tamils: Britain's Mistreatment of Refugees.* Manchester, Manchester Law Centre.

Cohen, S. (2002) 'Dining with the devil: The 1999 Immigration and Asylum Act and the voluntary sector.' In S. Cohen, B. Humphries and E. Mynott (eds) (2002) *From Immigration Controls to Welfare Controls.* London: Routledge.

Community Care (2003a) 'Student loan', 5 June.

Community Care (2003b) 'Campaign launched to support asylum-seekers', www.communitycare.co.uk, 4 June.

CPAG (2003) 'Asylum-seekers' milk tokens success', www.cpag.org.uk, 16 May.

DOH (2003) 'Guidance on accommodating children in need and their families. 'LAC (2003), 13.

Ferguson, N. and Barclay, A. (2002) *Seeking Peace of Mind: The Mental Health Needs of Asylum-seekers in Glasgow.* Sterling: University of Sterling.

Gibbons, A. (1999) *A Fight to Belong.* Save the Children.

Hayter, T. (2000) *Open Borders: The Case against Immigration Controls.* London: Pluto Press.

Jones, C. (1993) 'Social work and society.' In R. Adams, L. Dominelli and M. Payne. *Social Work: Themes, Issues and Critical Debates.* London: Macmillan.

Kundnani, A. (2003) 'Libraries rebuff police surveillance of asylum seekers.' *Institute of Race Relations News* 24 March, via website www.irr.org.uk

Mapstone, N. (2003) 'Human decency.' Editorial in *BASW* newsletter, February 2003.

Masters, S. (2003) 'Long way to go.' *BASW* newsletter, 2 June.

NCADC (2003) 'Tayyip Oruc campaign', 12 June.

Stanley, K. (2001) *Cold Comfort: Young Separated Refugees in England.* Save the Children.

Contributors

Chris Brown has been a social worker for the past 16 years having qualified at Manchester Metropolitan University, formerly Manchester Polytechnic, in 1986. In 1994 she gained an MA in Social Work Studies. She has been employed by several authorities within Greater Manchester, primarily in the field of child care. Latterly, she worked in adult services, specifically health care, but left local authority work in 2001 to pursue an interest in the area of immigration and asylum provision within social work. She has since provided a number of independent reports for immigration tribunals throughout the UK.

John Collett is a newly qualified social worker, graduating in 2002 from Manchester Metropolitan University. During his training he became aware of the lack of social work input for asylum seekers and completed his dissertation on the subject, as well as completing his final social work placement in a statutory asylum team. He has been employed as a statutory social worker in Manchester since July 2002 and in January 2003 took up the position of operations manager for Rochdale asylum-seekers team.

Bryan Fanning is a lecturer in the Department of Social Policy and Social Work at University College Dublin. He studied at the University of Limerick and at Birkbeck College, University of London. He is the co-author of a number of studies of asylum seekers in Ireland: *Regional Resettlement of Asylum Seekers: A Strategic Approach* (Cork: Irish Centre for Migration Studies 1999), *Asylum Seekers and the Right to Work in Ireland* (Dublin: Irish Refugee Council 2000) and *Beyond the Pale: Asylum Seeking Children and Social Exclusion in Ireland* (Dublin: Irish Refugee Council 2001). His most recent research has been on racism, ethnicity and poverty in Ireland. He is the author of *Racism and Social Change in the Republic of Ireland* (Manchester: Manchester University Press 2002).

Peter Fell qualified as a social worker in 2001 after teaching French and German for nearly 20 years. He currently manages the Revive project, which provides advocacy and support for asylum-seekers and refugees in Salford. He is author (with Heather Piper) of 'Framing and reframing fears of disorderly youth' (*Practice 13*, 2, 2000, 43–54).

Pete Grady qualified as a social worker in 1992; he worked in residential services for adolescents for eight years as a practitioner and manager, before becoming a senior lecturer at Manchester Metropolitan University. He has an interest in the way that children and young people are constructed and understood within a policy context, and the implications of this for social work practice. He is currently engaged in a number of international projects that focus on the way children and young people who are considered to be 'at risk' receive services in different policy arenas.

Jennifer Harris is senior research fellow in the Social Policy Research Unit at the University of York. Her first book, *The Cultural Meaning of Deafness* was published by Avebury Press (1995) and her second *Deafness and the Hearing* by Venture Press (1997). Jennifer has an international reputation in the field of Disability Studies. Her recent publications include *Disabled People in Refugee and Asylum Seeking Communities in Britain* (2002, Policy Press) (with Roberts).

Debra Hayes became interested in immigration issues whilst working as a practitioner in the probation service. She joined with others to set up the Campaign Against Double Punishment, which still supports black prisoners who are at risk of deportation as a result of their offending. She has worked jointly with the Greater Manchester Immigration Aid Unit and, in particular, with Steve Cohen on research into race, health and immigration. They jointly published *They Make You Sick: Essays on Immigration Control and Health* (MMU/GMIAU 1998). Debra has worked as a senior lecturer in the Social Work Department at Manchester Metropolitan University since 1991, where she has continued to write in this area, particularly concerning the relationship between immigration control and the welfare state. She is actively committed to opposing immigration controls and supporting those under threat of deportation.

Rachel Hek works at Birmingham University as a researcher with the National Evaluation of the Children's Fund team. She teaches social workers at Birmingham University and the Open University, and also works as an independent social work consultant, researcher and therapist for young people. She has undertaken independent research, service evaluation and audits for local authorities and health trusts and has published reports in relation to self harm amongst young people, attitudes of social workers to refugees, the aspirations of young refugees and young women's views on sex, contraception and pregnancy.

Susanna Hoikkala recently qualified as a MA of Social Sciences at the University of Helsinki, where she currently works as a researcher. She is interested in developing the methodologies and methods of participatory research with vulnerable adolescents and migrants, especially in the international context.

Beth Humphries is a reader in social work at Lancaster University. She has published and conducted research on welfare and immigration controls, the most recent of which is *From Immigration Controls to Welfare Controls* (edited with Steve Cohen and Ed Mynott).

Angela Montgomery is solicitor to Humberside Probation Service and is the Senior Manager responsible for High Risk Offenders. She is also an independent parole board member. Previously she was crime and disorder solicitor for Liverpool and Salford City councils. She has been a legal adviser for the Greater Manchester Immigration aid unit and a senior lecturer in criminal justice.

Keri Roberts worked as a research fellow in the Social Policy Research Unit at the University of York until recently, when she completed the research project 'Disabled Refugees in Britain: Entitlements to and Needs for Social and Welfare Services'. With wide ranging research interests in social experiences of impairment and ill health, Keri is now training to be a genetic counsellor at St Mary's Hospital, Manchester. Her recent publications include (2002) *Disabled People in Refugee and Asylum-seeking communities in Britain* (with Harris) and 'All doors are closed to us: A social model of analysis of the experiences of disabled refugees and asylum seekers in Britain' (*Disability and Society*) (forthcoming, with Harris).

Rosemary Sales is reader in Social Policy at Middlesex University. She teaches specialist modules on migration policy at both postgraduate and undergraduate level and has written widely on the subject. Recent publications include *Gender, Migration and Welfare in Europe* (Routledge 2000) (with E. Kofman, A. Phizacklea and P. Raghuram), 'Migrant women and exclusion in Europe' *The European Journal of Women's Studies* (1998) (with E. Kofman) and 'The deserving and the undeserving: Refugees, asylum-seekers and welfare in Britain' *Critical Social Policy 22,* 1. Rosemary has received funding for studies on migration and citizenship rights from the Economic and Social Research Council, the National Health Service and the International Organization of Migration. She is an active campaigner against deportations, and secretary of the Hackney Refugee Migrant Support Group.

Michael Wells is a recent graduate of Manchester Metropolitan University. His current work includes teaching, direct work with young people using statutory youth services, and developing participation based inclusion projects for young refugees and migrants. Although recently trained as a social worker, his practice experience has been with young refugees and migrant families within both voluntary and statutory sectors in Finland and England. His further research interests are European immigration controls and their impact upon the well-being of young separated refugees.

Subject Index

Author Index

Lightning Source UK Ltd.
Milton Keynes UK
UKOW051647280313

208356UK00001B/4/A